POCKET GUIDE
to the
EDIBLE GARDEN

Visit our How To website at www.howto.co.uk

At www.howto.co.uk you can engage in conversation with our authors – all of whom have 'been there and done that' in their specialist fields. You can get access to special offers and additional content, but most importantly you will be able to engage with, and become a part of, a wide and growing community of people just like yourself.

At www.howto.co.uk you'll be able to talk and share tips with people who have similar interests and are facing similar challenges in their lives. People who, just like you, have the desire to change their lives for the better: be it through moving to a new country, starting a new business, growing their own vegetables or writing a novel.

At www.howto.co.uk you'll find the support and encouragement you need to help make your aspirations a reality.

You can go direct to www.pocket-guide-to-edible-gardening.co.uk which is part of the main How To site.

How To Books strives to present authentic, inspiring, practical information in its books. Now when you buy a title from **How To Books**, you get even more than just words on a page.

POCKET GUIDE
to the
EDIBLE GARDEN

WHAT TO DO AND WHEN, MONTH BY MONTH

Joe Hashman

SPRING HILL

Published by Spring Hill, an imprint of How To Books Ltd.
Spring Hill House, Spring Hill Road
Begbroke, Oxford OX5 1RX
United Kingdom
Tel: (01865) 375794
Fax: (01865) 379162
info@howtobooks.co.uk
www.howtobooks.co.uk

How To Books greatly reduce the carbon footprint of their books by sourcing their typesetting and printing in the UK.

British Library Cataloguing in Publication Data
A catalogue record of this book is available from the British Library.

ISBN: 978 1 905862 46 7

Produced for How To Books by Deer Park Productions, Tavistock, Devon
Designed and typeset by Mousemat Design Ltd
Printed and bound in Great Britain by Bell & Bain Ltd., Glasgow

NOTE: The material contained in this book is set out in good faith for general guidance and no liability can be accepted for loss or expense incurred as a result of relying in particular circumstances on statements made in the book. Laws and regulations are complex and liable to change, and readers should check the current position with relevant authorities before making personal arrangements.

Contents

BACKGROUND

Until recently, growing vegetables in kitchen gardens and allotments was viewed largely as a preserve for old men and retirees, where the secret lives of gardeners carried on in make-do-and-mend shanty towns of sheds, dwellings and peaceful havens away from the noise, worries and trappings of modern times: a world of pipe-smoking, double-digging, giant-veg growing, moonshine-brewing, magic and mystery which was accessible only to the very young (as grandchildren, for a treat) or those approaching the autumn of their years.

As recently as the year 2000, allotment sites countrywide were neglected and falling into disrepair as their incumbents either gave up or took their seed packets to the great veg patch in the sky. Hotbeds of cultivation became overgrown wastelands, havens for the creatures that make their homes in long grass but hardly conducive to growing your own food. Surviving plots were tended by a hardy breed of gardener who, through the repetitive spirit of their actions, kept the fields and dreams they shared alive.

Something happened after 2001. Whether it was the 9/11 atrocity or something else is unclear, but suddenly reps in the gardening trade noticed sales of vegetable seeds starting to increase and, a few years later, outstripping those for ornamentals. In tandem was a renewed interest from ordinary people (that's you and me) in how to grow vegetables.

Suddenly folk were clamouring for allotments. Derelict land was being reclaimed by a new generation of gardeners. These were often younger people with families – frequently they were women! A revolution was happening and it carries on still, to this day.

The great thing about this revolution is that it is universally inclusive. It is not a club where you have to give funny handshakes or pass a dodgy induction ritual. It is a world of possibility which embraces anyone prepared to invest the time and effort which are the only demands.

Writing as 'Dirty Nails', through his weekly articles in local and regional newspapers, Joe Hashman has been demystifying the art of edible gardening to a public audience since February 2004. His urge to grow vegetables and fruit stems from a love of nature and good, locally-produced, wildlife-friendly food. He is now the author of several books which combine his passion for gardening with the natural pleasures of being outdoors 'in amongst it'.

Helen Lanchbery supplied the illustrations. They're based on scraps of paper and scribbled notes supplied by the author. With five grown-up children who were raised on food she grew and preserved herself from the family veg patch, Helen has drawn on her life-long experiences as a gardener to provide beautifully interpreted visual guidance for the reader.

INTRODUCTION

Your *Pocket Guide to the Edible Garden* holds green and not-so-green fingered hands through the fruit and vegetable gardening year. It answers those awkward but essential questions regarding how deep, how far apart, how to look after fruit and veggies, when to do this and that.

Your *Pocket Guide to the Edible Garden* is not meant to sit on the coffee table or be lost in your bookshelves. It's a practical manual which wants to live in your pocket or toolkit and be consulted throughout the seasons, just as you might turn to an experienced old friend for advice and guidance on edible gardening matters.

Your *Pocket Guide to the Edible Garden* sees the knowledge and experience of author Joe Hashman and illustrator Helen Lanchbery condensed into clear and concise language. This little book aims simply to empower you and enhance your chances of success on the plot.

Good luck. Growing your own food is a wonderful, soul-enhancing thing to do. We wish you every success and pleasure on the way.

HOW TO USE THIS BOOK

This book is divided up into the months of the year. The months are divided into related subjects. Each subject contains information some of which include a further reference. The first three letters of this reference point you to the month and the number directs you to where the entry lies within that month. Throughout the text you will be guided to references made earlier or subsequently which contain further (relevant) advice. Within the text, these references will always be bracketed and in bold print, e.g. **(Jul 54)**, which refers to potato blight.

The illustrations are numbered too. They are referred to in the text with their individual number and the page which you'll need to turn to see them, e.g. **(Fig. 62, p.76)**, which is called: *Cross-section of how to plant an asparagus crown.*

But before we begin...

UNDERSTANDING PROPRIETARY GROWING MEDIA

Don't make the mistake of purchasing cheap commercially produced potting composts for raising your veggies from seed or in containers. The results from such 'bargains' are often disappointing. Having failed miserably to muster my charges in the past, the lesson I've learned is that you get what you pay for. Nowadays I'm happy to dispense a fair price for a decent product.

In the greenhouse or potting shed, peat has long been the gardener's traditional compost of choice. It is long lasting and provides a stable, moisture-retentive, well-aerated medium. Peat is partially decomposed plant debris and occurs naturally in the cool, waterlogged environments of bogs and moors. It takes thousands of years to form and in the latter half of the 20th century, 94% of British peat lands were destroyed by the horticultural industry.

The repercussions for wildlife have been serious. Many rare or specialized plants and animals are declining rapidly due to habitat loss. There is also a global warming issue connected to peat extraction; being of plant origin, vast quantities of carbon dioxide are locked up in these bogs. The removal and use of peat liberates this CO_2 and the combined effect with other sources is to unnaturally alter the climate.

Happily, alternatives are now on the market which offer options to the home grower. Composts made from recycled timber residues and green waste are more environmentally friendly. Being precisely formulated with added ingredients for a natural balance of essential trace elements, they give veggies the best chance of maximizing their potential. Having tried and tested a number of different brands, I've found New Horizon Peat Free Multi-Purpose to be great value for money. It is perfect for sowing seeds, taking cuttings, potting up seedlings and growing edibles in containers.

John Innes (JI) potting composts

JI potting composts are loam-based but do contain a small percentage of peat and yet less of sand. Loam is prepared commercially by stacking turf for a minimum of six months before being sterilized with heat or chemicals. It contains a high degree of organic matter and provides a reservoir of food and trace elements for plants from seed to adult stages. With slightly differing amounts of added 'base fertilizer' JI Composts are specifically tailored to meet the needs of veggies throughout various stages of development:

JI Seed Compost has a low nutrient level which is ideal for germinating seeds and rooting cuttings.

JI Number 1 contains a small dose of base fertilizer matched with the requirements of young seedlings at the pricking out stage (when they are moved from communal trays to individual pots).

JI Number 2 is a good all-round general compost but with more base fertilizer for potting on young plants and cuttings.

JI Number 3 has extra fertilizer with chalk. It is perfect for use in containers where crops are to remain for a long period of time.

Other options

Coir is another possibility. Made from coconut husks, it is clean, easy to handle and completely renewable. Coir makes an excellent growing medium but crops cultivated in it long-term do need to be fed regularly because it is also quite free-draining.

You can also make your own seed compost. Flick forward **(Jan 1/Fig. 1, p. 9)** for instructions.

GREEN MANURES

Organic matter comprises a small but crucial percentage of most soils in this country. Soil organic matter, or SOM, is any part of the growing medium which once lived, either plant or animal, in various stages of decomposition.

SOM is at its best nutritionally when it becomes humus. In this very well-rotted state, humus can be identified as the dark brown, porous and spongy component of a soil. In a heap, it smells sweet and rich. It is as humus that the nutrients in SOM become most readily available to plants. Additionally, SOM reduces erosion on light and sandy soil by binding particles. In heavy clay, it breaks up the sticky clods and makes ground easier to work.

Home-made compost and animal dung are obvious examples of how SOM can be integrated into the plot but the reality is not always that simple. For instance, the quantity of kitchen and other waste required to produce sufficient compost to treat even a small garden is immense. Dung is often heavy, mucky and difficult to source reliably. This is when 'green manure' comes into its own.

Green manure is simply the name given to plants which are cultivated whenever ground lies empty for more than a few weeks specifically to benefit the soil and/or subsequent edible crops. A range of plants is available for this purpose these days, selected for one or more soil enhancing qualities. All are 'non-invasive', which means that they won't take over your growing space.

Members of the pea and bean family (such as alfalfa and red clover) are popular choices because they fix atmospheric nitrogen in their roots. This provides food for crops that follow. Some are especially deep-rooted. Lupins, for example, can plunge down two metres and dredge otherwise inaccessible minerals to the surface.

Others produce copious quantities of leafy top growth and extensive root systems which protect soil from wind erosion and nutrient leaching by winter rains; annual Italian ryegrass or buckwheat, for example. The dense foliage of mustard also suppresses weeds and shelters pest-eating animals such as frogs, toads and beetles. However, as a member of the cabbage family it would be unwise to grow mustard immediately before or after related edible species **(Fig. 183, p. 206)**.

Phacelia is a wildlife-friendly favourite. Feathery leaves provide lots of SOM. Some should always be allowed to mature and flower because they are beautiful and adored by bees.

Green manures sown from seed are easy to handle and relatively cheap. Good preparation is important, so make a seedbed which is weed-free and raked to a fine tilth. Then broadcast-sow the seed by hand, scattering handfuls in a controlled manner with a backwards sweep of your arm and flick of the wrist. Rake seeds a centimeter or so into the surface.

Green manures can be usefully chopped down with a hoe or spade at any point before they flower or become woody. Allow them to wilt before digging in to the top 15cm layer of soil. If you prefer not to dig, green manures can be allowed to decompose on the surface.

Most green manures are suited to employment throughout the growing period from spring to autumn. Field beans and perennial rye are exceptions. These grow in winter too, so can stand happily on vacant land from harvest time until the following spring. Big-seeded beans are best planted 5cm deep, at 15cm intervals, in rows 30cm apart.

Free green manure is available simply by hoeing a carpet of weeds before they set seed.

JANUARY

January is the month to firm up your planting plans for next season.

Sort out seeds. It makes really good sense to put them in alphabetical order, neatly in a box. Write down what you intend to sow (or plant) and when, in a year-planner. Resolve to keep notes of your successes or failures, the weather, tips from other growers and observations of the natural world.

Purchase and prepare seed potatoes. Invest in composts and other essential little bits and bobs.

If you have somewhere under cover then you can start to sow some seeds. Think of the cabbage tribe, salads, turnips and radishes in pots, or some more exotic vegetable fruits if you can provide a little heat.

There should be plenty of roots and greens still in the ground, in the store shed, or standing on the plot.

Provided the soil isn't locked up by frost, as you fetch in the dinner, clear and weed the ground as well. A little-and-often approach is the secret to ensuring that your well-cultivated patch remains under easily manageable control.

Daylight hours are short but already discernibly lengthening. By mid-month, give yourself an extra half-hour after work to exercise your back: do some productive bending and stretching whilst listening to bird life settling down in the hedges of an evening.

In January you can lay the foundations for your edible gardening year.

Think big, get excited and practical but, if the weather and circumstances are against you, don't panic – there is plenty of time yet!

General jobs to do

1. Prepare your own home-made potting compost **(Fig. 1, p. 9)**.
2. Wash dirty pots and trays in warm soapy water **(Nov 20)**.
3. Potter and tidy ready for the spring rush (which will be coming soon)!
4. Check over all veg in store. Discard any showing signs of going off **(Nov 16)**.
5. Dig out stinging nettle and willowherb roots where not wanted. Drown them in a bucket of water **(Nov 6)** or burn (and save the ashes).
6. Mulch the plot with well-rotted manure or compost **(Nov 10)**.
7. Tickle about here and there while harvesting.
8. Define plot edges by digging and weeding thoroughly **(Mar 11)**.
9. Take measurements for any planned alterations to the dimensions of

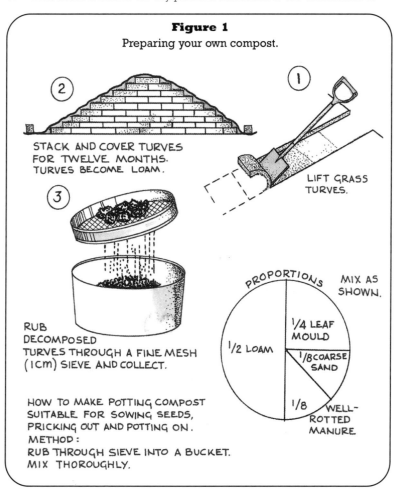

Figure 1
Preparing your own compost.

STACK AND COVER TURVES FOR TWELVE MONTHS. TURVES BECOME LOAM.

LIFT GRASS TURVES.

RUB DECOMPOSED TURVES THROUGH A FINE MESH (1cm) SIEVE AND COLLECT.

HOW TO MAKE POTTING COMPOST SUITABLE FOR SOWING SEEDS, PRICKING OUT AND POTTING ON.
METHOD:
RUB THROUGH SIEVE INTO A BUCKET.
MIX THOROUGHLY.

PROPORTIONS — MIX AS SHOWN.

1/2 LOAM
1/4 LEAF MOULD
1/8 COARSE SAND
1/8 WELL-ROTTED MANURE

your edible garden **(Fig. 2, p. 10)**.

10. Do some hedge trimming if the mood takes you and this job is not yet done **(Fig. 3, p. 11)**.

11. Tidy away junk and rubbish accumulations. Get rid of useless and broken 'litter' but find a place for useful bits and bobs.

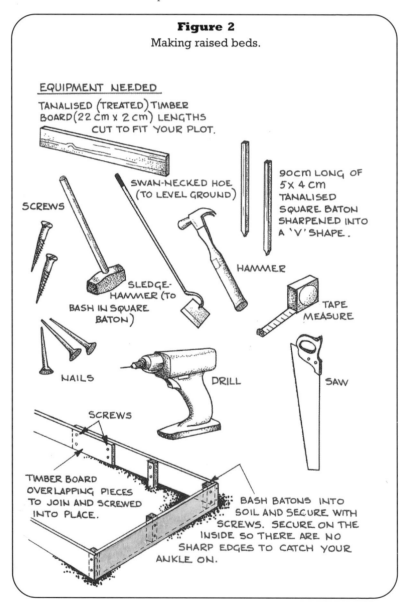

Figure 2
Making raised beds.

EQUIPMENT NEEDED

TANALISED (TREATED) TIMBER
BOARD (22 cm x 2 cm) LENGTHS
CUT TO FIT YOUR PLOT.

SCREWS

SWAN-NECKED HOE
(TO LEVEL GROUND)

90cm LONG OF
5 x 4 cm
TANALISED
SQUARE BATON
SHARPENED INTO
A 'V' SHAPE.

SLEDGE-
HAMMER (TO
BASH IN SQUARE
BATON)

HAMMER

TAPE
MEASURE

NAILS

DRILL

SAW

SCREWS

TIMBER BOARD
OVERLAPPING PIECES
TO JOIN AND SCREWED
INTO PLACE.

BASH BATONS INTO
SOIL AND SECURE WITH
SCREWS. SECURE ON THE
INSIDE SO THERE ARE NO
SHARP EDGES TO CATCH YOUR
ANKLE ON.

Figure 3
Hedge trimming.

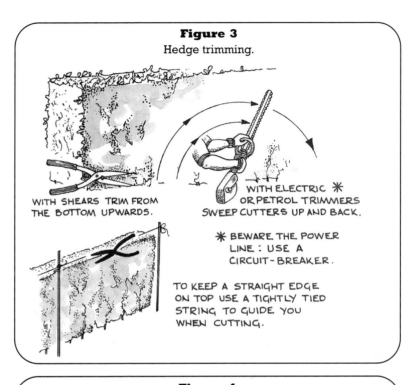

WITH SHEARS TRIM FROM
THE BOTTOM UPWARDS.

WITH ELECTRIC ✳
OR PETROL TRIMMERS
SWEEP CUTTERS UP AND BACK.

✳ BEWARE THE POWER
LINE : USE A
CIRCUIT-BREAKER.

TO KEEP A STRAIGHT EDGE
ON TOP USE A TIGHTLY TIED
STRING TO GUIDE YOU
WHEN CUTTING.

Figure 4
How to keep frost at bay in an unheated greenhouse.

DRAINAGE HOLE TO LET
FLAME BREATHE.

INVERTED CLAY POT :
WILL NOT CRACK BUT
WILL ABSORB AND
RADIATE HEAT FROM
BURNING CANDLE.

FIRE-PROOF HARD
SURFACE (e.g. CONCRETE).

SLOW-BURNING
CANDLE.

SUGGESTION: LIGHT CANDLE OVERNIGHT IN
HOURS OF DARKNESS, WHEN
GREENHOUSE HEAT IS LOWEST.

12. Pay allotment fees to the local council if you're fortunate enough to rent a plot.
13. Remove couch grass from comfrey bed while the latter has completely died down and the wiry underground stems can be easily extracted **(Jul 6)**.
14. Clear and dig over a sunny, south-facing bed for early crops to be planted in the near future. Putting down a sheet of black plastic will serve to hasten the warming process and enable big-seeded veggies like broad beans, peas and radishes to go in sooner.
15. Ventilate the greenhouse in the mornings, in mild weather **(Mar 3)**.
16. Keep night cold at bay in your greenhouse by covering a lighted candle with a clay pot and letting it burn during the hours of darkness **(Fig. 4, p. 11)**.
17. Ensure greenhouse gutters and fixings are in good working order **(Feb 18)**.

Leaves & greens
18. CABBAGE. Sow Summer cabbages such as Filderkraut, Hispi F1 or Greyhound. Pop seeds 1cm deep into trays of multi-purpose or JI Seed Compost with about 3cm between each one. Firm and moisten **(Feb 20)**. These will need 'pricking out' when large enough to handle comfortably **(Feb 27)**. With care (and a little luck) they should yield heavy, flame-shaped hearts before the main butterfly season in July and August – a 'cultural control' which avoids pests rather than playing into their hands, so to speak. Repeat a sowing in February and March to get a succession of vitamin-rich greens.
19. KALE. Clean yellowing leaves from kale and other brassicas to keep plants clean and fresh.
20. LETTUCE. Pot on Winter Density and other lettuces into fresh compost to give them a boost **(Apr 22)**.
21. Sow lettuce. Lobjoits Green Cos, Dynamite or Salad Bowl are suitable varieties to sow now **(Feb 20)**.
22. CORN SALAD. Sow corn salad **(Apr 41)**.
23. Maintain bird-scaring devices over crops, especially cabbages and greens **(Apr 18)**.
24. WINTER PURSLANE. Plant out winter purslane which has been nurtured in the greenhouse then hardened off **(Apr 2)**. Tap them out of their pots and tuck the undisturbed root-ball into a warm, preferably south-facing bed with 20cm all round. Do the same with corn salad plants which have been grown in pots.
25. LEAF BEET. Remove outside leaves from chards and beets. Give a little

feed to see if a fresh flush of edible portions can't be persuaded to sprout **(Jun 56)**.

Roots, tubers & stems

26. POTATO. Purchase seed potatoes and set them out to 'chit'. Healthy chits, or sprouted growths, are stout and rich in colour. If the chits appear drawn and pale then provide a more naturally illuminated position. At planting time, chits can be reduced to two or three to encourage fewer but bigger potatoes, or leave them all intact if you want lots of small spuds. Some gardeners don't bother but the fact is that chitted potatoes are already growing at planting time (March or April usually) and get going quicker than unchitted ones. This will be beneficial if blight strikes come high summer and all the tops have to be removed **(Jul 53/54)**. Subsequent swelling will stop so all growth made between now and then is important in terms of the weight of your haul at harvest **(Fig. 5, p. 13)**.

27. Cover chitting spuds with newspaper at night if temperatures threaten to go below freezing. Do not allow them to get frost-bitten **(Feb 34)**.

Figure 5
Setting out seed potatoes to pre-sprout, or 'chit'.

DARK PIMPLES INDICATE WHERE SHOOTS WILL SPROUT FROM.

PLACE 'CHITS' UPPERMOST (SHOOT AKA 'CHIT')

USE AN EGG BOX OR SIMILAR.

POSITION CHITTING POTATOES IN GOOD LIGHT OUT OF THE FROST.

A FEW CHITS: FEWER BUT LARGER POTATOES.

LOTS OF CHITS: LOTS OF SMALL POTATOES.

CONTROL YOUR CHITS TO INFLUENCE THE CROP.

28. JERUSALEM ARTICHOKE. Weed amongst crop while harvesting. Ensure every last piece of the Jerusalems is removed to completely clear the site because they are very invasive.

29. Plant selected healthy tubers in a freshly-prepared site. Blemish-free tubers plunged into fertile soil, 15cm deep, at 30cm intervals should be perfect. Fuseau is a smooth variety and much easier to deal with in terms of washing and preparation in the kitchen. Some Jerusalems can be knobbly beyond belief!

30. CELERIAC. Tend celeriac by stripping off limp outside leaves. Maintain a bracken or straw mulch to protect from frost if weather is extremely cold **(Fig. 6, p. 14).**

31. TURNIP & RADISH. In pots of multi-purpose compost, sow F1 Market Express turnip and French Breakfast radish. They will grow from seed to harvest in these, so pop them in 1.5cm deep at 4cm intervals. Keep moist and on a sunny shelf in the greenhouse or porch for small and early portions in a few weeks' time **(Apr 45)**.

32. SWEDE. Tidy lines of swedes while harvesting.

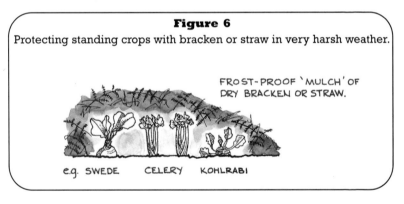

Figure 6

Protecting standing crops with bracken or straw in very harsh weather.

FROST-PROOF 'MULCH' OF DRY BRACKEN OR STRAW.

e.g. SWEDE   CELERY   KOHLRABI

Veg fruit

33. TOMATO, PEPPER & AUBERGINE. Sow in the house on a warm windowsill if 18–21°C can be consistently provided. Sow them 5mm deep in trays for future pricking out **(Feb 27)** into 9cm pots.

Onion tribe

34. LEEK. Sow leeks in a tray **(Feb 48)** for immature edibles in high summer or an early autumn crop of full size. Try Roxton F1 for the former or Carentan 2 for autumnal liftings.

35. Clear remaining leeks from the main bed and heel in near the house **(Mar 67)**.

36. ONION. Top dress winter onions with wood ash. Just sprinkle it along the rows to give your charges a little fillip.
37. Sow seeds of a maincrop onion such as Bedfordshire Champion. Sprinkle evenly and not too thickly over a tray of seed compost in exactly the same way as for leeks **(Feb 48)**. Keep moist but not wet with a little artificial heat, between 15–20°C.
38. SHALLOT. Firm in loosened shallots to encourage good root anchorage **(Fig. 7, p. 15)**.
39. GARLIC. Plant garlic, such as Printador **(Feb 50)**.

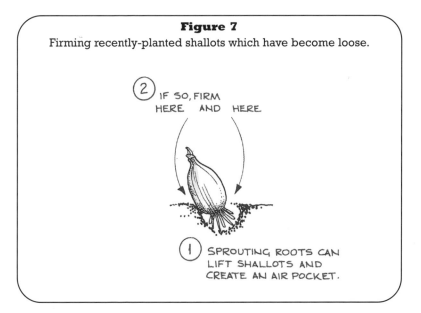

Figure 7
Firming recently-planted shallots which have become loose.

② IF SO, FIRM
HERE   AND   HERE

① SPROUTING ROOTS CAN
LIFT SHALLOTS AND
CREATE AN AIR POCKET.

Peas & beans
40. PEA. Sow Feltham First Early peas 4cm deep in pots or cardboard tubes full of potting compost **(Feb 52)**.
41. BROAD BEAN. Cover with fleece if the weather gets nasty.
42. RUNNER BEAN. Dig a trench for runner beans. Line it with flat newspapers to retain moisture then start to fill with green kitchen waste **(Apr 84)**.

Edible flowers
43. SUNFLOWER. Take down remaining sunflower stalks and sling on the compost heap.

44. GLOBE ARTICHOKE. Remove globe artichokes in pots from the greenhouse and place in a sunny spot outside to harden off, but do protect from frosts **(Apr 2)**.

Fruit garden

45. APPLE, PEAR & PLUM. Wassail all fruit trees with cider and toast on the evening of Twelfth Night **(Fig. 8, p. 16)**.

46. Prune apple and pear trees unless the air temperature is freezing, in which case delay until the temperature rises **(Mar 93a/93b)**.

47. Clear soil in vicinity of step-over apples and other 'restricted' **(Feb 63)** forms.

48. RED & WHITE CURRANT. Secure nets over red and white currant

Figure 8
Wassailing apple trees.

PUT TOAST IN THE BRANCHES TO FEED THE TREE GUARDIAN'S SPIRIT.

SPRINKLE CIDER ON THE ROOTS TO QUENCH THE THIRST OF THE SPIRITS.

TRADITIONALLY, DO THIS ON TWELFTH NIGHT.

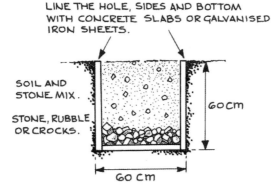

Figure 9
Preparing a planting pit for figs.

LINE THE HOLE, SIDES AND BOTTOM
WITH CONCRETE SLABS OR GALVANISED
IRON SHEETS.

SOIL AND STONE MIX.

STONE, RUBBLE OR CROCKS.

60 cm

60 cm

THIS IS A BIG JOB. DO IT NOW BUT DON'T
PLANT FIG TREE UNTIL MARCH.

cordons to stop bullfinches eating the buds. Keep in place until the discreet 'strigs' of pale flowers come out.

49. RASPBERRY. Prepare a site for raspberries. They are a long-term perennial crop (i.e. comes back year after year). Prepare thoroughly as soon after New Year as possible, when the soil is neither frost-bound nor waterlogged. A sheltered site that gets plenty of sun is ideal. This is especially important for raspberries that ripen in autumn – sunshine late in the year can make all the difference to your returns. Avoid sites prone to waterlogging. In scrupulously weeded ground, excavate a trench that is 75cm wide and 25cm deep. Work in as much leaf mould, compost or well-rotted manure as can be spared, by the barrow-load if possible. Lighten heavy soils with grit – thoroughly mix this with the soil whilst refilling the trench. Budget for 45cm of space between each plant. If preparing more than one row, allow 2m between them. Rows that run north to south will receive an even amount of sunshine as the sun moves across the sky. East to west orientation is liable to be shaded on the far side all day. Bear this in mind. Also, insert stout posts firmly at either end of the rows, 2m in height. Fix wires between these for any summer fruiting raspberries, at approximately 75cm, 1.35m and 1.95m intervals. These will support the canes so must be taut and secure. No need to erect supports for autumn varieties – they are bushier in habit. Do all this a month before planting to allow the ground to settle. Alternatively, for plants to be grown individually (i.e. not in a row), prepare the ground as described at the foot of single 2m posts.

50. Between now and the end of February, cut all canes from established autumn raspberries back to ground level. Mulch the rows with whatever bulky organic matter has been put aside for this job.

51. Clean either side of established raspberry rows. Both summer and autumn fruiting varieties are extremely invasive plants. They must be kept within the confines of their 75cm wide rows or else they are liable to take over. Dig deeply either side as far out as possible to lift and extract woody, fibrous roots. These can be burnt or used to propagate new plants.

52. STRAWBERRY. Apply wood ash top dressing to strawberry beds. Use whatever is available from winter fires this month and next. Sprinkle handfuls along the rows.

53. FIG. Prepare an enclosed planting hole for fig tree against a south or south-west facing shed **(Fig. 9, p. 17)**.

FEBRUARY

In February, why not have a good old tidy-up? Gather all the rubbish in your garden or allotment, stack it in a pile and – on one of those short, cold evenings – light a bonfire. Then you'll be like an artist about to paint a new picture on a fresh canvas.

This is the month to steal a march on spring. Prepare the ground now and then, in a month or two, when the rush and tear of planting-time is upon us, you'll be able to relax and enjoy the experience knowing that the hard work has already been done.

There's plenty to sow. A greenhouse or porch can become a seedling nursery. If it's mild and you're able to wait no more, big seeds may be sown direct.

Make a fuss of over-wintered veg like artichokes, purple sprouting broccoli and rhubarb but don't get carried away yet. Keep protective mulches in place a while longer.

February is prime time for planting, propagating and pruning most tree and soft fruits. Ideally, get these jobs done before the month's end. Sap will soon be rising. After that, things are on the up.

This can be a cruel month weather-wise *and* it's the Hungry Gap: when stores in the shed and ground are low and what's been newly planted has yet to fruitfully come up. But even during the harshest conditions, along hedge bottoms, in gardens and down in the woods, signs of emerging new life are everywhere.

Early birds like dunnock have begun a-courting and flit between the bushes playing kiss-chase.

General jobs to do

1. Potter about. Tidy away bits and bobs.
2. Clean the weeds from neglected corners. Turn soil along the edges **(Nov 13)**.
3. Tidy and sort out the shed.
4. Construct permanent and semi-permanent paths in the veg patch **(Fig. 10, p. 21)**.
5. Import bundles of twiggy hazel faggots. Store for various uses to come. Any hedge-layers in your area will be pleased to help you out. Alternatively, volunteer for a day or three down at your local woods doing coppicing. Take home a portion of the cut stems for personal use **(Fig. 11, p. 22)**.
6. Swill out and clean buckets, pots and such like which are loitering in corners or presenting trip hazards.
7. Trim privet and other hedges before the birds' nesting season starts **(Fig. 3, p. 11)**.
8. Hoe down crops grown deliberately as 'green manure' **(Jun 15)**.
9. Tease out as much couch grass as you are able, and burn it.
10. Stroll around your little piece of heaven and have a good think. Plan for the season to come in your head or (better still) on paper **(Dec 2)**.
11. Where straw was used to mulch an area for courgettes last summer **(Jun 66)**, turn this in to the soil.
12. Check over standing crops, areas of bare earth and recently sown seeds (on a daily basis).
13. Keep greenhouse ventilated in mild weather **(Mar 3)**.
14. Keep some newspaper or horticultural fleece handy in case temperatures plummet.
15. Light a long-burning candle in the greenhouse and place in a safe position under a clay pot at night to keep off any frosty chill **(Fig. 4, p. 11)**.
16. Cover early seedlings in the greenhouse with newspaper or fleece at night if the conditions outside are freezing.
17. Apply dribbles of water to seeds and seedlings where needed, but be careful not to soak the compost too much **(Fig. 12, p. 22)**.
18. Keep on top of running greenhouse repairs and maintenance jobs to gutters, seals, door hinges, glass, etc. **(Fig.13, p.23)**.
19. Purchase growing-bags and compost and keep ready for later in the season. Store these in a greenhouse or shed so that they don't get frosted and are pleasantly mild to touch when sowing seeds into.

Figure 10
Construct permanent and semi-permanent paths in the veg patch.

WITH BRICKS

BRICKS - SUNK INTO THE SOIL.
LOOKS GOOD AND SOLID BUT EASILY MOVED.

JUST LAY ON THE SOIL AND MOVE AT WILL.

WITH PLANKS OF WOOD.
SCAFFOLD PLANKS ARE GOOD. SPREAD YOUR WEIGHT AND PROTECT THE SOIL. FIT IN WELL WITH THE STRAIGHT LINES OF A VEG PATCH. A CINCH TO LIFT, MOVE AND ADJUST.

SLIGHTLY RAISED CAMBER TO SHED RAINFALL.

CONCRETE PERMANENT VERY HARDWEARING AND WILL LAST A LIFETIME. FUN IF YOU LIKE BUILDING ETC. BUT A CHORE OTHERWISE.

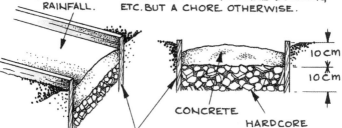

10 cm
10 cm

CONCRETE
HARDCORE

TANALIZED WOODEN BOARDS AS STRAIGHT EDGES.

Figure 11

Import bundles of twiggy hazel faggots.

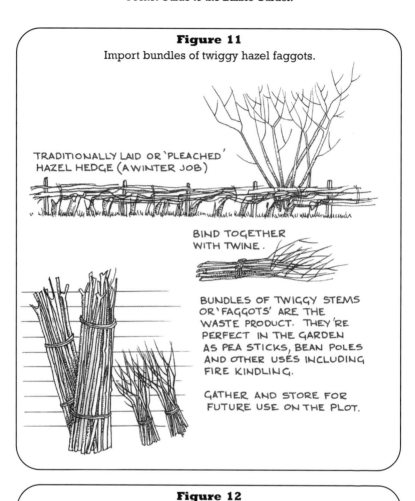

TRADITIONALLY LAID OR 'PLEACHED'
HAZEL HEDGE (A WINTER JOB)

BIND TOGETHER
WITH TWINE.

BUNDLES OF TWIGGY STEMS
OR 'FAGGOTS' ARE THE
WASTE PRODUCT. THEY'RE
PERFECT IN THE GARDEN
AS PEA STICKS, BEAN POLES
AND OTHER USES INCLUDING
FIRE KINDLING.

GATHER AND STORE FOR
FUTURE USE ON THE PLOT.

Figure 12

How to control water flow from a can.

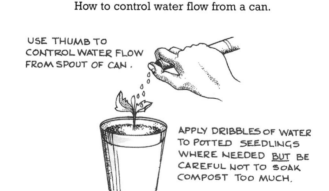

USE THUMB TO
CONTROL WATER FLOW
FROM SPOUT OF CAN.

APPLY DRIBBLES OF WATER
TO POTTED SEEDLINGS
WHERE NEEDED BUT BE
CAREFUL NOT TO SOAK
COMPOST TOO MUCH.

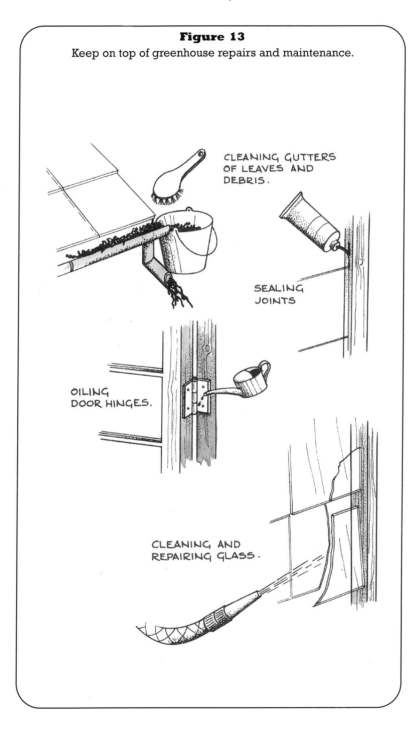

Figure 13
Keep on top of greenhouse repairs and maintenance.

CLEANING GUTTERS OF LEAVES AND DEBRIS.

SEALING JOINTS

OILING DOOR HINGES.

CLEANING AND REPAIRING GLASS.

February

Leaves & greens

20. CABBAGE, BRUSSELS SPROUT, KALE, LETTUCE, LEAF BEET. In pots and trays, sow summer cabbages (such as Spitfire, Hispi F1, Greyhound); lettuces (e.g. Trocadero, Buttercrunch, Tiger, Salad Bowl); kale (e.g. Pentland Brig, Habholer Grun Krausner); Swiss chard; rocket; summer cauliflower (e.g. Snowball); Brussels sprout (e.g. Egor and Wellington F1) **(Figs 14 and 15, p. 25)**.

21. Make pigeon-scarers from old shredded plastic bags tied to canes **(Fig. 16, p. 26)**.

22. If any red cabbages are not firming up just pick the leaves to eat individually, then bash the woody stems to a pulp before composting **(Feb 25)**.

23. Weed amongst purple sprouting broccoli, then secure netting over the top to keep pigeons off **(Dec 19)**.

24. Remove tattered, brown and yellowing lower leaves from Brussels sprouts and kale. These can fruitfully be placed in the bottom of a bean trench **(Apr 84)** or on the compost heap.

25. Harvest the last of the strap-leaved kale. Remove plants and bash tough, woody stems with a hammer before chucking on the compost heap or in a bean trench **(Apr 84)**. Alternatively, if the ground space is not urgently needed, allow spent plants to stand and flower later (April-ish). Early insects find the simple blooms of brassicas extremely useful and attractive **(Fig. 17, p. 27)**.

26. Compost spent Swiss chard or throw it in the bottom of a bean trench **(Apr 84)**.

27. Prick out Lobjoits Green Cos (or other varieties of) lettuce sown just after mid-January. This involves lifting them carefully from the seed tray and nestling them individually into 9cm pots. Take care not to damage the roots and handle by the leaf only (never the stem).

28. CORN SALAD, WINTER PURSLANE. Place winter purslane and corn salad (in pots) outside during the day to harden off **(Apr 2)**.

29. Re-pot winter purslane into larger containers for greenhouse cultivation **(Apr 22)**. This will encourage a new burst of productive energy. Those to go outside can be planted into their final positions now at 20cm spacings. Place up-turned glass jars over the top to act as mini greenhouses and provide extra warmth.

30. EDIBLE WEEDS. Weed out nettles and the first signs of germinating goosegrass (they are both edible so steam as greens or use in soups). Nettle roots can be submerged in a bucket of water. Use a stone or brick to weigh them down. They will drown in a month or two, when they may be safely added to the compost heap without any danger of re-growing there. The water becomes rich in nutrients and can be stored in bottles for future use as a liquid feed.

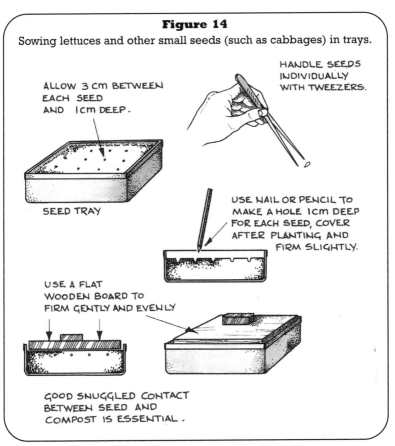

Figure 14

Sowing lettuces and other small seeds (such as cabbages) in trays.

HANDLE SEEDS INDIVIDUALLY WITH TWEEZERS.

ALLOW 3 cm BETWEEN EACH SEED AND 1cm DEEP.

SEED TRAY

USE NAIL OR PENCIL TO MAKE A HOLE 1cm DEEP FOR EACH SEED, COVER AFTER PLANTING AND FIRM SLIGHTLY.

USE A FLAT WOODEN BOARD TO FIRM GENTLY AND EVENLY

GOOD SNUGGLED CONTACT BETWEEN SEED AND COMPOST IS ESSENTIAL.

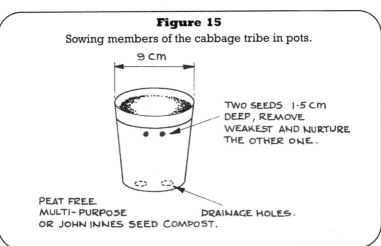

Figure 15

Sowing members of the cabbage tribe in pots.

9 cm

TWO SEEDS 1·5 cm DEEP, REMOVE WEAKEST AND NURTURE THE OTHER ONE.

PEAT FREE MULTI-PURPOSE OR JOHN INNES SEED COMPOST.

DRAINAGE HOLES.

Figure 16

How to make a bird-scaring device with an old compost bag.

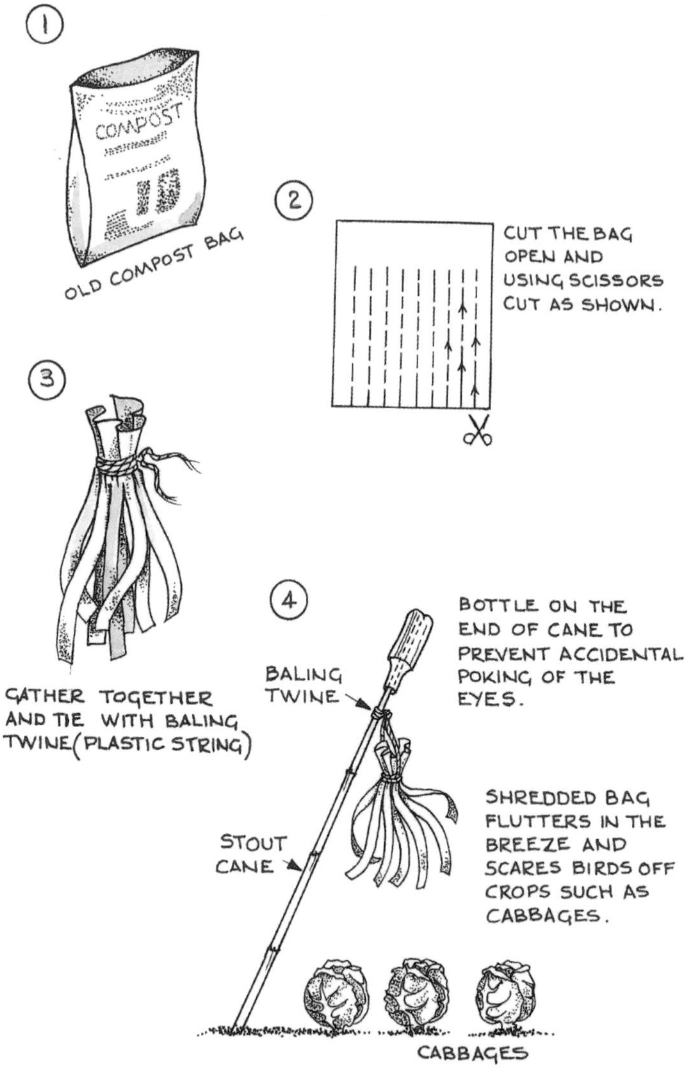

① OLD COMPOST BAG

② CUT THE BAG OPEN AND USING SCISSORS CUT AS SHOWN.

③ GATHER TOGETHER AND TIE WITH BALING TWINE (PLASTIC STRING)

④ BALING TWINE

STOUT CANE

BOTTLE ON THE END OF CANE TO PREVENT ACCIDENTAL POKING OF THE EYES.

SHREDDED BAG FLUTTERS IN THE BREEZE AND SCARES BIRDS OFF CROPS SUCH AS CABBAGES.

CABBAGES

Figure 17

Pulverising cabbage family members for the compost heap.

LUMP HAMMER

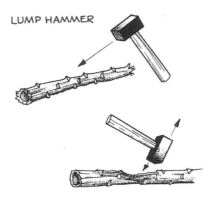

FLATTENED AND FIBROUS STEM ROTS
IN THE COMPOST HEAP QUICKER.

HARVEST THE LAST OF THE DWARF GREEN
CURLY KALE. REMOVE PLANTS AND BASH
TOUGH WOODY STEMS WITH A HAMMER
BEFORE CHUCKING IT ON THE COMPOST HEAP.

Roots, tubers & stems

31. TURNIP. Sow White Globe, F1 Market Express in trays. Pop seeds 5mm deep at about 3cm intervals. They'll be pricked out **(Feb 27)** when large enough to handle comfortably.

32. RADISH. Sow French Breakfast in pots. Pop seeds 5mm to 1cm deep with 3cm between. They'll grow from seed to harvest in the pots, so keep moist but not wet and in a sunny position to encourage fast development.

33. POTATO. Set up seed potatoes in trays or egg boxes to 'chit'. The chits are little sprouts that grow on the potatoes and should be facing uppermost in the light so that growth is stout and healthy as opposed to weak and drawn **(Jan 26)**.

34. In freezing weather take frost precautions with chitting potatoes in the greenhouse by covering at night with horticultural fleece or newspaper **(Fig. 18, p. 29)**.

35. Dig trenches in preparation for planting First Early potatoes next month. These are 'new potatoes' and will be ready in mid-summer.

Trenches should be 25cm deep and, if digging more than one, 60cm apart running parallel. Allow for 30cm between each seed potato so, for example, if cultivating ten plants you'll need 3m of trench. Enrich trenches with a 10cm thick blanket of compost or well-rotted manure.

36. Mark out rows for Second Early, Maincrop and Salad potatoes with canes and string. This really helps to orientate what is going where on the plot. Bear in mind that Second Earlies need to be placed at 38cm intervals in parallel rows 60cm apart. Maincrop and Salad potatoes demand more space; 38cm apart with 75cm between rows if planting more than one **(Mar 47)**.

37. RHUBARB. Weed carefully around emerging rhubarb. Tease out couch grass and perennial weeds before they have a chance to establish.

38. ASPARAGUS. Hand weed asparagus bed. Even though weeds will be few and far between (hopefully) it is important to keep asparagus scrupulously clean.

39. Use a swan-necked hoe to draw soil up into ridges over dormant asparagus crowns on established beds **(Fig. 19, p. 29)**.

40. Top-dress established asparagus bed with dusting of sea salt and organic fertiliser. Scatter it by the handful as if feeding grain to chickens to mimic the ancestral, maritime home of the forebears of this delectable crop.

41. JERUSALEM ARTICHOKE. Take care when digging. Meticulously remove every last tiny piece of tuber. Any bit left in the ground will grow again, which may interfere with subsequent crops. A special 'potato fork' with numerous long and closely positioned prongs (or 'tines') is helpful in this respect. Purchase specially or, a cheaper option, keep an eye open at the local tip where such tools turn up from time to time at a fraction of the cost.

42. CELERIAC. Lift remaining celeriac. 'Heel in' close to the kitchen. This involves just digging a trench, placing celeriac into this and almost-but-not-quite covering with loose soil **(Mar 67)**. Remember that a leaf or two makes an excellent celery substitute in soups.

43. Dig over ground where celeriac and parsnips have been harvested. Doing it now saves a panic later on when there are lots more jobs to keep you busy.

44. HORSERADISH. Plant pieces of root in large, deep pot **(Fig. 20, p. 30)**.

45. SWEDE. Hand weed around swedes which are still standing on the plot.

46. Use fleece or straw to protect standing crops such as swede from getting frost-bitten in really cold night temperatures. Lay it over the top or pack it around **(Fig. 6, p. 14)**.

Figure 18

Protecting 'chitting' seed potatoes.

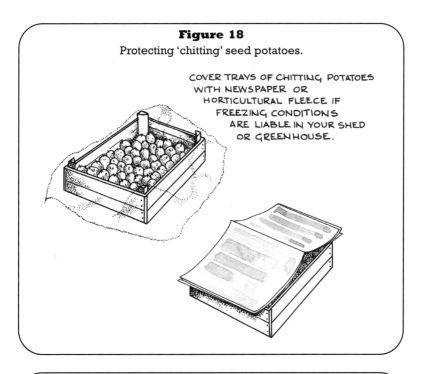

COVER TRAYS OF CHITTING POTATOES
WITH NEWSPAPER OR
HORTICULTURAL FLEECE IF
FREEZING CONDITIONS
ARE LIABLE IN YOUR SHED
OR GREENHOUSE.

Figure 19

Making ridges with a hoe over dormant asparagus crowns.

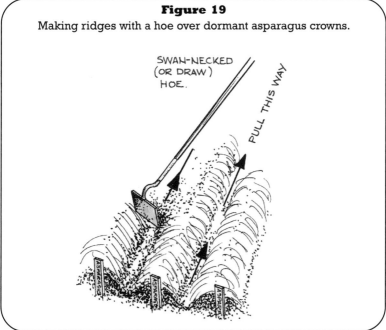

SWAN-NECKED
(OR DRAW)
HOE.

PULL THIS WAY

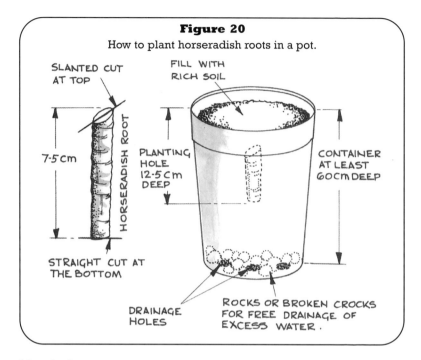

Figure 20
How to plant horseradish roots in a pot.

SLANTED CUT AT TOP

FILL WITH RICH SOIL

HORSERADISH ROOT

7·5 cm

PLANTING HOLE 12·5 cm DEEP

CONTAINER AT LEAST 60 cm DEEP

STRAIGHT CUT AT THE BOTTOM

DRAINAGE HOLES

ROCKS OR BROKEN CROCKS FOR FREE DRAINAGE OF EXCESS WATER.

Veg fruit

47. CUCUMBER. Prepare a sunny bed; erect chicken-wire against south-facing wall for them to scramble up. Apply ample well-rotted manure **(Fig. 21, p. 31)**.

Onion tribe

48. LEEK. Sow leeks (e.g. Musselburgh, Carentan 2) in trays. Also sow leek Roxton F1 for immature, super-sweet summer crops. Sprinkle them onto the surface of moist compost like you would apply salt and pepper to a plateful of food. Then cover with about 5mm of compost, shaken evenly through a sieve, and firm gently with a flat wooden board. Remember to stick a label in at the side with the variety name and date sown – it is easy to loose track of what's what when seedlings start jumping up! Keep the trays on a sunny greenhouse shelf or windowsill.

49. ELEPHANT GARLIC. Hand weed.

50. GARLIC. Split bulbs and plant each clove individually **(Fig. 22, p. 31)**. Or plant the whole bulb intact for lots of smaller cloves. Plant anything from 2.5 to 10cm deep, about 12.5cm apart. If cultivating more than one row, run them parallel about 30cm apart.

51. ONION. Hand weed through winter onions **(Sep 68)**.

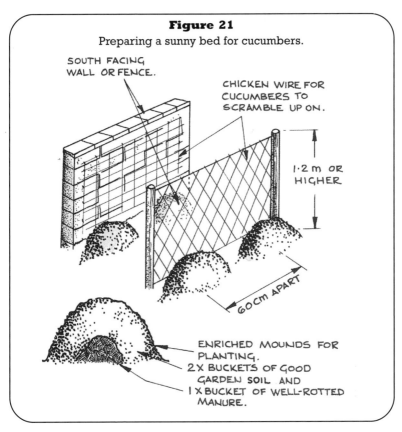

Figure 21

Preparing a sunny bed for cucumbers.

SOUTH FACING WALL OR FENCE.

CHICKEN WIRE FOR CUCUMBERS TO SCRAMBLE UP ON.

1·2 m OR HIGHER

60 cm APART

ENRICHED MOUNDS FOR PLANTING.
2 X BUCKETS OF GOOD GARDEN SOIL AND
1 X BUCKET OF WELL-ROTTED MANURE.

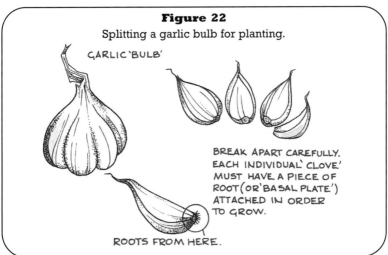

Figure 22

Splitting a garlic bulb for planting.

GARLIC 'BULB'

BREAK APART CAREFULLY. EACH INDIVIDUAL 'CLOVE' MUST HAVE A PIECE OF ROOT (OR 'BASAL PLATE') ATTACHED IN ORDER TO GROW.

ROOTS FROM HERE.

Peas & beans

52. PEA. Sow Feltham First Early individually in 9cm pots or cardboard tubes. Toilet roll inner tubes are perfect because they are long enough to accommodate a good development of roots. The young plants can then be planted in the ground without removing from the tube first, and then the tubes rot down to nothing. Pop in dried peas, one per pot/tube, 4cm deep, moisten and cover with compost.

53. Sow Mangetout and Sugar Snap **(Feb 52)**.

54. Prepare ground for early direct sowing of peas: dig a trench, fill with well-rotted manure, cover over with soil and put a cloche over the top to warm the ground slightly **(Fig. 23, p. 32)**.

55. Daily, remove autumn-sown Feltham First Early peas **(Oct 54)** to the outdoors during daytime to harden off and bring them back into the greenhouse (or a shed) at night.

56. BROAD BEAN. Remove fleece protection from autumn-sown broad beans **(Oct 53)** if the weather is improving.

57. Plant individual Aquadulce broad beans in the gaps where plants have succumbed to pests and harsh winter conditions. Pop them in 7.5cm deep at 15cm intervals.

58. Plant broad beans (e.g. Witkiem) and protect with cloches. Plant double rows, with 20cm between each row. Pop seeds in 5cm deep at 12cm intervals. Also plant a handful of beans at one end of the row. They'll come up and can be used to fill any further gaps in the future. You might need to cover with wire netting until the beans are about 15cm tall to thwart crows. If mice are a problem just swill the seeds in paraffin before planting to make them distasteful.

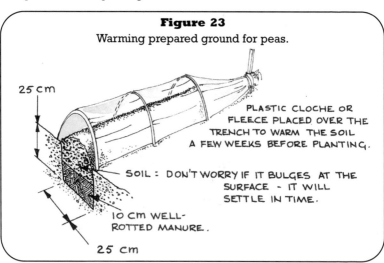

Figure 23
Warming prepared ground for peas.

25 cm

PLASTIC CLOCHE OR FLEECE PLACED OVER THE TRENCH TO WARM THE SOIL A FEW WEEKS BEFORE PLANTING.

SOIL : DON'T WORRY IF IT BULGES AT THE SURFACE - IT WILL SETTLE IN TIME.

10 cm WELL-ROTTED MANURE.

25 cm

Edible flowers

59. GLOBE ARTICHOKE. Sow Green Globe or other named variety. Pop in one seed per 9cm pot just 1.5cm deep. Keep warm, moist but not wet and in good light.

60. Hand weed around globe artichoke crowns on the plot, to stop perennial weeds becoming established.

61. Secure horticultural fleece over globe artichoke crowns if frost threatens. These are tough members of the thistle family but prefer a bit of shelter from really fierce weather. Dry bracken, leaves or straw are alternative swaddling materials. Even some twiggy, leafy prunings laid against a globe artichoke crown will help reduce the chill.

Fruit garden

62. Purchase and plant 'bare-rooted' fruit trees which have been grown in a field then dug up just prior to sale (apples and pears, maybe a Victoria plum, for example). Do this when there is no frost in the ground. Bare-rooted trees are much cheaper than specimens cultivated in pots (which can be planted any time).

63. APPLES are grown on 'rootstocks' which are adapted to suit local conditions and available space, from good soil to poor, large acreages to backyards and even pots. Apples (and pears) can be trained in all manner of so-called 'restricted' shapes or forms, e.g. espaliers – flat, single-stemmed trees with opposite branches which look like arms held out straight to the sides and are called 'laterals'; fan – two branches trained in a V shape above a short stem with other, smaller 'lateral' branches splaying off these like fingers on a hand; step-over – an espalier only one tier high **(Jun 92)**; bush – a cluster of branches held up from a short stem to look like a goblet. Notes 63a to 63e apply to trees grown as a single trunk with a spreading framework of branches.

    63a. M27, 'extremely dwarfing'. Grows not taller than an average man. Needs permanent staking and feeding with a well-rotted manure mulch annually. Suitable for pots. Fully cropping in five years. Can be planted 1.6m apart.

    63b. M9, 'very dwarfing'. 3m in height. Provide permanent support and feed with a manure mulch annually **(Nov 50)**. Fully cropping inside ten years. Ideal for small garden. Plant 3m each way.

    63c. M26, 'semi dwarfing'. 3m plus in height, support until established. Feed with a manure mulch annually **(Nov 50)**. Plant 3.6m apart.

    63d. MM106, 'semi vigorous'. Grown as 'half-standard' trees 6m high. Stake only until established. Fully cropping in eight years. Allow 6.6m between specimens.

63e. M25 (MM111), 'vigorous'. 6–9m eventually. No need for staking once established. Perfect as 'standards' for orchards and large gardens. Longer to crop than the others but can fruit prolifically. Allow 10m between trees.

63f. Older, so-called 'formatively pruned' trees (which have been partially trained to shape in the nursery) can be planted but they'll take longer to really get going than one-year-old single-stemmed 'maiden whips'. These have been growing in the nursery already for one year since being attached to their rootstock. They look like a slender twig but you'll have the pleasure (and pressure!) of training and pruning them all by yourself from the start **(see also Feb 64 to 70/Mar 90)**.

64. PEARS are grown on Quince C 'semi-dwarfing' or Quince A 'semi-vigorous' rootstock. Plant them as bare-rooted whips **(Feb 63/63f)** from 3.6m to 5.5m apart. Quince A might grow 5.5m tall, which could be too big for a small plot. Bear this in mind when planning the position of your trees.

    64a. Be warned, pear rootstock BA29 is a little more vigorous than Quince A and is inappropriate for all but the largest of gardens.

65. You'll need another compatible pear (or apple) to be certain of satisfactory cross-pollination at blossom time and subsequent fruit set. Ask for specific advice at the point of purchase. If unhappy, try elsewhere.

66. Prune maiden whips **(Feb 63f)** at planting time to the height at which you want the branches to grow from, or 'break'. For trees on dwarfing rootstocks **(Feb 63a, b, c/ Feb 64)**, and eventual 'bush' forms, this will be a little under 40cm in height at just above a strong bud, with at least three more below it **(Fig. 24A, p. 35)**. Vigorous rootstocks **(Feb 63d/63e/Feb 64/64a)**, where the trees will become 'standards', may be allowed to grow into their second year unhindered. Branches can then be encouraged to break by pruning above a strong bud at around 1.5m. Side branches, the so-called 'feathers', may be reduced by a half at this time and then removed altogether the following year (when the framework of branches above is forming). In this way a strong, clean trunk is established **(Fig. 24B, p. 35)**.

67. 'Winter prune' established pear trees grown as 'bushes' by removing all congested, diseased, dead or dying branches. Growth habit tends to be more upright than apples so keep the centre as open as possible to ensure light infiltration (to ripen fruits) and air circulation (to ward off fungal diseases). Cut summer-pruned **(Jul 93)** laterals (side stems) back to two buds only from the main stem. They then become the so-called 'fruiting spurs'. Prune main branches (leaders) by a third of the previous season's growth. This is the new wood arising from a concerti-

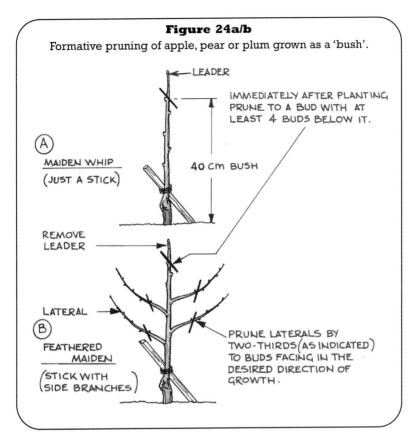

Figure 24a/b

Formative pruning of apple, pear or plum grown as a 'bush'.

LEADER

IMMEDIATELY AFTER PLANTING PRUNE TO A BUD WITH AT LEAST 4 BUDS BELOW IT.

(A)

MAIDEN WHIP
(JUST A STICK)

40 cm BUSH

REMOVE LEADER

LATERAL

(B)

FEATHERED
MAIDEN

(STICK WITH
SIDE BRANCHES)

PRUNE LATERALS BY TWO-THIRDS (AS INDICATED) TO BUDS FACING IN THE DESIRED DIRECTION OF GROWTH.

naed collar where pruned the year before. (See also **Mar 93b**).

68. 'Formatively prune' pears to be grown as 'bushes' and 'standards', as for apples **(Mar 93a)**.

69. PLUMS on Pixy rootstock are most suitable for a modest plot. Plant about 3.5m apart or closer if cultivated as a trained 'restricted' form **(Feb 63)**. Larger half-standards **(Feb 66)** can be achieved by planting on St Julien A rootstock at 4.5m intervals. Ensure suitable varieties exist nearby for cross-pollination at blossom time unless the variety is self-fertile, as in the case of the ever-popular Victoria. Ask at the nursery if in doubt.

70. MORELLO CHERRY. Tie in fan-trained Morello cherry to a network of canes against a north-facing wall **(Feb 63/Jul 107)**.

71. GENERAL. Clear weeds and grasses from around soft fruit bushes. Take care not to disturb any deeper than just below the soil surface. Blackcurrants and gooseberries especially are shallow-rooted and therefore easily damaged.

Figure 25
Preparing a tray with compost for sowing seeds.

① OVERFILL SEED TRAY WITH COMPOST. TAP IT DOWN TWICE ON A HARD SURFACE TO SETTLE.

② PUSH THIS WAY

STRIKE COMPOST LEVEL WITH A FLAT BOARD.

③ PRESS DOWN WITH A FLAT BOARD TO FIRM BUT DON'T FORCE IT.

(c) LARGE SEEDS: PREFER TO USE 9cm POTS/YOGHURT CARTON/TOILET ROLL.

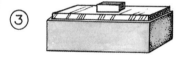

④ 1 cm

2 cm

(a) TINY SEEDS: COMPOST FLUSH WITH TOP OF SEED TRAY. e g STRAWBERRY, CELERIAC.

(b) SMALL SEEDS: COMPOST JUST BELOW RIM OF SEED TRAY. e g LETTUCE, CABBAGE.

eg SUNFLOWER BROAD BEAN.

72. GOOSEBERRY. Prune gooseberry bushes by cutting out half the number of old stems, including those that are weak, exhausted, dead or diseased

73. RED & WHITE CURRANT. Prune red and white currant 'cordons' (which are a restricted form grown with one main stem only): both recently planted and established cordons are pruned in almost exactly the

February

same way. Prune all side branches ('laterals'), and 'sub-laterals' (side branches coming from these) on an established cordon, to a bud about 2.5cm from main stem. These become the knuckle-like fruiting 'spurs'. Reduce main stem 'leader' by half of last season's growth on young plants. Ensure this is to a bud which faces in the opposite direction to the bud pruned back to the previous year so the stem keeps more or less straight. If the main stem has reached the desired height on an established cordon, then prune it back to within 2.5cm of the new growth. Completely remove all growth below 10cm to keep a clear 'leg'.

74. Propagate red and white currant cuttings in exactly the same way as for gooseberries **(Nov 60)**.

75. RASPBERRY. Plant bare-rooted raspberries ('canes') this month or March **(Jan 49)**. Dig a hole wide enough to easily accommodate the roots when well spread out, and about 7.5cm deep. Trim extra-long roots back a bit. Plant shallow, only about 5–8cm deep, and 45cm apart. Ensure the soil mark on canes matches the soil level at this point. Firm gently with the sole of your boot, not the heel. Cut all canes down, angled flush above a strong bud, between 15cm and 30cm high. Water well at this stage.

76. On established summer raspberries, either cut back canes growing beyond the top wire or weave them along it.

77. Raspberries in containers can be planted in any month.

78. STRAWBERRY. Sow strawberry (e.g. Temptation F1, Alpine or other choice varieties) **(Figs 25 and 26, pp. 36 and 37)**.

79. Put all over-wintered strawberry plants outside unless the weather is really cold. Drape a fleece over them as protection.

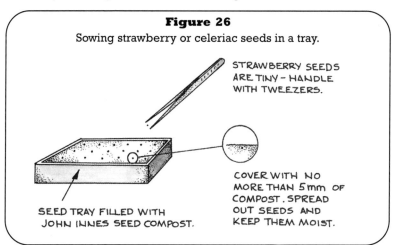

Figure 26
Sowing strawberry or celeriac seeds in a tray.

STRAWBERRY SEEDS ARE TINY – HANDLE WITH TWEEZERS.

SEED TRAY FILLED WITH JOHN INNES SEED COMPOST.

COVER WITH NO MORE THAN 5mm OF COMPOST. SPREAD OUT SEEDS AND KEEP THEM MOIST.

80. FIG. Check fastenings on horticultural fleece draped over fan-trained fig trees as protection from the elements. This should have been positioned before the first frosts and is sensibly left in place until March **(Oct 67)**.

81. GRAPE. At least a month before planting, prepare a site for grapes. Against a south or south-west facing shed or wall is ideal. Avoid thin chalk or clay soils, or waterlogged ground. Thoroughly mix grit and plenty of well-rotted manure or compost into a 60x60x60cm hole. Firm well. Provide securely tightened horizontal wires at 45cm, 75cm, 105cm spacings to bear the weight of the side branches ('laterals') and bunches of grapes. More wires can be secured at 30cm intervals if you plan to let your grape vine grow really tall. Wooden trellis is perfect also. A centrally-placed stick can be employed to support the single main stem. If planning to cultivate more than one vine allow at least 1.2m between each individual. The other best time to plant a bare-rooted (as opposed to pot-grown) grape vine is in late October. Be sure to spread the roots out well **(Mar 109/Oct 68)**.

82. COBNUT & FILBERT. Look out for male catkins dispensing clouds of yellow pollen and tiny female flowers, which are borne on short twigs as scarlet stars. Assist this pollination process by shaking branches gently when pollen is being shed **(Fig. 27, p. 38)**.

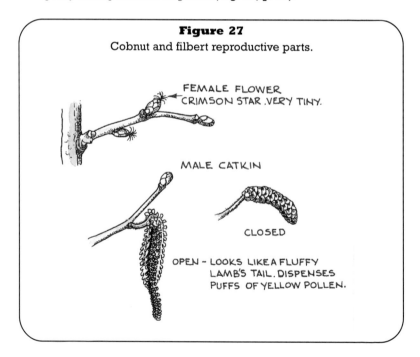

Figure 27
Cobnut and filbert reproductive parts.

FEMALE FLOWER
CRIMSON STAR .VERY TINY.

MALE CATKIN

CLOSED

OPEN – LOOKS LIKE A FLUFFY
LAMB'S TAIL. DISPENSES
PUFFS OF YELLOW POLLEN.

MARCH

Things really begin to take shape on the plot in March. If you grow potatoes in the ground as opposed to in sacks, cultivations associated with this springtime ritual significantly alter the lay of the land. Ridges and furrows appear. Planks are laid out as temporary paths that spread your weight and protect the soil.

Lines of greens and leeks stand amid a sea of rough-dug earth. In places, soil has been raked. If the weeds are growing so will the veggies. Touch the good stuff: when it's warm the time is right. Canes and string indicate where seeds have gone in.

The proximity to winter can make March feel cold and slow. Enjoy it! Potter at a steady and consistent pace. Finish groundworkings. Define your edges. Maybe even give grass paths a mow. Keep tools handy in the fruit garden.

Timetable in a gentle mooch around, tea-in-hand. Look forward. Conjure a vision of your patch of heaven in midsummer, brimming with a mix of delicious crops. Make your plans on paper.

Some of the potted salads which have served all winter in a protected environment will have a second wind if planted out. Position them in an easy to pick, sunny spot. In the greenhouse, you'll appreciate the extra space. There are pots of emerging seedlings and moist compost all over the place.

Be vigilant for slugs and snails. These big-footed monsters can wreak havoc under cover of darkness, especially when it's wet.

General jobs to do

1. Check and tend seedlings in the greenhouse or tunnel. This includes keeping them moist but not wet. Stroke emerging seedlings with the back of your hand to simulate the wind, strengthen stems and encourage strong rooting **(Fig. 28, p. 40)**.

2. In the greenhouse, take frost precautions with chitting spuds and seedlings if very cold at night. Cover with sheets of newspaper or horticultural fleece **(Fig. 18, p. 29)**.

3. Ventilate greenhouse in the mornings early in the month but for longer later on **(Fig. 29, p. 41)**.

4. Make seedling area cat-proof to stop felines from curling up on seed trays for a snooze or having a scratch and dig when helping with the chores! This will inevitably need to be some kind of barrier **(Fig. 30, p. 41)**.

5. If your seedlings are on a windowsill in the house and leaning to one side, be sure to turn the trays daily to encourage even development.

6. Clean and turn areas of the plot as crops are harvested. Keep clearing and preparing weedy ground.

7. Enlarge the plot by straightening out curved edges. Straight edges are most practical for veg production **(Fig. 31, p. 42)**. Use lines of string to mark a straight edge and a 'half-moon' edger to cut neatly.

8. Check over all areas and think about what will go where. Maybe make a planting plan on paper if not already done **(Dec 2)**.

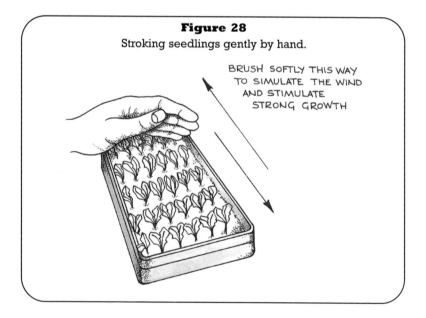

Figure 28

Stroking seedlings gently by hand.

BRUSH SOFTLY THIS WAY TO SIMULATE THE WIND AND STIMULATE STRONG GROWTH

Figure 29
Ventilation of the greenhouse during winter.

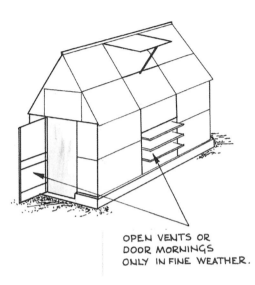

OPEN VENTS OR
DOOR MORNINGS
ONLY IN FINE WEATHER.

Figure 30
Simple cat-proof guard over seedlings in the greenhouse.

IN THE GREENHOUSE ...

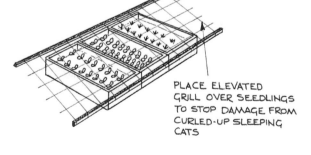

PLACE ELEVATED
GRILL OVER SEEDLINGS
TO STOP DAMAGE FROM
CURLED-UP SLEEPING
CATS

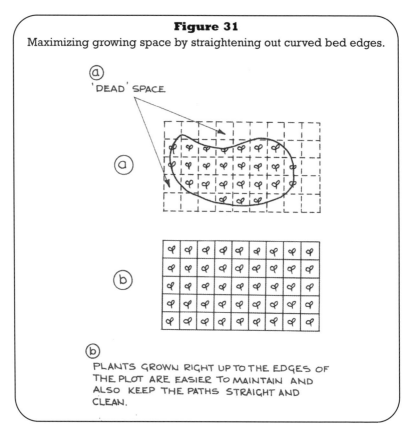

Figure 31
Maximizing growing space by straightening out curved bed edges.

(a)
'DEAD' SPACE

(a)

(b)

(b)
PLANTS GROWN RIGHT UP TO THE EDGES OF THE PLOT ARE EASIER TO MAINTAIN AND ALSO KEEP THE PATHS STRAIGHT AND CLEAN.

9. Have a good sorting and tidying session in the shed in preparation for the coming season. Organize the chaos! If everything has a place and there is a place for everything then less time will be wasted searching for the right tools for different jobs throughout the coming season. More time to enjoy the pleasures of growing!

10. Employ the hoe during dry sunny spells to annihilate weeds. Hoeing is a skill and, like anything, needs to be learnt. Tickle the blade back and forth through the soil surface with short but smooth jabbing motions. Work backwards so you leave a crumbly surface in your wake with severed weeds on top which can shrivel in the sun and wind **(Apr 7/May 6)**.

11. Tidy plot edges by removing wiry threads of encroaching couch grass and turning spoil inwards to create a shallow ditch between path and productive soil **(Fig. 32, p. 43)**.

12. Deliver sacks of horse manure to the plot. If it is fresh, put it away somewhere for six months to quietly rot down for future use **(Jun 13)**.

13. Wash dirty pots and trays to stop clutter accumulating. Like everything,

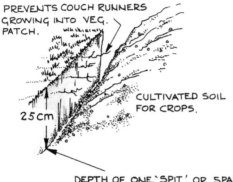

Figure 32

How to keep plot edges tidy and weed free.

TIDY PLOT EDGES BY REMOVING WIRY THREADS OF ENCROACHING COUCH GRASS AND TURNING SPOIL INWARDS TO CREATE A SHALLOW TRENCH BETWEEN PATH AND PRODUCTIVE SOIL.

PREVENTS COUCH RUNNERS GROWING INTO VEG. PATCH.

CULTIVATED SOIL FOR CROPS.

25 cm

DEPTH OF ONE 'SPIT' OR SPADE HEAD (APPROXIMATELY 25 cm)

a little and often is the way to avoid a log-jam **(Nov 20)**.

14. Have a cup of tea early each morning and listen to the birds. Quiet, reflective moments are priceless and integral to the joy of gardening.

15. Test the soil temperature. Old-timers swore by planting their bare bottoms on the earth. If it was comfortable to sit on then they deemed it acceptable to receive seeds. Nowadays a bare elbow might be more appropriate, especially on an allotment!

16. Prepare seed beds by turning weed-free soil. Then rake it level and break the lumps into crumbs. A sterile seedbed is one where a flush of weeds is allowed to germinate for two or three weeks after this raking and is then hoed into oblivion. With minimal disturbance subsequently, vegetable seeds can be sown into it without further competition.

17. Tidy away unused sticks, poles, plastic and other oddments. Useless bits should be disposed of; pieces which might prove useful again may be put aside somewhere convenient.

18. Collect hazel bean and pea sticks from the local countryside and store for future use. If any local hedge-layers are at work, offer to remove some of their cuttings **(Fig. 11, p. 22)**.

19. Scatter Phacelia seeds in plot corners for wildlife-rich green manure. Not only does the bulky plant enrich soil and add body, but if allowed to flower occasionally it will attract essential and beneficial pollinating insects that will also visit your beans and peas **(Jun 15)**.

Leaves & greens

20. BRUSSELS SPROUT, CABBAGE & KALE. Sow Brussels (e.g. Fl Hybrid
Millenium, Wellington F1, Evesham Special); cabbage (e.g. Derby Day,
Ormskirk Savoy, January King, Marner Gruwefi, Premier, Greyhound);
kale (e.g. Westland Winter, Pentland Brigg); cauliflower (e.g. Snowball)
(Figs 14 and 15, p. 25).

21. Harvest the last of the red cabbages and dig over this area.

22. LETTUCE. Prick out Dynamite and other seedlings plus kale sown in
trays during February **(Feb 27/Fig. 33, p. 44)**.

23. Sow Great Lakes, Talia, Red Merveille, Salad Bowl into trays in the
greenhouse or on a windowsill **(Fig. 14, p. 25)**.

24. Harden off Dynamite lettuces by putting outside in the day and bringing

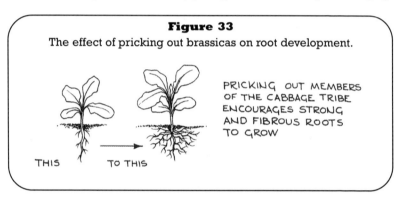

Figure 33
The effect of pricking out brassicas on root development.

PRICKING OUT MEMBERS
OF THE CABBAGE TRIBE
ENCOURAGES STRONG
AND FIBROUS ROOTS
TO GROW

THIS   TO THIS

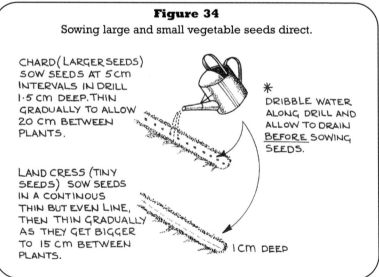

Figure 34
Sowing large and small vegetable seeds direct.

CHARD (LARGER SEEDS)
SOW SEEDS AT 5 cm
INTERVALS IN DRILL
1·5 cm DEEP. THIN
GRADUALLY TO ALLOW
20 cm BETWEEN
PLANTS.

＊
DRIBBLE WATER
ALONG DRILL AND
ALLOW TO DRAIN
BEFORE SOWING
SEEDS.

LAND CRESS (TINY
SEEDS) SOW SEEDS
IN A CONTINOUS
THIN BUT EVEN LINE,
THEN THIN GRADUALLY
AS THEY GET BIGGER
TO 15 cm BETWEEN
PLANTS.

1 cm DEEP

back into the greenhouse at night. Do the same with Hispi F1 and Greyhound cabbages and turnips for a fortnight or so before planting out. When ready to plant out, allow 20cm between lettuces which you want to form dense hearts, 45cm between cabbages and 8cm between turnips **(Apr 2)**.

25. ROCKET. Sow tiny seeds 3mm deep in plastic trays of a loam-based seed compost. They germinate swiftly, whereupon they'll need 'pricking out'.

26. Prick out rocket for growing in containers or plant out into their final resting places **(Feb 27)**.

27. KOHLRABI. Sow Partick F1 or other varieties to suit. Either sow in trays for future planting out **(Fig. 14, p. 25)** or sow direct towards month's end. Sow seeds into 1.5cm deep drills, in rows 30cm apart. Thin gradually, as the growing leaves touch their neighbours, to end up with 15cm between each plant **(May 67)**.

28. LEAF BEET. Sow Swiss chard, leaf beet, Rhubarb Leaf. Get them going in trays as for cabbages **(Fig. 14, p. 25)**, or if the weather is mild towards the latter half of March sow direct outside, 2.5cm deep in drills 30cm apart **(Fig. 34, p. 44)**. Seeds are large enough to handle individually. Plant them every 5cm or so and thin gradually until there is 20cm between plants. Use thinnings in salads or uproot carefully and plant them elsewhere. Or keep them growing tightly together and cut as 'baby leaves' when very small and young. Chard with colourful leaves can look beautiful in a flower border.

29. Remove spent Perpetual spinach plants to the compost heap or chop them up with a spade and sling them in trenches being enriched for future crops of beans **(Apr 84)**.

30. PARSLEY. Sow Moss Curled or Plain Leaved. This hardy perennial herb is suitable for growing in containers as well as a sunny position in the open garden. Soak seed overnight then sow 1cm deep direct into drills made in a fine tilth. Thin gradually to allow 23cm between individual plants **(May 67)**. If sowing more than one drill, make them 30cm apart. Alternatively, sow into trays, prick out into pots **(Feb 27)** and plant outside when roots fill their containers without being constricted.

31. CORN SALAD. Prick out D'Orlando **(Feb 27)**. This salad can be sown direct into weed-free soil or started in trays then planted out when large enough to handle at 10cm spacings. Pricking out from a seed tray allows you to keep plants in a greenhouse or on a sunny windowsill, one per 9cm pot, for earlier pickings than those left to fend for themselves outdoors. Keep moist but not wet. Harvest a leaf or three per plant each time.

32. LAND CRESS. Sow American land cress. Seeds are minute. They may

be scattered onto a seedbed and raked in, which is the easiest method. Alternatively, sow in shallow drills and barely cover with soil **(Fig. 34, p. 44)**.

33. RADISH. Sow French Breakfast. Drills need to be less than 2.5cm deep. Seeds are large enough to handle individually. Place one every 2.5cm along the drill. When they germinate and are showing a pair of seed leaves, remove every other plant or weak specimens. Keep moist **(Fig. 35, p. 47)**.

34. WINTER PURSLANE. Plant out over-wintered plants with protection. Cover plants with glass jars or plastic bottles which have had the bottoms cut off and removed **(Jan 24)**.

35. Liquid feed winter purslane once weekly a few days after planting out **(Jun 56)**.

36. KALE. Give a very diluted liquid feed to standing crops of Dwarf Green Curled kale **(Jun 56)**.

37. Clear spent plants to the compost heap. Bash the stems to a fibrous pulp with a hammer to hasten the rotting process **(Fig. 17, p. 27)**.

38. SWEDE. Clear standing swedes and 'clamp' if still usable. This is a simple process: dig a shallow trench, put the swedes into it, and cover them over. They'll be perfectly edible like this for a few weeks.

39. PEST CONTROL. Commence nightly torchlight slug patrols, both on the plot and in the greenhouse. Dispose of molluscs as you see fit **(Apr 3)**.

40. Set beer traps amongst leaves and greens to thwart slugs and snails **(Apr 3)**.

Roots, tubers & stems

41. CELERIAC. Sow Alabaster and Giant Prague. Celeriac seeds are absolutely minute so employ tweezers for ease of handling. Sow into trays when 16°C can be consistently reached. Barely cover them with compost, otherwise they'll run out of oomph before breaking the surface. Keep trays moist and shaded with glass and newspaper until seedlings have cracked the surface. Be aware that this may take some time as celeriac can be slow to germinate **(Figs 25 and 26, pp. 36 and 37)**.

42. BEETROOT. Sow Early Wonder, Detroit or Boltardy, direct into prepared ground in 2.5cm deep, pre-moistened drills. Allow up to 30cm between more than one drill **(Apr 49)**.

43. Plant out Early Wonder beetroot grown in trays at 10–15cm intervals in rows or a block.

44. JERUSALEM ARTICHOKE. Harvest the last Jerusalems, and top-dress site with compost to dig in later. Ensure every last fragment of 'choke is

Figure 35

How to sow and tend radishes from seed to harvest.

SOW RADISHES EVERY TWO WEEKS
'LITTLE AND OFTEN' FROM MID-MARCH.

(1) MARK A ROW FOR RADISHES WITH STRING TIED TIGHT BETWEEN TWO CANES. USE YOUR FINGER TO MAKE A SHALLOW TRENCH, OR 'DRILL' 2·5 cm DEEP.

(2) MOISTEN DRILL AND ALLOW TO DRAIN.

(3) SOW SEEDS EVERY 2·5cm ALONG THE DRILL.

(4) COVER SEEDS WITH SOIL AND FIRM (OR TAMP) GENTLY WITH BACK OF RAKE.

(5) REMOVE EVERY OTHER SEEDLING TO ALLOW 5 cm BETWEEN PLANTS.

(6) KEEP MOIST. PULL WHEN RED SHOULDERS ARE PLUMP AND SHOWING ABOVE THE SOIL. PULL SMALL RATHER THAN TOO BIG; LARGE RADISHES ARE WOODY.

removed otherwise they'll re-grow and disrupt the following crop. Jerusalems can be allowed to occupy a specific patch as a perennial vegetable but there is great merit in establishing them on fresh, enriched ground each year. They will perform in even the poorest soils but repay a little care and attention famously. Also, this way they won't take over the plot!

45. PARSNIP. Prepare a bed by turning and raking in a top dressing of dry wood ash (if there is any spare) to a fine tilth **(Mar 16)**. Then, if the weather is not too cold, sow parsnip seeds of your choice, such as White King. Sow where they are to crop in drills 1.5cm deep, rows 30–40cm apart. Parsnips can be sown any time between late February and May, depending on conditions of soil and weather. Parsnip seeds are very light and confetti-like so sow on a calm day or else they'll literally blow out of your hand **(Apr 60)**.

46. Clear away the last parsnips and salsify. Clamp in the garden close to the kitchen **(Mar 67)**.

47. POTATO. Deposit well-rotted manure close to a proposed potato patch. Potatoes are very hungry plants and will benefit from any fertile bulky organic matter which can be spared. Getting it close to hand is the first stage. Then calculate the space required for spuds and mark out rows with canes and string. First Early potatoes will yield from midsummer as what we call 'new' potatoes. Allow 60cm between rows and 30cm between individual seed potatoes. Second Early potatoes are ready in July and require 38cm between them. Maincrop potatoes will be dug in September/October for storage over winter to supply the dinnertime kitchen. They need more room: rows 75cm apart and each seed potato 38cm in the row **(Fig. 36, p. 50)**.

48. Commence digging and lining trenches for spuds. Excavate to a 'spit', or spade head, deep (25cm). Use string tied tight between two canes to keep the trenches straight. Enrich these spud trenches with well-rotted leaf mould, compost, manure, or whatever good stuff is to hand (avoid cooked kitchen waste which may attract rodents). Just flop a layer into the bottom.

49. If mild, plant out First and Second Early potatoes, all at 15cm deep. Remember they're liable to being nipped by frost so if any greenery is proud of the soil and a cold night is forecast, have a horticultural fleece or similar handy to drape over. Alternatively, draw a little soil over the top with a hoe.

50. HORSERADISH. Plant 15cm lengths of horseradish root into deep pots of a rich, soil-based compost **(Fig. 20, p. 30)**.

51. SCORZONERA & SALSIFY. Deeply dig a bed in preparation. These are deep-rooting vegetables so ensure soil is broken up to a generous depth to allow easy penetration **(Mar 16)**.

52. Dig out and store remaining roots from last year in boxes of barely moist compost. They'll be good to eat for a few weeks kept like this.

53. CARROT. Plan where to sow carrots and prepare this area. Merely turn the soil and rake to a fine tilth **(Mar 16)**. Do not add any organic matter, especially not manure. The idea is to get roots to plunge deep and straight in search of goodness. Having manure freshly applied near the surface simply encourages misshapen roots that 'fork and fang'. Ground enriched for a previous crop (such as cabbages or potatoes) is perfect.

54. Sow carrots of your chosen Early or Maincrop variety (e.g. Early Nantes or Autumn King) if the soil is not cold. It should be pleasant to the touch. Employ a bare elbow to check this. Sow seeds thinly along 1.5cm deep drills. Allow up to 30cm between drills if sowing more than one. Alternatively, can sow in 15cm-plus deep pots or boxes year-round for continual crops. Barely cover seeds with a light compost and keep moist. Out of the growing season put containers in the greenhouse or porch. Stump-rooted varieties, such as Paris Market, will succeed in shallow containers **(Apr 45)**.

55. TURNIP. Succession sow **(May 52)** lines of F1 Market Express, or other swift-growing variety, 1cm deep in drills up to 30cm apart. Thin gradually **(May 67)** to allow 10cm between roots. Keep moist.

56. Plant out F1 Market Express turnips sown in early February, 10cm apart, in rows or blocks.

57. RHUBARB. Keep well watered.

58. ASPARAGUS. Hand weed the bed. Ongoing and important! Don't let deep-rooted perennial weeds establish because digging later will damage the asparagus roots **(May 75)**.

59. FLORENCE FENNEL. Sow Zefa Fino or Romanesque at month's end in a warm spring, or delay until April. A sunny bed is best. Sow direct, 1cm deep with 30cm between rows. Sow thinly and evenly. The aim is for 30cm between bulbous plants later in the summer but remember that thinnings are aromatic and delicious salad additions so use wisely.

60. RADISH. Sow into moist, weed-free soil in rows about 25cm apart. Sow seeds 1.5cm deep with 2.5cm between seeds, which are large enough to handle individually **(Fig. 35, p. 47)**.

Veg fruit

61. PEPPER. Sow varieties like Ring o Fire, Long Red Marconi, Bedigo F1, Yolo Wonder or whatever varieties you fancy depending on the heat desired. Peppers need 18–21°C to germinate well. Sow in loam-based

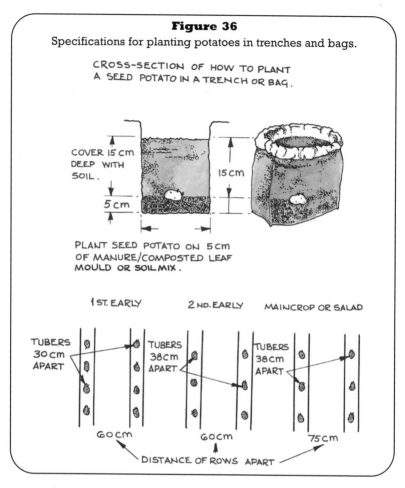

Figure 36

Specifications for planting potatoes in trenches and bags.

CROSS-SECTION OF HOW TO PLANT
A SEED POTATO IN A TRENCH OR BAG.

COVER 15 cm DEEP WITH SOIL.

15 cm

5 cm

PLANT SEED POTATO ON 5 cm
OF MANURE/COMPOSTED LEAF
MOULD OR SOIL MIX.

1 ST. EARLY   2 ND. EARLY   MAINCROP OR SALAD

TUBERS 30 cm APART

TUBERS 38 cm APART

TUBERS 38 cm APART

60 cm   60 cm   75 cm

DISTANCE OF ROWS APART

potting compost, barely covering the seeds. Keep moist and shaded until shoots are showing.

62. TOMATO. Sow varieties like Early Pak 7, Britain's Breakfast, Tumbler, Gardener's Delight. Sow as for peppers with similar heating requirements **(Mar 61)**. Germination should take 8–12 days, after which shading should be removed.

63. Pot on tomatoes which were sown earlier in the year **(Jan 33)**. Never let roots become tightly constricted in their pots. Knock them out from time to time carefully to check on progress. Pot on to a bigger container if necessary **(May 36)**.

64. AUBERGINE. Sow varieties such as Long Tom **(Mar 61)**.

65. TOMATILLO. Pot on Verde. Treat as for tomatoes at this stage. Use good quality peat-free multi-purpose compost or JI Number 2 **(Apr 22)**.

Onion tribe

66. LEEK. Sow varieties of your choice (e.g. Axima and Mammoth, Carentan 3). Sprinkle the tiny black seeds like salt and pepper on to the surface of a lightly-firmed tray of moistened compost. Then cover with 5mm of compost which has been rubbed through a sieve. Firm again gently, label and date. If the compost was thoroughly dampened before sowing there is no need to add any more water for a fortnight or so, until germination has commenced.

67. Harvest and use remaining leeks. Heel in the last of the crop near to the house – simply dig a trench, lean the leeks into this and cover their roots with a loose dollop or three of soil. Or, put them in a bucket and pack soil or compost around the sides and roots. This is very handy when positioned right outside the back door **(Fig. 37, p. 51)**.

68. ONION. Turn and rake proposed onion bed. Rake and re-rake. Do the Gardener's Shuffle **(Fig. 38, p. 53)**. The idea is not to tread it all down hard, but just to close the air spaces between soil particles so that roots snuggle down in close contact with the soil.

Figure 37
Heeling in leeks.

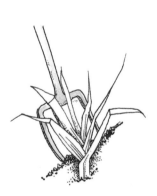 

LIFT LEEKS BY INSERTING A FORK UNDERNEATH AND LEVERING UPWARDS. PULL GENTLY UP.

MAKE A TRENCH ONE 'SPIT' DEEP AND 'HEEL' THE BUNCHED LEEKS IN, PACKING THE SOIL AROUND FIRMLY. TO BE USED WHEN NEEDED IN THE KITCHEN.

69. Plant onion sets. Red Baron and Stuttgarter Giant are two widely available varieties. Firm the bed with the Gardener's Shuffle **(Fig. 38, p. 53)**. Mark rows with string tied tight between two canes, 30cm apart if planting more than one row. Lay the miniature onions out at 10–15cm intervals then make a little nest in the soil with your finger. Nestle each set in, making sure the roots are at the bottom (!) and firm two-handed, with thumbs and first fingers. Take care not to crush or otherwise damage the onion set at this stage. Check them over daily if possible for a week to ten days and re-plant any dislodged by disturbance or pushed out by their own roots **(Fig. 39, p. 53)**.

70. Keep over-wintered onions weeded with hand and hoe. They won't look like much more than thin green shoots at this stage but fear not – bulbous swelling occurs around late April/early May. Mulch winter onions with compost, if any is available, to give them a fillip.

71. Plant out grass-like seedlings **(Jan 37)**. Space seedlings between 10 and 15cm in the row, or less if you want smaller onions. Allow 30cm between rows. Ensure the roots are fully extended at planting time rather than being scrunched up. The easiest way is to use two straight fingers to make a narrow, deep hole and caress the roots down into this. Firm the soil well around them. Avoid planting the base of the actual seedling too deep.

72. Sow spring onion (e.g. Guardsman, Toga or other varieties). There is no need to thin if not sown in clumps. For direct sowing in soil, ensure a weed-free seedbed raked to a fine tilth **(Mar 16)**. Mark drills with 15cm between and cover to a depth of 1.5cm. Ishikura is a non-bulbing variety which can be sown either on the plot, in pots or containers every few weeks for a succession of crops. They are happy when growing densely together.

73. SHALLOT. Prepare and plant a bed. This is done in the same way as for onions: rake a weed-free bed to a crumbly tilth, do the Gardener's Shuffle and rake once more to a fine tilth **(Mar 68)**. Nestle the bulbs in at 23cm intervals in rows 30cm apart.

74. Top dress shallots planted on winter solstice with wood ash. Just sprinkle handfuls between the rows. Rain will soon wash it down to the roots.

75. GARLIC. Plant garlic cloves. Break bulbs into separate cloves. Make sure a piece of the root 'basal plate' is attached to every clove or else it won't grow. Pop them in lines or blocks with 12.5cm between each. 6cm in depth is fine for spring-sown garlic **(Fig. 22, p. 31)**.

76. If shoots of autumn-sown garlic are growing erect and green, remove twigs from garlic beds (placed to keep off cats).

March

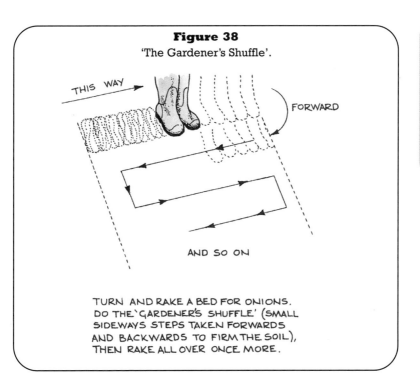

Figure 38
'The Gardener's Shuffle'.

THIS WAY

FORWARD

AND SO ON

TURN AND RAKE A BED FOR ONIONS.
DO THE 'GARDENER'S SHUFFLE' (SMALL
SIDEWAYS STEPS TAKEN FORWARDS
AND BACKWARDS TO FIRM THE SOIL),
THEN RAKE ALL OVER ONCE MORE.

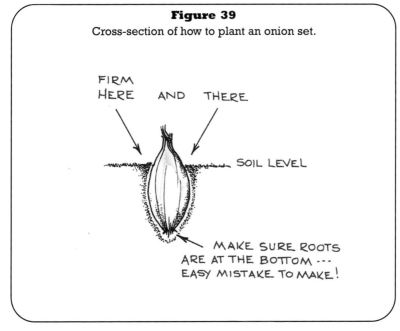

Figure 39
Cross-section of how to plant an onion set.

FIRM
HERE   AND   THERE

SOIL LEVEL

MAKE SURE ROOTS
ARE AT THE BOTTOM ---
EASY MISTAKE TO MAKE!

Peas & beans

77. PEA. Sow Sugar Snap peas in pots or containers to nurse them on undercover **(Feb 52)**. 5cm is the right depth. One per pot is fine if the pot is small. In due course the young plant can go out into the main garden with minimal disturbance to the roots, which all peas prefer **(Apr 88)**. However, don't be afraid of sowing close together (3–5cm apart) in a big pot or container, then teasing the seedlings apart when they are showing a couple of sets of leaves, taking great care not to damage the roots. Alternatively, just sow direct in a fertile drill as for normal peas at the very tail end of the month if it's mild **(Apr 86)**.

78. Prepare sunny ground for receiving Feltham First Early peas that were sown in protected pots during early December. This involves digging a one-spit deep trench (25cm) about 30cm wide, lining it with a blanket of well-rotted manure, compost or leaf mould and covering back over,

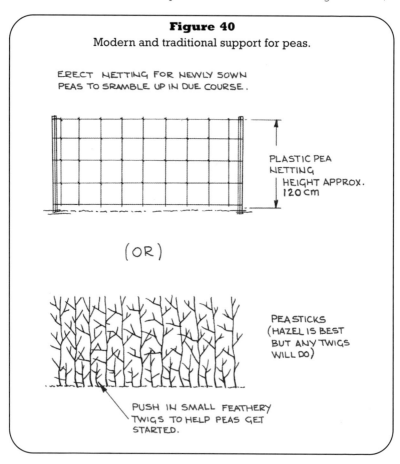

Figure 40

Modern and traditional support for peas.

ERECT NETTING FOR NEWLY SOWN
PEAS TO SRAMBLE UP IN DUE COURSE.

PLASTIC PEA
NETTING
HEIGHT APPROX.
120 cm

(OR)

PEA STICKS
(HAZEL IS BEST
BUT ANY TWIGS
WILL DO)

PUSH IN SMALL FEATHERY
TWIGS TO HELP PEAS GET
STARTED.

then raking to a neat level. This is properly called a 'bottom dressing' and will subsequently nourish the roots as they delve deep **(Fig. 23, p. 32)**.

79. Erect something for newly-sown peas to scramble up in due course. Pea netting is available in gardening outlets. Alternatively, use hazel 'pea sticks' like they did in the Olden Days **(Fig. 40, p. 54)**.

80. Plant out Feltham First Early peas into prepared ground as soon as it is pleasantly mild to the touch **(Apr 88)**. The other way of telling if soil is ready to receive seeds and young plants is to look for germinating weeds. When they're up and at 'em, the time is right!

81. BROAD BEAN. Mulch over-wintered broads with compost.

82. Pinch away side growth from autumn-sown broad beans to encourage a strong single stem. This should be done carefully so as not to damage the main stem. Use scissors or a strong thumbnail **(Fig. 41, p. 55)**.

83. Sow broad beans, variety of your choice. All being well, a crop should yield at around midsummer. Sow the chunky seeds 5cm deep at 12cm intervals in parallel rows, with 20cm between rows. Broads can go in a single row but are more stable and easier to prop up when heavy with pod when done in double rows **(Jun 83)**. Protect freshly-sown seed with a wire mesh covering, or similar, if local jackdaws have learnt to

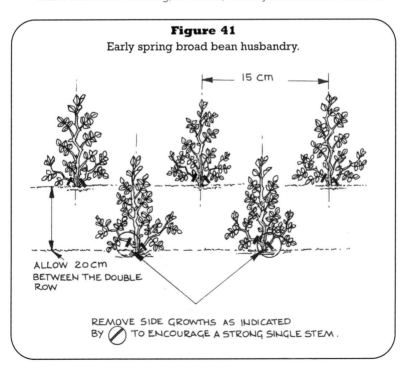

Figure 41
Early spring broad bean husbandry.

15 cm

ALLOW 20 cm
BETWEEN THE DOUBLE
ROW

REMOVE SIDE GROWTHS AS INDICATED
BY ⊘ TO ENCOURAGE A STRONG SINGLE STEM.

poke around in the soil for a hearty snack. If mice are a problem, and they can be, simply dunk the beans in paraffin prior to sowing. That should put them off!

84. RUNNER BEAN. Erect poles for runner beans. Hazel poles or bamboo canes should be positioned 20cm apart to give the plants plenty of root room. Keen builders might like to make elaborate rows, tied together at the top. But you can keep it simple too – four poles, lashed together high up, are perfectly adequate. Before runner beans become too tall you can pinch the growing tips out. It is inconvenient to let pods form beyond reach. You can't easily pick them and the development of beans inside will subdue further flowering, so use your personal reach as a guide for how high poles should be **(Apr 85)**.

Edible flowers

85. POT MARIGOLD. Broadcast-sow seeds around plot edges. Really easy – just sprinkle them along where desired to grow and rake them in to moist soil.

86. GLOBE ARTICHOKE. Remove winter protection from crowns as they start in to growth but be ready to replace it over them if frost is forecast. This may seem slightly labour-intensive but is well worth the effort. New shoots don't like being frost-nipped and will benefit in the long run from some tender loving care now.

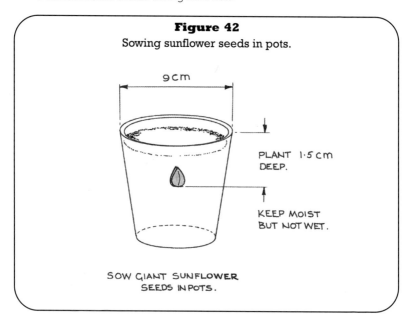

Figure 42
Sowing sunflower seeds in pots.

9cm

PLANT 1·5cm DEEP.

KEEP MOIST BUT NOT WET.

SOW GIANT SUNFLOWER SEEDS IN POTS.

87. Water globes well if there is a spring drought as they start in to growth.

88. NASTURTIUM. Sow in trays for planting out later. Very easy to grow, the big seeds can go into trays of moist compost at 2.5cm deep and 5cm apart for planting out when a pair of circular leaves have formed. Or try them individually in pots and plant out when they're a bit bigger. Or sow direct next month.

89. SUNFLOWER. Sow Giant Single in pots. These are the monsters which can reach over 3m if you're lucky. Pop the black and white striped seeds individually into 9cm pots of loam-based seed compost to a depth of 1.5cm. Keep moist but not wet. Slugs love sunflowers, so beware of these big-footed blighters from the moment a shoot emerges **(Fig. 42, p. 56)**.

Fruit garden

90. Last chance to sensibly plant out bare-rooted apples, pears, plums and other 'top fruit' on the plot or orchard **(Fig. 43, p. 58)**.

91. Apply water generously to newly-planted fruit trees if the month is dry. One or two buckets per tree is not excessive. Pour it on slowly so that run-off and wastage is minimalized. You could mould a raised ring to contain the puddle until it has soaked in **(May 126)**.

92. Top dress pears with any spare wood ash from home or bonfires. 'Top dressing' just means sprinkling the ash over the surface above where the roots will be **(Dec 36)**.

93. Prune apples and pears early in the month, before trees start into growth and their sap begins to rise.

    93a. *Formative pruning for 'bush' trees* **(Feb 63)**

        For 'maiden whips' **(Feb 63f)** which have completed their first year after planting: prune back the leading stem to the height where you want the stem to break, or split, from the buds which will burst below. Therefore, ensure at least four strong buds are beneath your cut. Leave any side shoots ('laterals'), which at this stage are also known as 'feathers'.

        Second year: select the best three or four shoots which have sprouted from buds below last year's pruning cut. These are now called 'leaders'. Reduce these leaders by a third each, flush above an outward-facing bud **(Fig. 44, p. 58)**. These leaders will now form the framework of your tree. Remove right back to the stem any others which may have sprouted below the framework.

        Third year: prune leaders by about a third to a bud which faces the direction you want growth to take. Newly-formed side shoots, or 'laterals', should be trimmed back to four buds to encourage

Figure 43
Planting a bare-rooted tree.

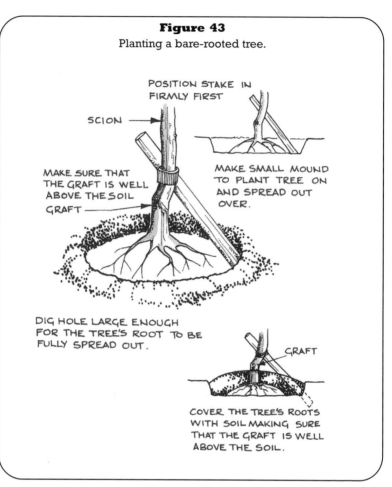

POSITION STAKE IN FIRMLY FIRST

SCION

MAKE SURE THAT THE GRAFT IS WELL ABOVE THE SOIL
GRAFT

MAKE SMALL MOUND TO PLANT TREE ON AND SPREAD OUT OVER.

DIG HOLE LARGE ENOUGH FOR THE TREE'S ROOT TO BE FULLY SPREAD OUT.

GRAFT

COVER THE TREE'S ROOTS WITH SOIL MAKING SURE THAT THE GRAFT IS WELL ABOVE THE SOIL.

Figure 44
Correct and incorrect pruning cuts.

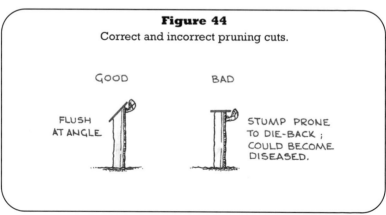

GOOD

BAD

FLUSH AT ANGLE

STUMP PRONE TO DIE-BACK ; COULD BECOME DISEASED.

the future formation of fruit-bearing spurs **(Mar 93b)**.
Subsequently: nip back the strongest, tallest leaders by a third to a bud facing in the direction you want future growth to go. Laterals can go back by half of the previous season's growth. Take out crossing and poorly-placed branches completely.

93b. *Pruning once established*

Look at the buds. Apples are 'tip bearers' or 'spur bearers'. This refers to where blossom, then fruits, form. Fruit buds are full of blossom. They are plump and fairly round. Growth buds have only leaves inside. They hug the branch and are small, compact and tight. Tip bearers tend to have fruit buds further apart and few or no spurs. Spurs form as stumpy knuckles along a branch with fat fruit buds in their midst. Some apples, confusingly, produce on tips and spurs! Observe closely. Avoid pruning out too many fruit buds for obvious reasons.

93c. 'Maintenance pruning' of older trees means removing dead, diseased, dying or crossing branches to keep an open framework which allows light and air to circulate around a ripening crop. Any amount of whippy, young stems can go back to a fruit bud but take care not to be too drastic with bigger branches. Serious dismemberment will shock the tree into producing lots of unproductive shoots. Once it's gone it can't be put back so err on the side of caution. If in doubt, remove one big branch this year and another the next. It is a gradual balancing act.

94. MORELLO CHERRY. Water newly-planted specimens liberally every month if rain is scarce.

95. GOOSEBERRY. Early in the month, plant then prune gooseberry bushes, as an alternative to doing it in October or November **(Nov 58/59)**. Ideally, select a sunny and well-drained site which is not over-prone to being frosted. Enrich the planting ground with compost or well-rotted manure and make sure the roots are well spread out. Ensure specimens show 10–20cm of 'leg' (clear stem) and four or five small branches. Imagine the bush in your mind's eye as fully grown and looking like a wine glass. Allow 1.2m between bushes. This may seem excessive in the early days but they'll soon fill the void. If growing as a cordon treat as for red and white currants **(Oct 60)**.

96. Prune newly-planted gooseberries which have enjoyed one season of growth. Reduce leaders (main stems) on each branch by half. Reduce any laterals (side shoots) to four or five buds. Completely cut out any shoots coming from the stem base (called 'suckers').

97. RED & WHITE CURRANT. Have a fleece handy to drape over red and white currant cordons **(Feb 73)** if frost is forecast while they are in flower.

98. Mulch red and white currants with well-rotted manure or compost, 5cm thick and 45cm all round, as an annual feed.

99. BLACKCURRANT. Last chance to plant, prune or sensibly propagate blackcurrant bushes **(Oct 62/63/64)**.

100. Mulch blackcurrants with old dung or compost, 5cm thick over the area of the roots if possible. Grass clippings can be mixed in too.

101. Take frost precautions for blackcurrants from month's end. Keep an ear to the forecast. Be ready to throw horticultural fleece over your crop for the night if frost threatens.

102. RASPBERRY. Mulch raspberries late in the month with a thick dressing of bulky organic matter, right along the row. Preferably use manure or compost **(Nov 50)**.

103. Water newly-planted raspberry plants generously, monthly if rainfall is in short supply **(Feb 75)**.

104. BLUEBERRY. Plant two- or three-year old 'American high bush' specimens sourced from a specialist nursery. There are a few named varieties to choose from. Selecting more than one variety will ensure maximum cross-pollination of flowers and then fruits, provided the birds don't beat you to it! Cultivate either in 45cm deep containers with

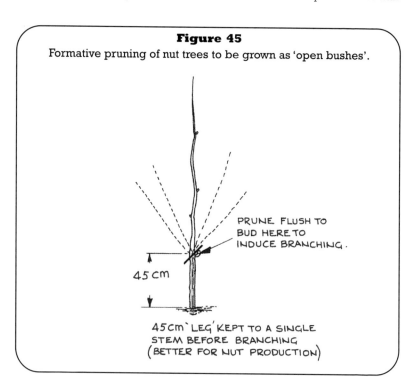

Figure 45

Formative pruning of nut trees to be grown as 'open bushes'.

PRUNE FLUSH TO BUD HERE TO INDUCE BRANCHING.

45 CM

45CM 'LEG' KEPT TO A SINGLE STEM BEFORE BRANCHING (BETTER FOR NUT PRODUCTION)

gritty, acidic ('ericaceous') compost, or direct into the ground if your garden naturally grows handsome specimens of rhododendron and azalea. If in the ground, allow 1.5m betwixt bushes. A sunny and sheltered site is ideal. Water well, especially those in pots, with rainwater only, throughout the season. Feed annually with a balanced all-round fertilizer. Pot-grown blueberries should have the top 10cm or so of compost replaced every year and receive a mulch of pine needles for their acidic and moisture-retaining qualities. Start with a two-litre pot but re-pot and increase the size every couple of years to a maximum of 50 litres.

105. STRAWBERRY. 'Spring-clean' strawberry plants. Pinch or cut off old outer leaves, weed thoroughly, snip out any old, mummified fruits and make room for a new season of productive growth.

106. FIG. Remove horticultural fleece protection from figs at month's end. Store it, clean and dry, until this coming October or November.

107. Water fig generously, as for other fruit trees **(May 126)**.

108. Snip off any dead bits from Brown Turkey fig which have been lost in a cold winter. Cut back into living wood just above a bud **(Fig. 44, p. 58)**.

109. GRAPE. Plant grape vines against a south or south-west facing wall **(Feb 81)** if possible, to be trained as a 'single cordon'. Prune all side shoots back to one bud. Cut the main shoot at 60cm just above a strong bud and tie stem to supporting, centrally-placed cane **(Oct 68)**.

110. Early in the month, nip back established cordon vines to just below the top wire. Lower the main stem (leader) to 45 degrees to stimulate bud break. When buds start popping out green growth tie the leader back on the vertical.

111. Mulch all vines with well-rotted manure or compost.

112. COBNUT & FILBERT. Formatively prune back newly-planted cobnuts and filberts for training as a 'bush' **(Fig. 45, p. 60)**.

113. Prune established bushes immediately after catkins have finished shedding pollen **(Feb 82)**. Cut brutted laterals **(Aug 85)** off completely, flush above the third or fourth buds. Reduce all main branches by one-third of growth made last year, to an outward-facing bud. Cut unbrutted side shoots back to about 10cm unless they are weak, in which case leave untouched. These often have the female flowers on them. Completely and cleanly get rid of inward-growing branches to keep the goblet-shaped bush open.

APRIL

Technically it's been spring for a few weeks now but at last, during brighter spells, you can really feel it.

Traditional lore states that the season of renewal has arrived when a maiden can place her dainty foot on seven daisies. There should be places on the lawn where you can put your boot over many more than that.

Soft and persistent rain can be reasonably expected for April. It's a beautiful thing, rain which falls like a heavy mist for hours and thoroughly moistens the soil down deep without pummelling it and flash-flooding, as a brisk and heavy deluge is wont to do. Perfect rain for sowing seeds, perfect conditions for pulling weeds. An ideal time to step outside and smell the magic on the breeze.

But sometimes this month is dry. If so, don't be shy with the watering can where flowering fruit bushes and emerging seedlings are concerned.

Indoors, this is the time to sow all those 'half-hardy' veggies that can't survive a frost but will provide earlier harvests if you get them started in pots now: think beans and members of the marrow family like courgettes, cucumbers and squashes, for example.

'Hardening off' vegetables simply means acclimatising them to the rigours of outdoor life. Before planting greenhouse-raised specimens on the plot, spend at least a week putting them outside in a sunny spot in the daytime and returning them indoors, or covering them up, at night. This induces cellular changes within the plants and will toughen them up.

General jobs to do

1. Keep all seedlings moist but not wet **(Fig.12, p.22)**.
2. Harden off plants on the verge of being planted out. Either place them outside in the sun in the daytime and put them in a greenhouse, cold frame or porch at night, or drape horticultural fleece over them at night. Hardening off induces cellular changes in plants which makes them more able to withstand the rigours of outdoor life **(Fig. 46, p. 63)**.
3. Set beer traps in the greenhouse amongst pots and trays to control slugs and snails. After dark, torchlight patrols are a good idea too and will definitely prove worth the effort. Do the same outdoors as well **(Figs 47 and 48, p. 64)**.
4. Trim grass around plot edges. Neat and tidy edges make a huge psycho-

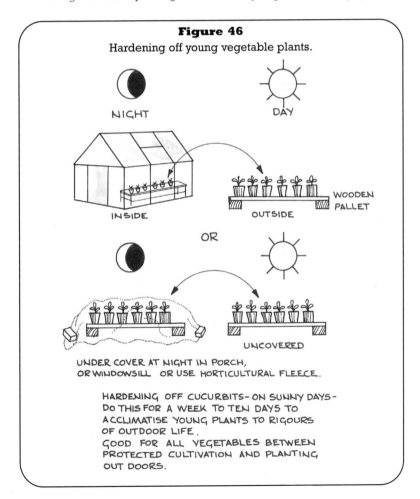

Figure 46

Hardening off young vegetable plants.

NIGHT   DAY

INSIDE   OUTSIDE   WOODEN PALLET

OR

UNCOVERED

UNDER COVER AT NIGHT IN PORCH,
OR WINDOWSILL OR USE HORTICULTURAL FLEECE.

HARDENING OFF CUCURBITS- ON SUNNY DAYS-
DO THIS FOR A WEEK TO TEN DAYS TO
ACCLIMATISE YOUNG PLANTS TO RIGOURS
OF OUTDOOR LIFE.
GOOD FOR ALL VEGETABLES BETWEEN
PROTECTED CULTIVATION AND PLANTING
OUT DOORS.

Figure 47
Searching for slugs and snails by torchlight.

COMMENCE NIGHTLY
TORCHLIGHT PATROLS
FOR SLUGS AND SNAILS.
DON'T FORGET TO LOOK
IN THE GREENHOUSE !

Figure 48
Mechanics of a beer trap.

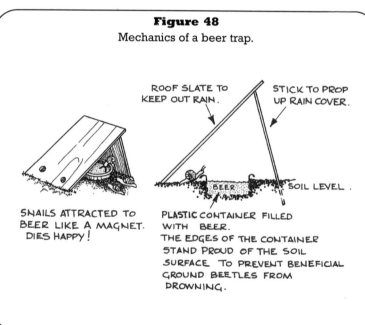

ROOF SLATE TO
KEEP OUT RAIN.

STICK TO PROP
UP RAIN COVER.

BEER

SOIL LEVEL.

SNAILS ATTRACTED TO
BEER LIKE A MAGNET.
DIES HAPPY !

PLASTIC CONTAINER FILLED
WITH BEER.
THE EDGES OF THE CONTAINER
STAND PROUD OF THE SOIL
SURFACE TO PREVENT BENEFICIAL
GROUND BEETLES FROM
DROWNING.

logical difference and inspire more work! Long-handled edging irons are quiet, sustainable (no fuel) and comfortable to use. Evenings are a good time to do this as it's a very relaxing and mellow job **(Fig. 49, p. 65)**.

5. Check all areas and crops: an ongoing year-round job, best done with a cup of tea in hand.

6. Rake level remaining rough-dug areas.

7. Hoe open ground if the soil surface is dry and the sun is shining. Don't let weeds get out of control. The best time to exercise your hoe is before a carpet of seedling weeds is visible **(Fig. 50, p. 66)**.

8. Clean out the old wormery, which is perfect for making liquid plant food with fresh comfrey and nettles. Strain off all remaining liquid into a bottle and store. Remove soggy contents and flop them around fruit trees as a mulch. Then stuff it choc-full with nettles and comfrey and start the process all over again **(Jun 8)**.

9. Keep on weeding. A little and often. Don't look at a weed and think, 'I'll have it out later,' especially if it's in flower. Do it now! Remember the old saying: 'One year's weed means seven years' seed.'

10. Potter, tidy and enjoy this fantastic time of the year! Whenever you visit the plot do something useful on the way even if it is only just fetching and carrying.

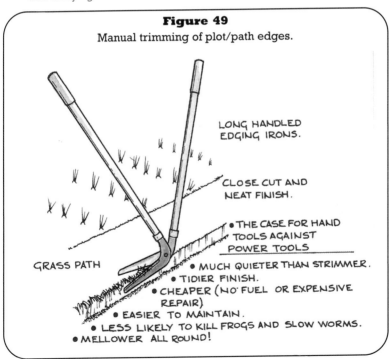

Figure 49
Manual trimming of plot/path edges.

LONG HANDLED EDGING IRONS.

CLOSE CUT AND NEAT FINISH.

THE CASE FOR HAND TOOLS AGAINST POWER TOOLS

GRASS PATH

• MUCH QUIETER THAN STRIMMER.
• TIDIER FINISH.
• CHEAPER (NO' FUEL OR EXPENSIVE REPAIR)
• EASIER TO MAINTAIN.
• LESS LIKELY TO KILL FROGS AND SLOW WORMS.
• MELLOWER ALL ROUND!

11. Slash back encroaching brambles. They grow rampantly. Wherever a spiny shoot touches the soil it will produce roots and have renewed energy. In that way a bramble patch can encroach on vacant land very quickly. Hack 'em back with a slasher, shears or a hedge trimmer. But don't get rid completely – remember that brambles produce food for free in the shape of autumnal blackberries and protect all sorts of wild creatures **(Fig. 51, p. 67)**.

12. Mow grass paths. Once-weekly attention keeps this job easy. Use a hand-pushed cylinder mower if possible. The exercise is healthy, no fossil fuels get burned and they are much more friendly on your neighbours' ears **(May 14)**.

13. Be ready to throw horticultural fleece over newly planted-out crops if the forecast is for frost. April weather and temperatures can be deceptive. Frost is a threat throughout the month, even in the English south.

14. Prepare seed beds. Beat lumpy soil with the back of a rake then turn the tool over and run the teeth over your soil, back and forth, reducing it to breadcrumb-sized particles. A sterile seedbed can be prepared three weeks in advance of sowing: prepare as described, then wait for a flush of weeds to create a green baize as they germinate. Hoe this off on a sunny morning and you remove all the immediate competition for the veggie seeds that will be sown in a few days, when weather and time permits.

15. Ventilate greenhouses and tunnels well in the day but close at night as temperatures can still be very chilly.

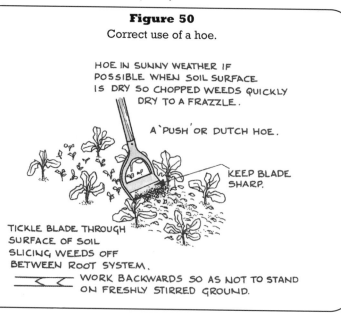

Figure 50
Correct use of a hoe.

HOE IN SUNNY WEATHER IF POSSIBLE WHEN SOIL SURFACE IS DRY SO CHOPPED WEEDS QUICKLY DRY TO A FRAZZLE.

A 'PUSH' OR DUTCH HOE.

KEEP BLADE SHARP.

TICKLE BLADE THROUGH SURFACE OF SOIL SLICING WEEDS OFF BETWEEN ROOT SYSTEM.

WORK BACKWARDS SO AS NOT TO STAND ON FRESHLY STIRRED GROUND.

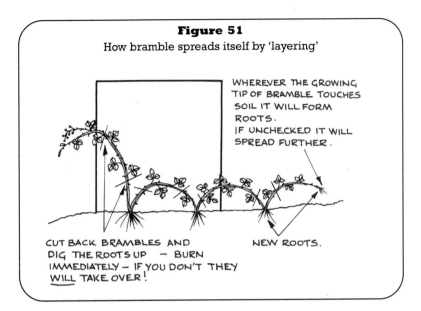

Figure 51

How bramble spreads itself by 'layering'

WHEREVER THE GROWING TIP OF BRAMBLE TOUCHES SOIL IT WILL FORM ROOTS.
IF UNCHECKED IT WILL SPREAD FURTHER.

CUT BACK BRAMBLES AND DIG THE ROOTS UP — BURN IMMEDIATELY — IF YOU DON'T THEY WILL TAKE OVER!

NEW ROOTS.

16. Amongst the whoosh of April growth, don't panic! Take your time and enjoy precious moments in the greenhouse tending your charges.

17. If your cat enjoys the greenhouse as much as you do be sure to keep her off the shelves where seedlings are growing. Puss can accidentally cause chaos in her quest for a warm spot to curl up in **(Fig. 30, p. 41)**.

Leaves & greens

18. String up take-away cartons on sticks to keep pigeons off brassicas. Unlikely to be 100% successful but well worth the effort. Looks quite pleasing too, like a tinfoil washing line **(Fig. 52, p. 68)**.

19. LETTUCE. This is a great crop to sow now **(Fig. 34, p. 44)**. Different varieties can be sown year-round – try Dynamite, Lobjoits Green Cos (so-called 'Romaine' types), Butterhead, Talia (an 'iceberg') or Salad Bowl (also called a 'cut-and-come-again'). As ever, read the blurb on the back of seed packets before making your choice. Red-leaved lettuces seem less prone to slug predation, though are never immune!

20. Plant out lettuces that are big and strong enough to cope with outdoor life. Clear plastic bottles, with their bottoms cut off, placed over your little charges provide welcome protection. Upturned jam jars do the job too, like a mini greenhouse **(Fig. 53, p. 69)**.

21. BRUSSELS SPROUT. Sow Brussels sprouts, as for winter cabbage **(Fig. 15, p. 25)**.

22. Pot on. Get earlier sowings into bigger containers with JI Number 2

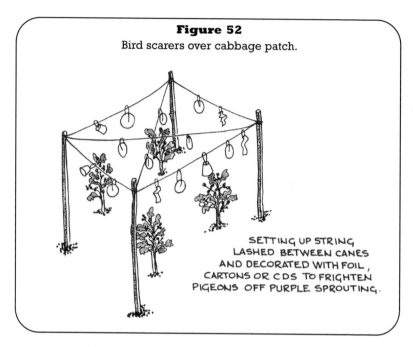

Figure 52
Bird scarers over cabbage patch.

SETTING UP STRING
LASHED BETWEEN CANES
AND DECORATED WITH FOIL,
CARTONS OR CDS TO FRIGHTEN
PIGEONS OFF PURPLE SPROUTING.

prior to planting out, or get them into the soil if there is growing space available **(Figs 54 and 55, p. 70)**.

23. CABBAGE. There is still time to sow summer cabbage (e.g. Greyhound and Hispi F1) for autumnal cropping. Sow into a seedbed **(Apr 14)** 1.5cm deep. Transplant to 30cm spacings when large enough to handle.

24. Sow winter cabbage outdoors (e.g. January King, Ormskirk Savoy or red varieties – massive choice, so look around). Sow into a seedbed 1.5cm deep. Transplant into fertile, well-dug soil at 60cm spacings when five or six leaves have formed and they're large enough to handle. Specimens sown earlier in the year might be ready to go out now. Plant deeply, up to the first set of leaves, firmly (tread down carefully) and fit a collar **(Apr 28)**.

25. Cut tops off remaining spring cabbages and cut cross slits on the stump end to encourage new growth **(Fig. 56, p. 71)**.

26. Cut anti-cabbage root fly collars from carpet underlay and store for use **(Fig. 57, p. 71)**.

27. Plant out summer cabbages such as Greyhound, sown earlier in the year **(May 37)**.

28. Plant out members of the cabbage tribe (brassicas) into firm ground and fit with collars. These are 10cm squares of carpet underlay which create a barrier and stop hatching cabbage root fly grubs from burrowing down to feast (fatally) on the roots **(May 37/Fig. 58, p. 73)**.

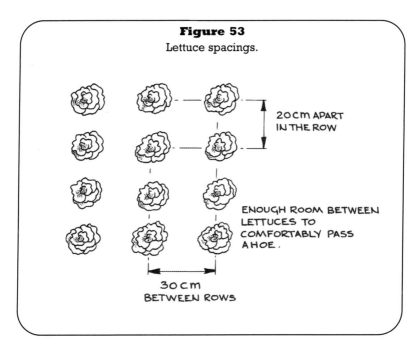

Figure 53
Lettuce spacings.

20CM APART IN THE ROW

ENOUGH ROOM BETWEEN LETTUCES TO COMFORTABLY PASS A HOE.

30CM BETWEEN ROWS

29. KALE. Try sowing Pentland Brig, Thousandhead, Westland Winter and Dwarf Green Curled, for example, but there are lots of choices regarding leaf shape, colour and taste. Shop around for seeds of a type which excites those who will grow and eat them. Start your charges off in trays **(Fig. 14, p. 25)**, prick out into pots **(Feb 27)**, then harden off **(Fig. 46, p. 63)** and plant outside in June **(May 37/Fig. 58, p. 73)**.

30. Pot on early March sowings of kale, Brussels sprouts and cabbage **(Fig. 55, p. 70)**.

31. CALABRESE. Sow Green Sprouting for late summer/autumn heads. Sow seeds 2cm deep in drills. Thin seedlings to 7cm spacings after they've emerged, then transplant with 45cm all round when five or six leaves have formed. If sowing multiple drills, allow 15cm between each drill.

32. PARSLEY. Pot on Green Curled. Make sure the roots have plenty of room to develop unrestricted. Use JI Number 2 compost or a peat-free alternative **(Fig. 55, p. 70)**.

33. LEAF BEET. Pot on Swiss chard seedlings if still making growing space available, or plant them out in final resting places at 20cm intervals. Leaves will grow big and luscious but you can pick as soon as they look good enough to eat in salads.

34. ROCKET. Sow one or more of the many rocket varieties for a quick harvest of tasty salad leaves. 'Succession sow' a little and often every fortnight **(May 52)** just 1cm deep in rows 30cm apart. Thin to 10cm

Figure 54

Removing a pot-grown specimen before planting out.

TAP HERE AND THE
POT SHOULD SLIDE
OFF EASILY.

STEM HELD GENTLY
BETWEEN MIDDLE
AND INDEX FINGER,
PALM SIDE UP.

OR

TAP THE POT ON
A HARD SURFACE
AS ILLUSTRATED.

Figure 55

Potting on young veggies.

FRESH MULTI-
PURPOSE
COMPOST OR
JOHN INNES N°2

REMOVE SMALL PLANT
WITH COMPOST AND ROOTS
INTACT, NESTLE INTO
BIGGER POT WITH ROOM
TO SPREAD SOME MORE.

TOO SMALL FOR HEALTHY
GROWTH ONCE ROOTS
ARE PUSHING OUT OF
THE DRAINAGE HOLES.

1   2

HOW TO GET A ROOTBALL OUT OF A POT INTACT.
INVERTED POT WITH SEEDLING
SUPPORTED BETWEEN FIRST AND MIDDLE
FINGER AND TAPPING POT ON BOTTOM.

Figure 56

How to get more from a spent cabbage.

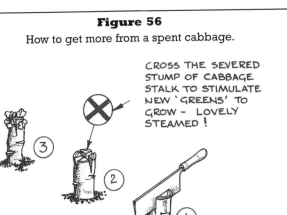

CROSS THE SEVERED STUMP OF CABBAGE STALK TO STIMULATE NEW 'GREENS' TO GROW - LOVELY STEAMED !

CUT TOPS OFF REMAINING SPRING CABBAGES AND CUT CROSS SLITS ON THE STUMP END TO ENCOURAGE NEW GROWTH.

Figure 57

Thwarting the cabbage root fly without chemicals.

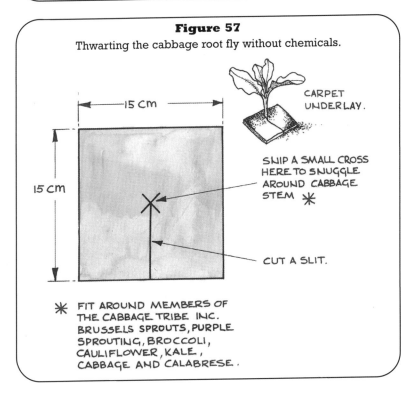

CARPET UNDERLAY.

SNIP A SMALL CROSS HERE TO SNUGGLE AROUND CABBAGE STEM *

CUT A SLIT.

15 CM

15 CM

* FIT AROUND MEMBERS OF THE CABBAGE TRIBE INC. BRUSSELS SPROUTS, PURPLE SPROUTING, BROCCOLI, CAULIFLOWER, KALE, CABBAGE AND CALABRESE.

and keep moist at all times. In dry soil they 'bolt' (run to flower then seed). Mind you, both blooms and seedpods are delicious in a sandwich **(Jun 29)**.

35. BROCCOLI. Sow Early and Late purple sprouting broccoli **(Fig. 15, p. 25)**.

36. Apply a manure mulch around the bases of Nine Star Perennial broccoli. Flop it down at least 5cm thick to feed the roots as rain and watering washes the goodness down below. This is called a 'top dressing' **(Fig. 59, p. 73)**.

37. Remove dead and brown leaves from purple sprouting broccoli. They'll come into harvest any time now. Keeping plants clean and removing pest hiding places is always a sensible thing to do. Cut heads of unopened flower buds carefully with a knife. Be sure to leave the next flush of budding portion intact, so look at what the plants are doing before you get stuck in with a knife!

38. Pull up and compost spent white sprouting plants. Bash stems with a hammer to pulverise before composting **(Fig. 17, p. 27)**. If you have the growing space you might like to let them flower. Bees and hoverflies flock to the simple blooms which are produced en masse. Treat spent kale and other cabbage family members in the same way.

39. TURNIP. Harden off greenhouse or tunnel-raised leaves and greens on the cusp of planting outside **(Fig. 46, p. 63)**.

40. LAND CRESS. Sow land (American) cress. Sprinkle seeds in a shady bed and rake in as a useful salad addition later in the year. No need to thin if scattered frugally.

41. CORN SALAD (Lamb's Lettuce). Sow in the same way as land cress **(Apr 40)**. These plants will flower and seed themselves if not hoiked out and it is helpful to let them do so in out-of-the-way places. Alternatively, sow thinly in 1.5cm deep drills and thin gradually to about 10–15cm between plants. Allow 15cm between drills if sowing more than one **(May 51)**.

42. CORIANDER. Succession sow **(May 52)** coriander either outdoors or in containers, 1.5cm deep. Most advice says not to transplant but you can so long as disturbance to the roots is minimal. Sowing one seed per compost-filled cardboard toilet tube works brilliantly and seedlings can be planted in the soil with no fuss once risk of frost has diminished. Pick regularly and sow often. Outside sowings in drills or clumps should prove successful. Keep moist. Also, save seeds and use in cooking.

Figure 58

Using cabbage collars on the plot.

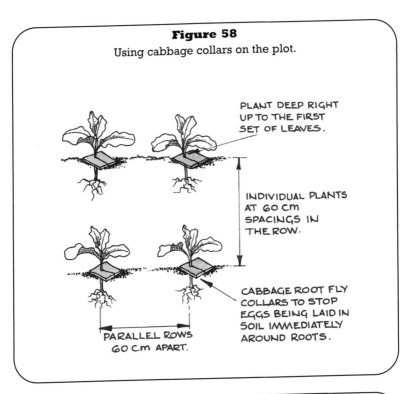

PLANT DEEP RIGHT
UP TO THE FIRST
SET OF LEAVES.

INDIVIDUAL PLANTS
AT 60 CM
SPACINGS IN
THE ROW.

CABBAGE ROOT FLY
COLLARS TO STOP
EGGS BEING LAID IN
SOIL IMMEDIATELY
AROUND ROOTS.

PARALLEL ROWS
60 CM APART.

Figure 59

Boosting Nine Star Perennial broccoli.

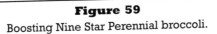
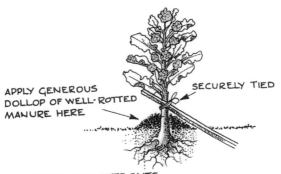

APPLY GENEROUS
DOLLOP OF WELL-ROTTED
MANURE HERE

SECURELY TIED

GOODNESS AND NUTRIENTS
WILL FILTER DOWN TO THE
ROOTS - AN IMPORTANT SPRINGTIME BOOST.

Roots, tubers & stems

43. KOHLRABI. Also known as 'turnip-rooted cabbage'. Different varieties of this flavoursome vegetable deliver green or purple-pink swollen stems. Can be succession sown **(May 52)** from February to April indoors, 1.5cm deep in trays at 13°C, pricked out into pots when large enough to handle then planted outside for cropping at 15cm intervals. Or sow a short row every fortnight, 1.5cm deep direct into a seedbed **(Mar 16)**, March to July. Thin to 15cm intervals. Thinnings can be lifted carefully and transplanted too. Keep moist, but will tolerate drought better than many other veggies. Harvest when golf ball-sized, small and crunchy rather than too big and woody.

44. TURNIP. Sow turnips (e.g. Purple Top Milan, Snowball or F1 Market Express) –1.5cm deep in drills up to 30cm apart should suffice. Keep moist, especially early on when leaf-nibbling Flea beetles are a

---

Figure 60
Sowing and growing carrots in pots and containers.

USE TWEEZERS TO HANDLE SEEDS INDIVIDUALLY. PLACE SEEDS IN CIRCLES AROUND THE OUTSIDE WITH 2 CM BETWEEN EACH ONE AND BARELY COVER. KEEP MOIST BUT NOT WET.

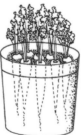

USE A DEEPER POT FOR LONG, FINGER-THIN ROOTS. eg AMSTERDAM FORCING

CAN USE A SHALLOW CONTAINER FOR 'STUMP ROOTED' CARROTS eg PARIS MARKET.

menace, and thin gradually to 10cm spacings (or closer for smaller roots). Given fertile, slightly alkaline soil, turnips should perform famously.

45. RADISH. In pots, sow French Breakfast radishes and CARROTS (Amsterdam Forcing). Radishes are very rapid developers when kept warm and moist. Sow seeds 1.5cm deep and 4cm apart. Carrots are brilliant in deep pots for long-rooted types like Amsterdam Forcing or boxes for intermediate (e.g. Berlicum) and stump-rooted types (e.g. Paris Market). Remember to provide drainage holes in the bottom. A sandy compost is best. Sow individual seeds with tweezers 1cm deep

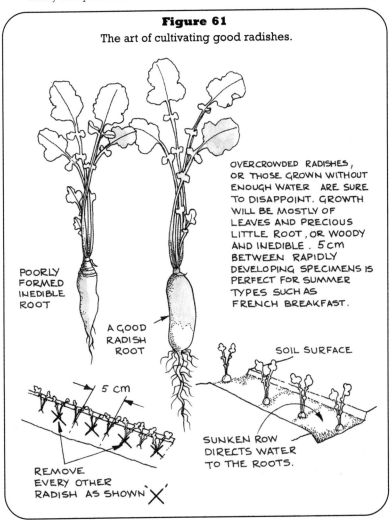

Figure 61
The art of cultivating good radishes.

OVERCROWDED RADISHES, OR THOSE GROWN WITHOUT ENOUGH WATER ARE SURE TO DISAPPOINT. GROWTH WILL BE MOSTLY OF LEAVES AND PRECIOUS LITTLE ROOT, OR WOODY AND INEDIBLE. 5cm BETWEEN RAPIDLY DEVELOPING SPECIMENS IS PERFECT FOR SUMMER TYPES SUCH AS FRENCH BREAKFAST.

POORLY FORMED INEDIBLE ROOT

A GOOD RADISH ROOT

5 cm

REMOVE EVERY OTHER RADISH AS SHOWN ✗

SOIL SURFACE

SUNKEN ROW DIRECTS WATER TO THE ROOTS.

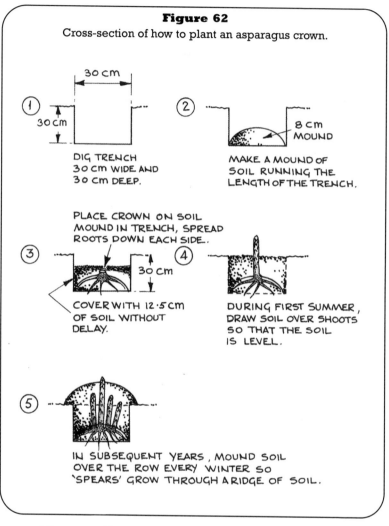

Figure 62

Cross-section of how to plant an asparagus crown.

① 30 cm / 30 cm
DIG TRENCH 30 cm WIDE AND 30 cm DEEP.

② 8 cm MOUND
MAKE A MOUND OF SOIL RUNNING THE LENGTH OF THE TRENCH.

③ PLACE CROWN ON SOIL MOUND IN TRENCH, SPREAD ROOTS DOWN EACH SIDE.
30 cm
COVER WITH 12·5 cm OF SOIL WITHOUT DELAY.

④ DURING FIRST SUMMER, DRAW SOIL OVER SHOOTS SO THAT THE SOIL IS LEVEL.

⑤ IN SUBSEQUENT YEARS, MOUND SOIL OVER THE ROW EVERY WINTER SO 'SPEARS' GROW THROUGH A RIDGE OF SOIL.

and 2cm apart. Time-consuming but worth it and very relaxing. Thin every other developing root for tender, aromatic salads or let them jostle and plunge. Pull at any stage you like once roots start forming. A couple of pots prepared like this keep clean and fresh homegrown carrots on the menu year-round (can be brought into a greenhouse or porch in freezing conditions during winter). Only thin out if sown in dense clumps or you accidentally dropped a load of seeds (easily done) **(Fig. 60, p. 74)**.

46. Thin out radishes sown towards the end of March **(Fig. 61, p. 75)**.

47. ASPARAGUS. Plant asparagus crowns. The bed must be prepared in advance **(Oct 36)** because crowns need planting as soon as purchased or delivered through the post from a reputable supplier. They dry out really easily so soak them for an hour in water immediately prior to planting. Make a ridge along the middle of the trenches and sit the crowns atop this, spreading the rubbery roots down either side. Cover with 12.5cm of earth straight away before positioning and planting the next crown. There is little further to do for the first year except keep scrupulously weed-free by hand **(Fig. 62, p. 76)**.

48. Keep a newly-planted asparagus bed well watered.

49. BEETROOT. Sow beetroot (e.g. Detroit 2 or Boltardy), in 2.5cm deep drills. Moisten the drill prior to sowing thinly along the bottom and

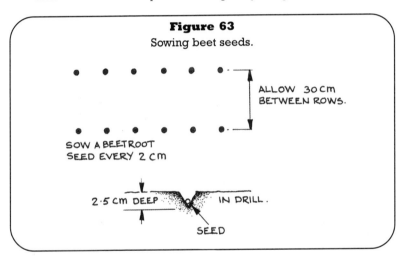

Figure 63
Sowing beet seeds.

ALLOW 30 cm BETWEEN ROWS.

SOW A BEETROOT SEED EVERY 2 cm

2·5 cm DEEP   IN DRILL.

SEED

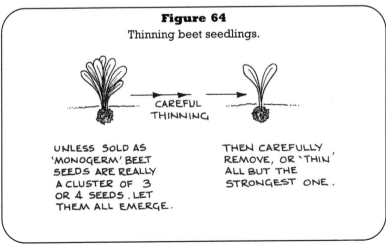

Figure 64
Thinning beet seedlings.

CAREFUL THINNING

UNLESS SOLD AS 'MONOGERM' BEET SEEDS ARE REALLY A CLUSTER OF 3 OR 4 SEEDS. LET THEM ALL EMERGE.

THEN CAREFULLY REMOVE, OR 'THIN' ALL BUT THE STRONGEST ONE.

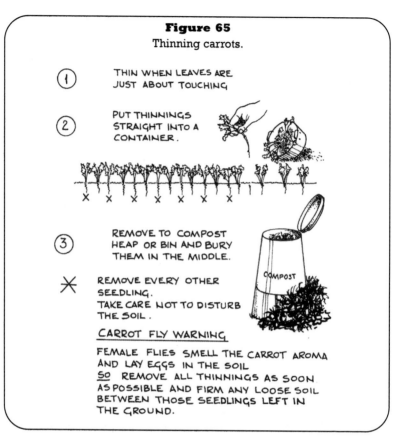

Figure 65
Thinning carrots.

① THIN WHEN LEAVES ARE JUST ABOUT TOUCHING

② PUT THINNINGS STRAIGHT INTO A CONTAINER.

③ REMOVE TO COMPOST HEAP OR BIN AND BURY THEM IN THE MIDDLE.

✳ REMOVE EVERY OTHER SEEDLING.
TAKE CARE NOT TO DISTURB THE SOIL.

CARROT FLY WARNING

FEMALE FLIES SMELL THE CARROT AROMA AND LAY EGGS IN THE SOIL
SO REMOVE ALL THINNINGS AS SOON AS POSSIBLE AND FIRM ANY LOOSE SOIL BETWEEN THOSE SEEDLINGS LEFT IN THE GROUND.

covering over. 'Tamp' down with the flat end of a rake (i.e. firm it gently and evenly). Remember to mark your row with an identification label and the date. If sowing more than one row, allow 30cm between **(Fig. 63, p. 77)**.

50. Thin beetroot when clusters of seedlings have germinated. Select the strongest one to nurture and pull or pinch out the rest. Do this in stages, as leaves are touching, so that eventually 13–15cm separates each plant **(Fig. 64, p. 77)**.

51. CARROT. First thinning required for Armetis carrots sown early March **(Fig. 65, p. 78)**.

52. Sow carrots in pots **(Apr 45)**.

53. POTATO. Plant Second Early and Maincrop potatoes. Individual Second Early seed potatoes should go in at 38cm intervals in previously prepared rows, with rows 60cm apart if planting more than one. Maincrops need the same distance in the row, but rows should be 75cm apart as they need more room **(Fig. 36, p. 50)**.

54. Dig trench for Pink Fir Apple or other 'salad' potatoes (the varieties best boiled and allowed to cool before eating). Treat as for Maincrop potatoes **(Fig. 36, p. 50)**.

55. Dig out any overlooked spuds from last year that are sprouting as weeds. Known as 'volunteers', they can transmit disease from one year to the next. You might well get a harvest in due course, but in the interests of biosecurity it's best to pull and burn the tops ('haulm') of volunteers as soon as possible.

56. SALSIFY & SCORZONERA. 'Station sow' early in the month. Popping three or four seeds in a cluster no more than 2cm deep at anything up to 15cm intervals is fine. The term 'station sow' refers to this practice of sowing a pinch of seeds together in precise positions as opposed to sprinkling them along the drill in a line (which is also perfectly acceptable) **(Fig. 66, p. 79)**.

57. Thin seedlings. When grass-like shoots have arched up and out of the soil it is time to select the strongest and best-looking for nurturing and eventual harvest. Discard the others by pulling and composting. Take care not to disrupt the soil surface too much. Aim for anything up to 15cm between plants eventually.

58. Last season's plants which have not been dug for roots can be allowed

---

Figure 66
Two ways of sowing parsnip seeds.

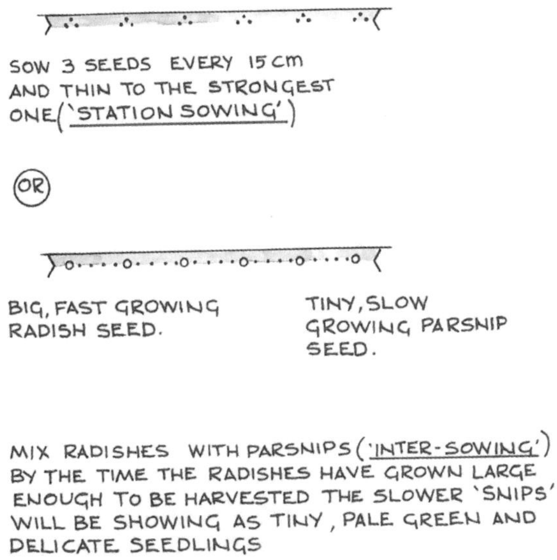

SOW 3 SEEDS EVERY 15 CM
AND THIN TO THE STRONGEST
ONE ('STATION SOWING')

BIG, FAST GROWING
RADISH SEED.

TINY, SLOW
GROWING PARSNIP
SEED.

MIX RADISHES WITH PARSNIPS ('INTER-SOWING')
BY THE TIME THE RADISHES HAVE GROWN LARGE
ENOUGH TO BE HARVESTED THE SLOWER 'SNIPS'
WILL BE SHOWING AS TINY, PALE GREEN AND
DELICATE SEEDLINGS

---

to flower in late spring/early summer. The unopened buds are remarkably similar to asparagus in taste when cut with a length of stem, steamed for a minute and served with a knob of margarine.

59. PARSNIP. Check over parsnips for signs of a fledgling crop amongst the weeds. They're notoriously slow germinators and can quickly be overwhelmed by weeds so stay busy and focused. Weed by hand, not hoe, at this delicate stage.

60. Re-sow parsnips if germination has been patchy. This job can be done right up until mid-May **(Fig. 66, p. 79)**.

61. JERUSALEM ARTICHOKE. Weed amongst new shoots of Jerusalem artichoke. And keep weeding around all fledgling crops. Weeds compete for moisture, nutrients, light and space. Freedom from this competition helps all vegetables grow handsome and strong.

62. Plant a row of Fuseau Jerusalem artichokes. 10cm deep at 30cm intervals in straight lines is perfect. This variety is much smoother than some of the knobbly types available, and thus much easier to cope with in the kitchen (less hassle and waste). If planting more than one row, allow 90cm between rows.

63. FLORENCE FENNEL. Sow Florence fennel direct into a sunny prepared bed **(Mar 16)**. 1cm deep with 30cm between rows should do. Sow thinly. Gradually remove seedlings then young plants until there is 20–25cm between specimens. Keep moist to avoid running to seed **(Mar 59)**.

Veg fruit

64. SQUASH. Sow after the middle of the month in a protected environment (greenhouse, windowsill or cold frame). There are dozens of different varieties. Summer squashes such as Custard White are more like marrows in that they need eating in summer and autumn rather than being kept for later. Winter squashes (e.g. Hubbard, Uchiki Kuri and Butternut Waltham) can be stored for several months in a cool, frost-free shed. Read the seed packet blurb to see what suits your needs. Some warmth is desirable, 20–25°C if possible. Pop in one seed per 9cm pot – plant the seeds on their edges to avoid collecting water on the upper surface and rotting. 2cm deep is perfect. Let them germinate and grow on in their pots. Planting outside is only safe after the risk of frost has passed in mid-May, or later in the north, so it may be necessary to pot on once more before then into a larger container. Have something suitable just in case this happens **(Fig. 67, p. 81)**.

65. Take a delivery of straw for mulching marrows and squashes later in the summer. It will suppress weeds and keep the fruits clean. Old

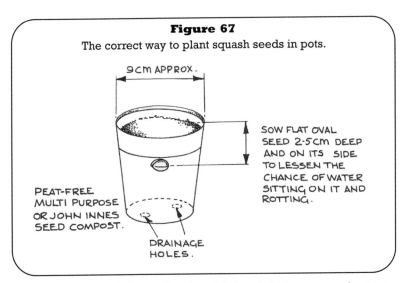

Figure 67

The correct way to plant squash seeds in pots.

9CM APPROX.

SOW FLAT OVAL SEED 2·5CM DEEP AND ON ITS SIDE TO LESSEN THE CHANCE OF WATER SITTING ON IT AND ROTTING.

PEAT-FREE MULTI PURPOSE OR JOHN INNES SEED COMPOST.

DRAINAGE HOLES.

thatching straw is free and perfect if that sort of thing goes on in your neighbourhood.

66. TOMATO. Sow tomatoes if you missed the boat in March or earlier **(Mar 61/62)**.

67. Start to pot up tomato seedlings. Prick them out of trays **(Feb 27)** and plant in 9cm pots of multi-purpose compost or JI Number 1.

68. Pot on tomatoes that are growing fast and need more root room. Bigger pots and JI Number 2 should suffice **(Fig. 55, p. 70)**.

69. Plant out Early Pak 7 tomatoes or other varieties for outdoor cultivation into rich soil in a sunny position. Use glass cloches for extra protection. Allow 45cm betwixt each plant.

70. COURGETTE, MARROW, CUCUMBER. Sow one or more varieties of the dozens available for all these fruiting veggies. If planning to grow cucumbers outside then make sure it is a 'ridge' variety suitable for outdoor cultivation and not specially bred for greenhouses only. Read the blurb on the seed packet! Sow seeds in exactly the same way as for squash **(Apr 64)**.

71. AUBERGINE. Sow seeds this month. Long Tom is a good one for indoors but there are plenty to choose from. In a hot summer, crops will bear outside in a sunny bed. Temperature required for germination is between 16–21°C. Can nestle them into trays, 1cm deep, for pricking out into pots when large enough to handle, or sow two seeds per 9cm pot and remove the weaker of the two. Will need bigger pots in due course **(Mar 61)**.

72. PEPPER. Sow peppers **(Mar 61)**.

73. TOMATILLO. Sow tomatillo in trays of seed compost. Handle the disc-like seeds with tweezers and pop in 1cm deep on their edges, 3cm apart. Prick out into 9cm pots when large enough to handle **(Feb 27)**. Can be sown direct into warm soil during a fine spring but will need plenty of room as they are bushy plants eventually.

Onion tribe

74. LEEK. Sow leeks in trays or the ground if none have been sown earlier. Musselburgh is a reliable variety. Barely cover the seeds with compost or soil. For sowing directly on the plot, 1.5cm deep drills can be as close as 10cm parallel because the grass-like seedlings will be moved to another place before they start competing with each other.

75. Plant out leeks sown in trays during February into a nursery bed. Rake weed-free soil to a fine tilth. Thoroughly moisten with water. Use a bamboo cane or narrow stick to create 5cm-deep holes at about 8cm intervals in a line or grid. Tease seedling leeks from their tray. Handle by leaf tips only. Pop them in one per hole. Roots might need slight trimming. Ensure roots are not doubled up and sticking proud of the surface. Don't fill the holes, but do water with a fine rose on your can. Let the holes close naturally after a daily water for three to four days. Keep moist and weed-free until leeks are of pencil thickness **(Fig. 68, p. 83)**.

76. ONION. Sow spring onions. 1cm deep in drills as close as 10cm apart will suffice. Or sow them between rows of carrots because they complement the health of each other. Avoiding sowing too thickly will mean there is no need to do any thinning out later. They can grow well very close together, but not on top of each other! Sprinkle seeds into a pot if you have no soil available.

77. Hoe winter onions. They'll be swelling soon so remove all competition from weeds **(Fig. 50, p. 66)**.

78. Check recently planted maincrop onions daily until their roots have anchored into the soil. Replace any turfed out by the weather, birds or cats **(Dec 29)**.

79. Hoe between onion sets with a bent kitchen knife for close control **(Jul 8)**.

80. SHALLOT, GARLIC. Water well. A thorough decent soaking every now and then is most helpful as bulbs swell, rather than an occasional light sprinkling. Keep the hoe busy.

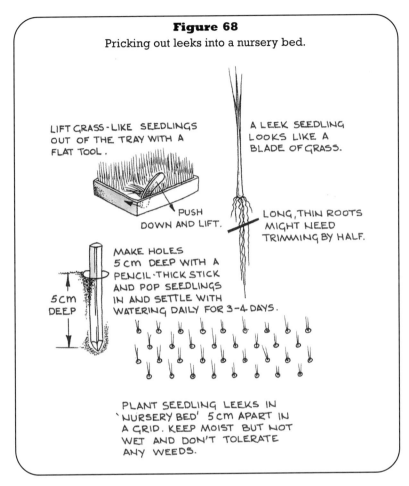

Figure 68

Pricking out leeks into a nursery bed.

LIFT GRASS-LIKE SEEDLINGS OUT OF THE TRAY WITH A FLAT TOOL.

A LEEK SEEDLING LOOKS LIKE A BLADE OF GRASS.

PUSH DOWN AND LIFT.

LONG, THIN ROOTS MIGHT NEED TRIMMING BY HALF.

MAKE HOLES 5cm DEEP WITH A PENCIL-THICK STICK AND POP SEEDLINGS IN AND SETTLE WITH WATERING DAILY FOR 3-4 DAYS.

5cm DEEP

PLANT SEEDLING LEEKS IN 'NURSERY BED' 5cm APART IN A GRID. KEEP MOIST BUT NOT WET AND DON'T TOLERATE ANY WEEDS.

Peas & beans

81. Pop down to the woods and collect some hazel pea sticks and bean poles for future use **(Fig. 11, p. 22)**.

82. RUNNER & FRENCH BEAN. Sow runner, dwarf and climbing French beans, varieties to suit you. They are unable to cope with frost but sowing now, one seed per 9cm compost-filled pot at 4-5cm deep, will get you an earlier crop. Keep moist and in good light on a windowsill or in the greenhouse, ready to plant outside in mid-May (in the south) or at the end of that month in the north. Flowers and pods of these nutritious veggies can be a range of single or mixed colours so consult the seed packet or catalogue blurb before selecting. If birds have been a problem flowers then remember that white-flowered runner beans often suffer less (try White Emergo) **(Fig. 69, p. 84)**.

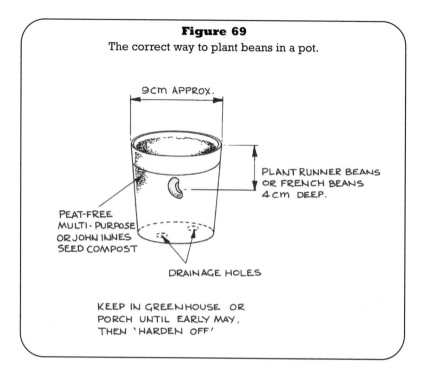

Figure 69
The correct way to plant beans in a pot.

9cm APPROX.

PLANT RUNNER BEANS
OR FRENCH BEANS
4cm DEEP.

PEAT-FREE
MULTI-PURPOSE
OR JOHN INNES
SEED COMPOST

DRAINAGE HOLES

KEEP IN GREENHOUSE OR
PORCH UNTIL EARLY MAY,
THEN 'HARDEN OFF'

83. Borlotti beans can be sown the same way as above **(Apr 82)**. These should be given a framework to climb up and left to dry in the autumn. Beans can then be collected and stored in air-tight jars for winter stews.
84. Dig a trench for planting runner beans in May. Fill it with well-rotted manure or green waste, cover over and allow to settle. Mark the position with canes and string.
85. Erect runner bean poles with 20cm between poles **(Fig. 70, p. 85)**.
86. PEA. Sow Sugar Snap peas where they are to crop. Use a swan-necked hoe to take out a 15cm wide, 5cm deep drill **(Fig. 71, p. 86)**.
87. Place cloches or other frost-proof covering over Sugar Snap peas at night if a frost is forecast; remove in the daytime.
88. Plant out Sugar Snap peas sown in containers or cardboard tubes at the end of March **(Mar 77)**. They can go as close together as 5cm apart. Make sure that pea sticks or netting is already in place for them to clamber up **(Figs 40 and 72, pp. 54 and 86)**.
89. Adjust and tend to pea plants trying to get a grip up their supports.
90. Sow Greenshaft and Mangetout peas in deep pots, toilet roll tubes, or direct **(Fig. 71, p. 86)**.
91. Erect wigwam of hazel twigs for peas in pots to climb up.
92. Plant out Feltham First Early peas planted in toilet rolls early April. Have

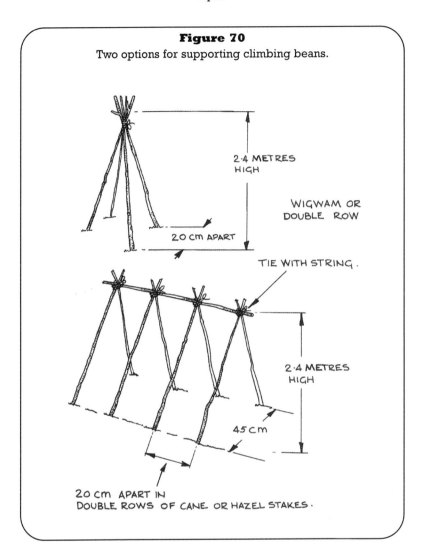

Figure 70
Two options for supporting climbing beans.

2·4 METRES HIGH

WIGWAM OR DOUBLE ROW

20 cm APART

TIE WITH STRING.

2·4 METRES HIGH

45 cm

20 cm APART IN DOUBLE ROWS OF CANE OR HAZEL STAKES.

a climbing frame already erected **(Apr 88)**.

93. BROAD BEAN. Hand weed autumn-sown Aquadulce broad beans **(Oct 53)**.

94. Mulch autumn-sown Aquadulce broad beans with fresh grass mowings. Thoroughly moisten the ground first, then lay the grass mowings down.

95. Sow more broad beans for a succession of crops. If you want to be technical, bear in mind that the Windsor varieties are best for spring or early summer sowing. Pods are shorter than autumn types (the Longpods, which are hardier) but their flavour is superior. If space is tight, go for a dwarf variety. The Sutton is classic in this respect **(Mar 83)**.

Figure 71

How to sow peas in a sunken drill.

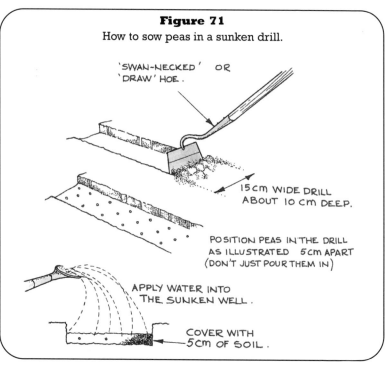

'SWAN-NECKED' OR 'DRAW' HOE.

15cm WIDE DRILL ABOUT 10 cm DEEP.

POSITION PEAS IN THE DRILL AS ILLUSTRATED 5cm APART (DON'T JUST POUR THEM IN)

APPLY WATER INTO THE SUNKEN WELL.

COVER WITH 5cm OF SOIL.

Figure 72

Planting peas raised in toilet roll tubes.

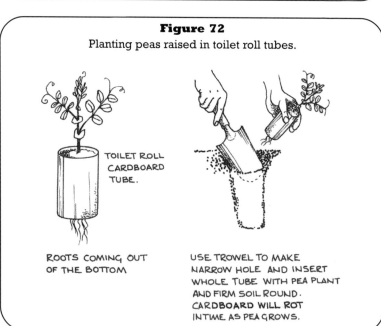

TOILET ROLL CARDBOARD TUBE.

ROOTS COMING OUT OF THE BOTTOM

USE TROWEL TO MAKE NARROW HOLE AND INSERT WHOLE TUBE WITH PEA PLANT AND FIRM SOIL ROUND. CARDBOARD WILL ROT IN TIME AS PEA GROWS.

Edible flowers

96. SUNFLOWER. Pot on sunflower, Giant Single, into larger containers **(Fig. 73, p. 87)**.

97. Plant out sunflowers if the weather is kind, but watch out for slugs and snails in the wet **(Fig. 48, p. 64)**.

98. GLOBE ARTICHOKE. Plant out potted-up globe artichokes that have been carefully nurtured through the winter. Give them 90cm of clear space all round as they will grow quite big. Water generously.

99. POT MARIGOLD. Prick out seedlings where they are to grow, or as specimens in pots close to the back door (where petals can be harvested for a colourful salad garnish).

100. Sow seeds direct, 2cm deep around the plot edges. If growing in rows, allow 30cm either side.

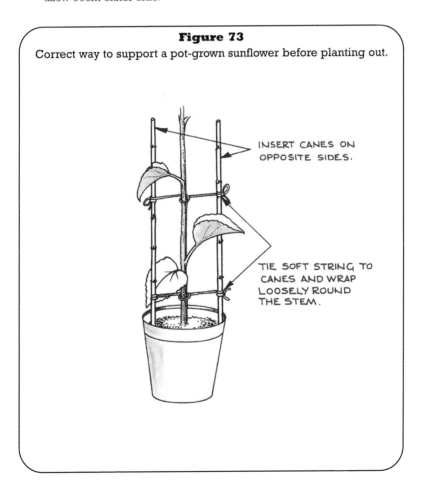

Figure 73

Correct way to support a pot-grown sunflower before planting out.

INSERT CANES ON OPPOSITE SIDES.

TIE SOFT STRING TO CANES AND WRAP LOOSELY ROUND THE STEM.

Cereals

101. SWEETCORN. Sow 2cm deep in 9cm pots or cardboard tubes. Moisten but don't soak.

Fruit garden

102. APPLE & PEAR. Rub off unwanted buds from the trunks of recently-planted apple and pear trees to keep the trunk clean until the point where you want it to 'break' **(Feb 66)**.

103. Early in the month, tidy and mulch around top-fruits (apple, pear, plum). Thoroughly weed, then apply a 5cm-thick mulch of well-rotted manure in a 60cm or so circumference around the stem base. Be sure that the mulch does not touch the stem or bury the swollen kink near the base of the stem **(Nov 50)**, which is the grafted junction of rootstock **(Feb 63 to 63e)** and the named variety ('scion').

104. Plant container-grown apple, pear and plum trees. This can be done in any month as long as the ground is not frozen or waterlogged. Dig a hole slightly wider and deeper than the pot your trees are growing in. Fill with water, allow to drain. Then line the hole with compost or well-rotted manure. Remove tree from pot, keeping root-ball intact. If it is tightly congested tease out the roots slightly. Otherwise, slip it into the hole snugly. Firm soil around the sides but be sure to keep the top of the compost level with the surface of the soil. In other words, don't plant it too deep. Also, don't have the root-ball standing proud of the soil! Take care to ensure a good fit. If extra support is needed, knock in a stout stake at an angle to avoid puncturing the root-ball. Position this stake on the side of the stem which is away from prevailing winds to avoid accidental rubbing against the bark, which may cause damage **(Fig. 74, p. 89)**.

105. PLUM. Early in the month, formatively prune young plums and other 'stone fruits' as the buds begin to open. Never prune in winter as fatal fungal diseases can result. Formatively prune a young tree as for apples to encourage a well-balanced head **(Mar 93a)**.

106. MORELLO CHERRY. On a fan-trained specimen **(Feb 63)**, prune out shoots facing directly in or outwards.

107. BLACKCURRANT & GOOSEBERRY. Frost precautions **(Mar 101)**.

108. Cut back encroaching brambles from blackcurrant and gooseberry bushes to keep future fruits accessible. Bramble can spread fast and become a nuisance **(Apr 11)**.

109. RED & WHITE CURRANT. Take frost precautions on red and white currant cordons **(Mar 101)**.

110. RASPBERRY. When new green shoots are showing well around newly-

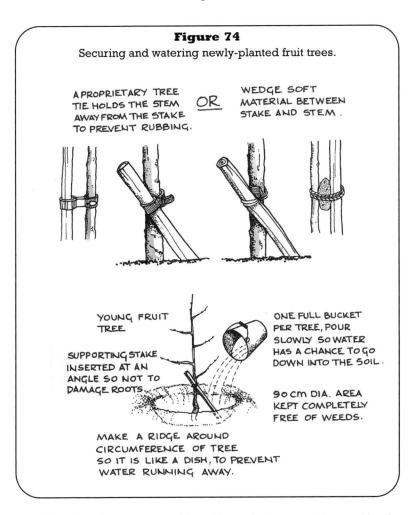

Figure 74

Securing and watering newly-planted fruit trees.

A PROPRIETARY TREE TIE HOLDS THE STEM AWAY FROM THE STAKE TO PREVENT RUBBING.

OR

WEDGE SOFT MATERIAL BETWEEN STAKE AND STEM.

YOUNG FRUIT TREE

SUPPORTING STAKE INSERTED AT AN ANGLE SO NOT TO DAMAGE ROOTS

ONE FULL BUCKET PER TREE, POUR SLOWLY SO WATER HAS A CHANCE TO GO DOWN INTO THE SOIL.

90 CM DIA. AREA KEPT COMPLETELY FREE OF WEEDS.

MAKE A RIDGE AROUND CIRCUMFERENCE OF TREE SO IT IS LIKE A DISH, TO PREVENT WATER RUNNING AWAY.

planted raspberry canes cut the old, woody stump out at ground level.

111. BLACKBERRY, TAYBERRY, LOGANBERRY & RELATIONS. Water copiously every month on thin, dry ground. Mulch with compost or well-rotted manure if feeling especially generous **(Mar 100)**.

112. Start training the canes in whatever way is convenient, such as spread-out fans on a wall, upright against a post, over an arch, on wires as for raspberries **(Jan 49)**. Can be allowed to ramble but will not be easy to manage in the long run!

113. Plant out specimens propagated by tip layering **(Jul 103)**. Just snip off the original cane cleanly with secateurs at about 30cm, lift the root-ball which has magically sprouted, plus any new growth, and plant where desired.

114. STRAWBERRY. Mulch strawberries at month's end instead of waiting until May **(May 133)**.

115. Prick out Alpine and other strawberries into pots **(Feb 27)**. 9cm pots will give roots room to settle and spread.

116. GRAPE. Newly-planted vines being trained as a cordon must develop fruit bearing 'spurs' alternately up the stem at 30cm intervals. So, rub out any side shoots which won't be needed before they get too big and tie the others to their horizontal supports **(Feb 81)**.

117. Towards month's end, on established single stem or 'cordon' vines, thin shoots on knuckle-like 'spurs' to the two strongest. Look for embryonic flower bunches (future grapes). Tie the stronger shoot with flowers on to the wire or trellis. Use the other only if this first one fails for any reason (prune out before it gets longer than 10cm). If neither show flowers, retain the stronger.

118. COBNUT & FILBERT. Water all fruit and nut trees thoroughly, especially youngsters yet to fully establish **(Mar 91)**.

MAY

May is arguably one of the most exciting months of the year –
midsummer is still weeks away. The air hangs thick with the
promise of magic, dreams to come and be fulfilled.

Things should be rocking and rolling in the
edible garden by now.

Potatoes will need attention.

Young plants in pots should be hardened off and planted out.
Many of the cabbage tribe will be well on the way, full of lust for
life and strapping of leaf from soft spring rains.

Peas and broad beans could be flowering, but runners, French
beans, courgettes, their relatives and others are wisely held back
indoors until around the 15th of the month in the south, or the
end of May up north – a sharp late frost will nip them and lay a
lot of your hard work to waste.

Salad days are here again! Individual leaves can be plucked a
few per plant before they heart up. They'll taste better than
anything money could buy from the shops, pre-packed, pumped
full of chemicals and air. 'Cut-and-come-again' lettuces have the
added bonus of re-growing harvested portions almost daily.

Asparagus is on the menu all month long. Just before you want to
eat them, cut the spears with a sharp knife and care, slightly
below the soil surface. Steam in minimal water and splash with a
dressing to suit your taste.

Exercise the hoe regularly when the soil surface is dry to keep
rampant weeds at bay. Cut paths and edges weekly from now on.

Think ahead. It's still the season for sowing winter roots.

General jobs to do

1. Keep water butts filled via a hosepipe if there's a natural shortage. Having bodies of water stored strategically to minimize carrying distances is very encouraging at the end of a long day.
2. Keep crops moist but not wet.
3. Keep refreshing beer traps every few days when the beer goes stale. Slosh it, and the mollusc bodies, on to the compost heap **(Fig. 48, p. 64)**.
4. Undertake nightly slug and snail patrols with a torch in greenhouse and open garden. Collect pests and deal with as you prefer **(Fig. 47, p. 64)**.
5. Check over seedlings and developing crops. Watching them grow is amazing. Signs of pests and diseases can be detected, and treated, early **(Jun 58/Fig. 75, p. 92)**.
6. Keep on top of the weeding, especially horsetail and bindweed. Keep your hoe busy. Do a little bit every time you visit the plot. This is the secret to keeping ground clear for the vegetables **(Figs 76 and 77, pp. 93 and 94)**.
7. Cut edges of plot to keep clear and tidy **(Fig. 49, p. 65)**.
8. Tidy out the shed. Save valuable time and keep organized: put tools away, cleaned, after use; sort out essential bits and bobs, take pride in the fact that you know where 'stuff' is as and when you might need it **(Nov 2)**.
9. Keep paths clear. Put trip hazards somewhere that they are not a nuisance.

Figure 75
Wildlife-friendly methods to encourage natural slug control.

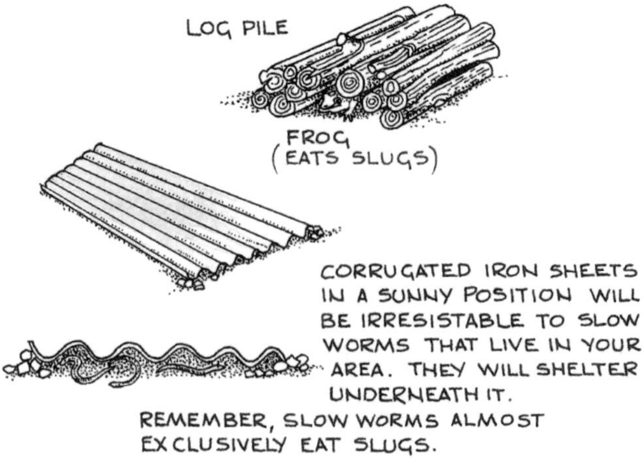

LOG PILE

FROG
(EATS SLUGS)

CORRUGATED IRON SHEETS IN A SUNNY POSITION WILL BE IRRESISTABLE TO SLOW WORMS THAT LIVE IN YOUR AREA. THEY WILL SHELTER UNDERNEATH IT.
REMEMBER, SLOW WORMS ALMOST EXCLUSIVELY EAT SLUGS.

Figure 76
Don't let those weeds go to seed!

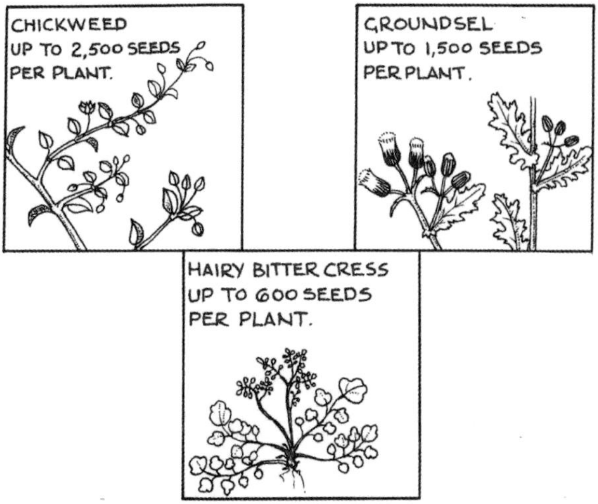

CHICKWEED
UP TO 2,500 SEEDS
PER PLANT.

GROUNDSEL
UP TO 1,500 SEEDS
PER PLANT.

HAIRY BITTER CRESS
UP TO 600 SEEDS
PER PLANT.

10. Water seedlings if conditions are dry. Give a weekly thorough soaking rather than daily sprinkle **(May 27)**.
11. Once past the seedling stage, vegetables benefit from a drop of home-made nettle and comfrey feed added to the watering can. Add just a drop, enough to slightly taint the water **(Fig. 78, p. 95)**.
12. Cut more nettles and comfrey. These plants are at their potent best in early summer so keep topping up your liquid-feed bin.
13. Water all young fruit trees and bushes with a watering can to get water where you want it – at the roots. Apply the water slowly so it gets a chance to absorb in and not just run off. Making a mounded ring around the stem, about 50cm away, will contain water like a bowl and make sure it goes where you want it to. One whole can or bucket per plant is not excessive.
14. Keep grass paths cut on a weekly basis. The longer grass gets, the harder work this job becomes **(Fig. 79, p. 96)**.
15. Deliver sacks of horse manure for later use. Put them out of the way. Well-rotted manure is full of worms and extremely valuable to edible gardeners for feeding crops **(Jun 13)**.
16. Keep thinning rows of seedling veggies. Follow specific guidelines for different crops (information which should be found on the seed packets, so always keep and file these for future reference) but as a guide, when one plant's leaves are touching their neighbour's that is the time to remove every other seedling **(May 67)**.

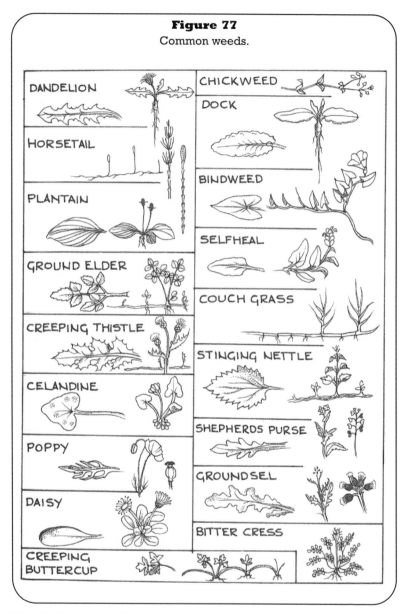

Figure 77
Common weeds.

17. Cut back vegetation which lolls over the path sides. Easy access, especially in wet weather, often makes the difference between thinking, 'Yes, I'll do so-and-so,' as opposed to, 'Nah, leave it 'till tomorrow.'

18. Hoe between lines of veg at every opportunity. If you can see barely a weed and the soil surface is dry, that's the time to do it **(Fig. 50, p. 66)**.

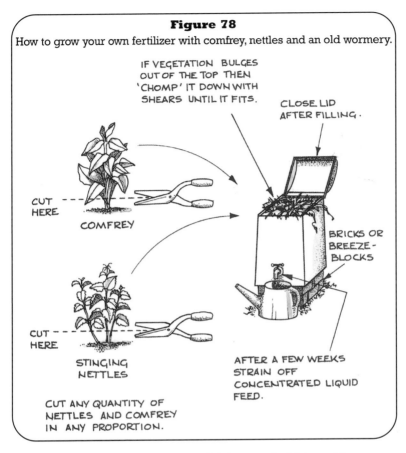

Figure 78

How to grow your own fertilizer with comfrey, nettles and an old wormery.

IF VEGETATION BULGES OUT OF THE TOP THEN 'CHOMP' IT DOWN WITH SHEARS UNTIL IT FITS.

CLOSE LID AFTER FILLING.

CUT HERE

COMFREY

BRICKS OR BREEZE-BLOCKS

CUT HERE

STINGING NETTLES

AFTER A FEW WEEKS STRAIN OFF CONCENTRATED LIQUID FEED.

CUT ANY QUANTITY OF NETTLES AND COMFREY IN ANY PROPORTION.

19. Take time to just stand and stare. This is a wonderful time of the year. Enjoy May while it lasts.

20. Strain off concentrated liquid nettle and comfrey juice from old wormery and decant into storage bottles for future use **(Fig. 78, p. 95)**.

21. Water all potted veg and seedling crops. Containers can become dry very quickly. Daily watering is required.

22. Enjoy priceless moments on the plot with young relations, showing them the amazing things that happen. Get the nervous or inexperienced to do some watering. Those with more confidence can get their hands dirty with some thinning or weeding. Collect manure from common land with youngsters to show them the magical life in piles of poo!

23. Have a summer bonfire with young friends and neighbours after a session watering and weeding on the plot to inspire their interest in gardening and the great outdoors.

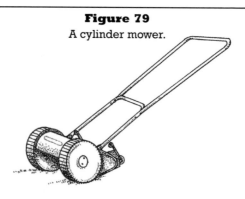

Figure 79
A cylinder mower.

VIRTUES: NO EXTERNAL POWER SOURCE OR FUEL NEEDED.
GOOD HEALTHY EXERCISE.
LIGHT AND EASY TO HANDLE. IF USED
REGULARY THE JOB IS NEVER TOO
STRENUOUS : ONCE A WEEK IN THE
GROWING SEASON (LATE MARCH – OCT.) IS IDEAL.

CAUTION! ALWAYS WALK THROUGH GRASS FIRST TO
CLEAR FROGS, TOADS AND SLOW WORMS.

24. Clean out dirty water butts and refill. Stale water can harbour diseases which might affect tender seedlings.

25. Use shears to tame rank grasses and weeds around the compost bins. It's no fun getting stung by nettles when you're trying to do the right thing with kitchen and garden waste **(Jul 2)**.

26. Sweep concrete paths. Only takes five minutes but is very pleasing to the eye.

27. Monitor watering demands of seedlings and developing crops in pots and grow bags. Drying out can be fatal for seedlings, wasting much time and effort **(Fig. 80, p. 97)**.

28. Ventilate the greenhouse well, especially in hot weather.

29. In the greenhouse, check tomatoes and other crops daily for pests and diseases **(Jun 58)** and also watering needs.

Leaves & greens

30. BROCCOLI. Still time to sow purple sprouting (indoors March to May, see **Fig. 14, p. 25**, outside April to June). For outside sowings, take out a 1.5cm deep drill in a weed-free seedbed **(Mar 16)**. Fill with water and allow to drain. Sprinkle seeds along this, not too thickly, cover and firm soil gently ('tamp') with the back of a rake or your hand. Keep

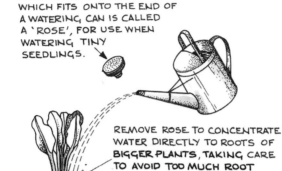

Figure 80

Effective watering direct to plant roots in dry weather.

PERFORATED ATTACHMENT
WHICH FITS ONTO THE END OF
A WATERING CAN IS CALLED
A 'ROSE', FOR USE WHEN
WATERING TINY
SEEDLINGS.

REMOVE ROSE TO CONCENTRATE
WATER DIRECTLY TO ROOTS OF
BIGGER PLANTS, TAKING CARE
TO AVOID TOO MUCH ROOT
DISTURBANCE.

seedlings well moistened once they're up (14–21 days). When about 10cm tall, lift and transplant to final resting places with 60cm of space all round.

31. Clear away spent purple sprouting plants to the compost heap. Bash up the stems to hasten rotting **(Fig. 17, p. 27)**. Pick up and remove any old carpet underlay put down at planting-out time to thwart the cabbage root fly.

32. Harvest Nine Star Perennial broccoli. Cut heads when they look like small white cauliflowers. Take care not to remove embryonic florets which will get bigger and take over from the main heads after they've been cut.

33. Sow Nine Star Perennial broccoli to replace tired plants in the future. Treat as for broccoli and other green-leaved brassicas **(May 30)**.

34. BRUSSELS SPROUT, CALABRESE, CABBAGE, KALE. Clear last year's exhausted cabbage plants to the compost heap. Weed, hoe and rake soil to a fine and level tilth **(Fig. 17, p. 27)**.

35. Sow calabrese, January King and Savoy cabbages. Pop the pinhead-sized seeds 1.5cm deep and about 4cm apart, in trays **(Fig.14, p.25)**. Those sown early in the month will need pricking out **(Feb 27)** by month's end. Keep moist and in a good light position.

36. Pot on kale, Brussels sprouts and cabbages if roots are constricted in their pots (look underneath at the drainage holes – if white, thread-like roots are showing then it's time to go into something a little bigger) **(Fig. 55, p. 70)**.

37. Alternatively, plant outside in their final resting places. Prepare a bed

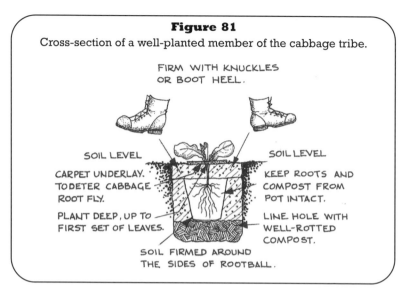

Figure 81

Cross-section of a well-planted member of the cabbage tribe.

FIRM WITH KNUCKLES
OR BOOT HEEL.

SOIL LEVEL

SOIL LEVEL

CARPET UNDERLAY.
TO DETER CABBAGE
ROOT FLY.

KEEP ROOTS AND
COMPOST FROM
POT INTACT.

PLANT DEEP, UP TO
FIRST SET OF LEAVES.

LINE HOLE WITH
WELL-ROTTED
COMPOST.

SOIL FIRMED AROUND
THE SIDES OF ROOTBALL.

by doing the Gardener's Shuffle **(Fig. 38, p. 53)** and raking to a level. Use a trowel to excavate planting holes 60cm apart in rows or blocks. Thoroughly soak then enrich planting holes with a generous dollop of well-rotted manure. Plant firmly and deep – up to the first set of leaves for all brassicas **(Fig. 81, p. 98)**.

38. Pot on red cabbage then place outside to harden off for a week to ten days **(Fig. 46, p. 63)**.

39. CAULIFLOWER. Pot on cauliflowers very carefully, with minimal disturbance to roots. Or nestle into their final resting places with 60cm between plants **(Fig. 81, p. 98)**.

40. LETTUCE. Pot on Salad Bowl lettuce for growing in containers **(Fig. 55, p. 70)**.

41. Sow lettuces of the Iceberg varieties (e.g. Sandringham) direct in pre-moistened 1.5cm deep drills (30cm apart if sowing more than one) for cropping later in the summer **(May 30)**.

42. Remove cloches from protected salads and lettuces so you can get in amongst them for a thorough weeding session. No need to replace now.

43. Plant out lettuces **(Fig. 53, p. 69)**.

44. Keep an eye on lettuce seedlings (from a mid-April sowing) and thin out to give developing plants room to grow without undue competition for space, water, nutrients and light. And sow more lettuces, varieties of your choice, for successional crops of baby leaves, big leaves or hearts **(May 41)**.

45. Plant out various lettuces amongst the Brussels sprouts as a 'catch crop'. Especially helpful if space is at a premium. Lettuces will be

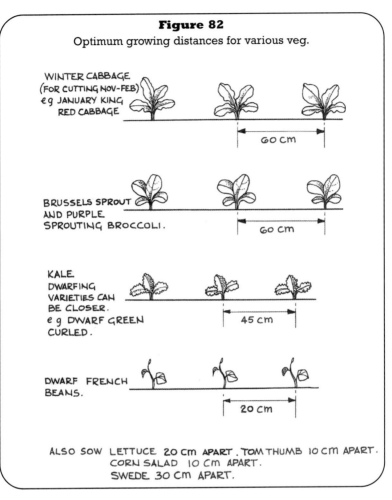

Figure 82

Optimum growing distances for various veg.

WINTER CABBAGE
(FOR CUTTING NOV-FEB)
eg JANUARY KING
RED CABBAGE

60 cm

BRUSSELS SPROUT
AND PURPLE
SPROUTING BROCCOLI.

60 cm

KALE.
DWARFING
VARIETIES CAN
BE CLOSER.
e g DWARF GREEN
CURLED.

45 cm

DWARF FRENCH
BEANS.

20 cm

ALSO SOW LETTUCE 20 cm APART. TOM THUMB 10 cm APART.
CORN SALAD 10 cm APART.
SWEDE 30 cm APART.

harvested well before they start adversely competing with their slower-growing neighbours.

46. LAND CRESS. Sow American land cress in trays or outside, where it is to grow **(Apr 40)**.

47. Liquid feed for broad beans, established lettuces, greens, spinach and chard. Put a capful of nettle and comfrey concentrate **(Fig. 78, p. 95)** into a watering can, just enough to taint the water. Do not apply to seedlings. Even like this it'll be too rich and can kill them; seedlings don't need feeding.

48. LEAF BEET. Sow Swiss chard and leaf beet for successional crops **(May 52)** of mature leaves or young salad pickings. For mature crops sow 1cm deep in pre-moistened drills and allow 30–45cm between rows (they get big). For baby leaf salads rows can be much closer, 10cm or so.

49. Sow spinach. Be aware that this leafy crop will run to seed rapidly in dry weather so keep moist at all times. Succession sow **(May 52)** March–July in 2.5cm deep drills, 30cm apart. Thin **(May 67)** to allow up to 15cm between plants. Pick regularly.

50. CORN SALAD, WINTER PURSLANE. Clear away spent corn salad and winter purslane plants unless they are to be allowed to flower and set seed.

51. Plant out corn salad seedlings. Space is not really an issue with these so pop them in wherever you have a bit of spare ground, or plant in containers (10cm apart is fine) **(Fig. 82, p. 99)**.

52. ROCKET. Sow one or more of the many rocket varieties for a quick harvest of tasty salad leaves. 'Succession sow' a little and often every fortnight just 1cm deep in 30cm apart rows. Thin to 10cm and keep moist at all times. In dry soil they 'bolt' (run to flower then seed). Mind you, both blooms and seedpods are delicious in a sandwich **(Jun 29)**.

Roots, tubers & stems

53. CELERIAC. Harden off **(Fig. 46, p. 63)**, then plant out celeriac. Allow 30–40cm between plants for generous swelling. Celeriac does not want to be planted too deep at this stage. Make sure the small swelling at the top of the stem (below the leaves) is proud of the soil surface. Celeriac responds well to generous applications of water so it is a good idea to plant a row in a sunken drill, made with a draw hoe, which retains all artificial watering within close confines of the celeriac roots **(Fig. 83, p. 101)**.

54. Pot on celeriac which is not ready yet to go out. By now roots should be fibrous and well developed. Lift carefully from small pots or modules and ease into something bigger with fresh potting compost. Handle by the leaf tips only and use a flat spatula to position the roots (a wooden lolly stick is perfect).

55. Prick out later-sown celeriac seedlings into individual pots **(Feb 27)**.

56. Make another sowing of celeriac as insurance **(Fig. 26, p. 37)**.

57. POTATO. Earth-up spuds. It's important to cover the leafage ('haulm') as it grows. This action encourages formation of more tubers in the darkness of underground. A light covering of soil will also afford some protection from frost, so if a nip is forecast use a swan-necked hoe to draw some soil over the top. Fresh grass mowings will do the same and feed the soil subsequently **(Fig. 84, p. 102)**.

58. Water potatoes generously if rain is not forthcoming. They need

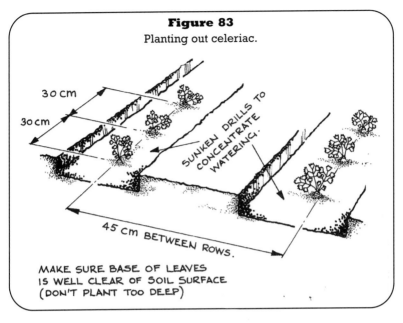

Figure 83
Planting out celeriac.

30 cm

30 cm

SUNKEN DRILLS TO CONCENTRATE WATERING.

45 cm BETWEEN ROWS.

MAKE SURE BASE OF LEAVES
IS WELL CLEAR OF SOIL SURFACE
(DON'T PLANT TOO DEEP)

moisture to swell. Don't employ a sprinkler system which might encourage fungal diseases. Plus, a lot of water will evaporate before getting into the soil anyway. Instead, thoroughly drench the bed in sections with an open-ended hose laid out on the ground.

59. Keep hoiking out last year's spuds which are sprouting as weeds and could pass on disease. They are called 'volunteers' and, although you might well get a modest crop, the danger they pose as vectors for disease is not worth the risk **(Fig. 85, p. 103)**.

60. SCORZONERA & SALSIFY. Hand weed. Seedlings are grass-like. Take care not to mistakenly pull them up. Remove the weakest and nurture the strongest **(Apr 56)**.

61. PARSNIP. Tend tiny parsnips. It is important to keep competition from weeds down as emergent parsnip seedlings get easily swamped by them.

62. CARROT. Sow carrots in pots, one seed every 2cm and just 1cm deep **(Apr 45)**. Or sow into pre-moistened drills at 1.5cm depth, rows at 30cm apart if more than one **(Fig. 60, p. 74)**.

63. Thin carrot seedlings (from a mid-April sowing). Be sure to dispose of the thinnings immediately. Bury them in the middle of your compost heap to avoid pests sniffing them out (carrot root fly specifically). Firm the soil around remaining carrots for the same reason **(Fig. 65, p. 78)**.

64. Thin out carrots sown in pots. Use tweezers instead of clumsy fingers.

65. Re-sow carrots if germination has been patchy. Failures are part and

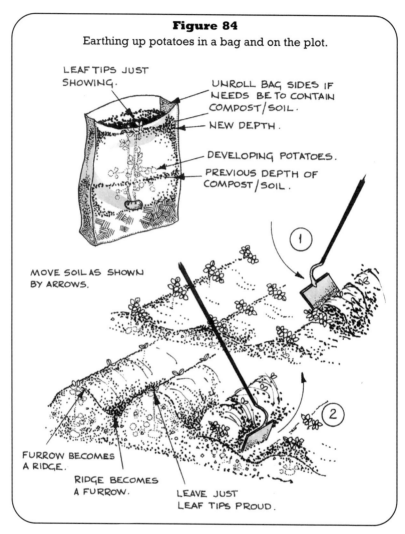

Figure 84

Earthing up potatoes in a bag and on the plot.

LEAF TIPS JUST SHOWING.

UNROLL BAG SIDES IF NEEDS BE TO CONTAIN COMPOST/SOIL.

NEW DEPTH.

DEVELOPING POTATOES.

PREVIOUS DEPTH OF COMPOST/SOIL.

MOVE SOIL AS SHOWN BY ARROWS.

FURROW BECOMES A RIDGE.

RIDGE BECOMES A FURROW.

LEAVE JUST LEAF TIPS PROUD.

parcel of gardening life – try not to become disheartened.

66. BEETROOT. Sow beetroot thinly in drills, 2.5cm deep. Allow 30cm between drills if sowing more than one. Water the drill before sowing the seeds if conditions are dry. Cover with fine soil and firm gently **(Fig. 63, p. 77)**.

67. Thin beetroot seedlings as and when leaves are touching **(Fig. 86, p. 103)**.

68. JERUSALEM ARTICHOKE. Weed amongst Jerusalem artichokes and beets. Use a hoe between the rows **(Fig. 50, p. 66)**.

69. Dig out 'volunteer' overlooked Jerusalem artichokes from last year's

Figure 85

How to deal with 'volunteer' potatoes.

WEED POTATO FROM LAST
YEAR IS CALLED A 'VOLUNTEER'.

REMOVE OVERLOOKED POTATOES FROM LAST YEAR
WHICH ARE SPROUTING AS
WEEDS AMONGST THE ONIONS, THEY CAN SPREAD
DISEASE AND SHOULD BE PULLED UP THEN BURNED.

Figure 86

Thinning veg seedlings.

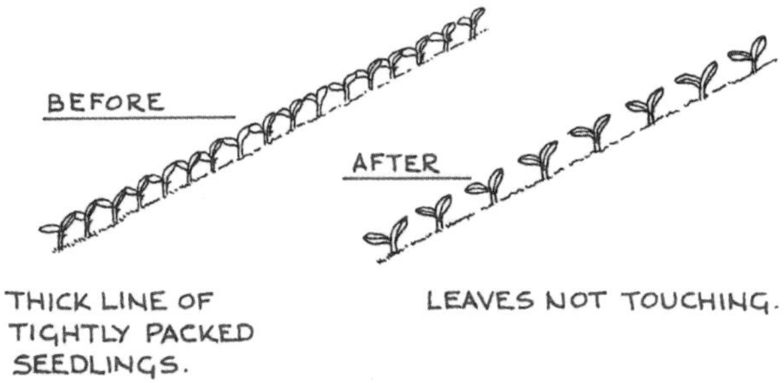

BEFORE

AFTER

THICK LINE OF
TIGHTLY PACKED
SEEDLINGS.

LEAVES NOT TOUCHING.

planting position to make room for something else. Jerusalems are notoriously invasive. It will almost certainly take more than one sifting session to clear a crop.

70. RHUBARB. Cut out rhubarb flower spikes if they start to issue forth from the middle of leafy crowns. Although beautiful in a champagne-spray kind of way, their production will weaken the plant and diminish subsequent crops.

71. Hand weed close in and around the rhubarb crowns so as not to damage them.

72. HORSERADISH. Hand weed.

73. ASPARAGUS. Do not cut any spears on crowns less than two years old. Cut no more than a couple of spears per two-year-old asparagus plant.

74. Water generously if rain is scarce. Better to let a hose soak the ground

Figure 87
Hand weeding the asparagus bed.

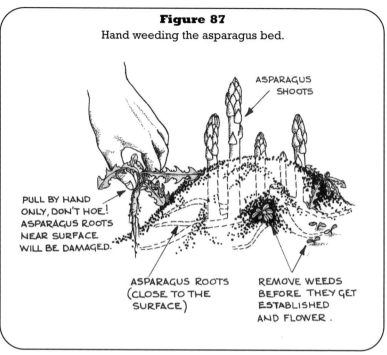

ASPARAGUS SHOOTS

PULL BY HAND ONLY, DON'T HOE! ASPARAGUS ROOTS NEAR SURFACE WILL BE DAMAGED.

ASPARAGUS ROOTS (CLOSE TO THE SURFACE)

REMOVE WEEDS BEFORE THEY GET ESTABLISHED AND FLOWER.

Figure 88
Flea beetles on turnip and radish leaves.

THE FLEA BEETLE. THEY SPRING OFF LEAVES WHEN DISTURBED. THEY EAT SMALL ROUND HOLES IN THE TOP SURFACE OF THE LEAF TURNING THE LEAVES BROWN AND CRISP.

KEEP PLANTS WELL WATERED DURING DRY SPELLS.

directly than fixing a spray attachment.

75. Keep weeding asparagus bed a little and often **(Fig. 87, p. 104)**.

76. Check over asparagus and cease cutting a young bed to boost strength for next year.

77. SWEDE. Sow early in the month. Marian is a reliable, disease-resistant variety. They like rich soil which is weed-free and raked to a fine tilth. Sow seeds in pre-moistened drills 1.5cm deep. Allow 30–45cm between rows if sowing more than one row. Thin out in stages after seedlings emerge in two to three weeks, aiming for about 25cm between plants eventually. Protect sowing from pigeons with strings criss-crossed over the top. Another option is to sow swedes between rows of ripening winter onions. The onion tops will hide the emerging seedlings from birds until harvested themselves in a month's time. Then fit protection from pigeons. A good space-saver at a time when productive ground is at a premium.

78. Keep well-watered to jolly them along and dissuade the flea beetle.

79. TURNIP. Check turnips for flea beetle damage and take preventative measures where it is severe. Light nibbling of leaves won't affect the crop but more than that will weaken plants. Prevention includes keeping soil moist at all times. Control could involve brushing along the leaves with double-sided tape to catch the insects as they jump to avoid the disturbance. Other crops commonly affected include radishes, rocket, young swedes and oriental salads like Pak Choi and Komatsuna **(Fig. 88, p. 104)**.

80. FLORENCE FENNEL. Sow 1cm deep with 30cm between rows. Sow thinly. Gradually remove seedlings, then young plants, until there is 20–25cm between specimens. Keep moist to avoid running to seed.

81. RADISH. Succession sow radishes **(May 52)**, 1.5cm deep in rows 23cm apart **(Fig. 35, p. 47)**.

Veg fruit

82. MARROW FAMILY. Put cucurbits (members of the marrow family, including cucumbers, courgettes, squashes and marrow) outside during daytime for hardening-off **(Apr 2)**. Take them back undercover at night. Or drape a horticultural fleece over them at night and unswaddle in the day. Do this for a week to ten days **(Fig. 46, p. 63)**.

83. Sow marrow and butternut (or other) squashes either in 9cm pots (2.5cm deep) or direct into enriched 'planting pockets'. This involves digging out 30cm squares of soil, one per plant to cultivate, and refilling with a soil/well-rotted manure or compost mix. Do this at 60cm intervals for marrows and up to 90cm spacings for butternuts, which

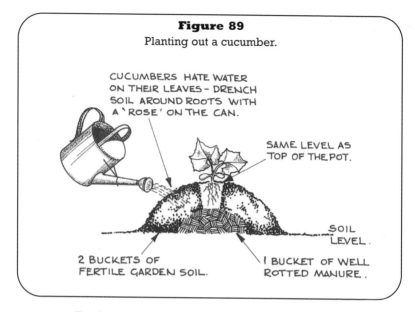

Figure 89
Planting out a cucumber.

CUCUMBERS HATE WATER
ON THEIR LEAVES - DRENCH
SOIL AROUND ROOTS WITH
A 'ROSE' ON THE CAN.

SAME LEVEL AS
TOP OF THE POT.

SOIL
LEVEL.

2 BUCKETS OF
FERTILE GARDEN SOIL.

I BUCKET OF WELL
ROTTED MANURE.

are trailing by nature. Pop in two seeds per planting pocket and thin out the weaker one as they develop.

84. Keep a fleece handy to sling over tender squashes and courgettes if a late frost is forecast.

85. Plant outdoor, or 'ridge', cucumbers in the sunny places prepared for them beforehand **(Fig. 89, p. 106)**.

86. Replace courgette plants which may have been eaten by slugs with specimens purchased from the market. Or raise more than you anticipate needing to allow for natural wastage and, if you end up not needing them, they'll provide a nice gesture when given to friends.

87. PEPPER. Pot on peppers for protected cultivation in a sunny place. Give them 28cm diameter pots to be sure of enough root space **(Fig. 55, p. 70)**.

88. TOMATILLO. Pot on tomatillo if the roots are too cramped (look at the drainage holes on the bottom to check if they're growing through) or harden off **(Fig. 46, p. 63)** and plant out with 60cm between individuals. They become very bushy and will benefit from support in due course.

89. TOMATO. Plant out tomatoes in the sunniest, most sheltered bed available. Allow 45cm between plants in rows 75cm apart. Keep well watered and give a weekly liquid feed of nettle and comfrey fertilizer **(Fig. 78, p. 95)**.

90. If the weather is very wet then erect some kind of tent-like shelter over outdoor tomatoes to save them from getting wrecked.

91. Remove covering from outdoor tomatoes when it seems that summer has really arrived.

92. Tie in outdoor tomatoes for raising as a single stem 'cordon' to supporting (1.5metre) canes. Pinch out growth from between leaf nodes and stem **(Jun 54/55)**.

93. Plant indoor cucumbers, peppers, aubergines and tomatoes into pots or grow-bags. Don't be tempted by really cheap 'bargain' bags – they are cheap because usually they're of poor quality and your crops will reflect this. Don't overstock the bags (follow the advice given on the bag, two or three plants maximum). In pots, use JI Number 3 or top quality peat-free multi-purpose compost **(Fig. 90, p. 108)**.

94. PEST CONTROL. Pot up French marigolds from the market into individual pots and place throughout the greenhouse to naturally deter whitefly **(Fig. 91, p. 108)**.

95. Conduct nightly torchlight slug and snail patrols **(Fig. 47, p. 64)**.

Onion tribe

96. LEEK. Tend nursery beds. Keep moist and weed-free **(Apr 75)**.

97. Prepare a bed for maincrops. Completely weed and turn the bed. Rake to a crumbly tilth. Doing this now allows for a flush of weeds to germinate which can be hoed into oblivion before planting takes place next month. The bed is said to be 'sterile'.

98. Plant out Roxton leeks for midsummer consumption as pencil-sized babies. 10cm apart in rows with 20cm between is fine **(Feb 48)**.

99. ONION. Sow spring onion. There are many different varieties. Some are colourful too, so browse and select imaginatively. Sowing seed thinly should negate the need for subsequent thinning out, especially of the non-bulbing types **(Apr 76)**.

100. Weed onions and shallots. Use a hoe between the rows and a bent knife to get in tight between the actual plants **(Jul 8)**.

101. GARLIC. Weed garlic patch. No members of the onion tribe like to compete for space, moisture, nutrients and light with their neighbours. Observing correct planting distances **(Mar 75)** may lessen the occurrence of fungal rust, which shows as orange pustules on leaves. Garlic is prone. Unless the rust is a thick gelatinous mass then its negative effects are usually only cosmetic.

Figure 90

Correct way to cultivate tomatoes in a grow-bag.

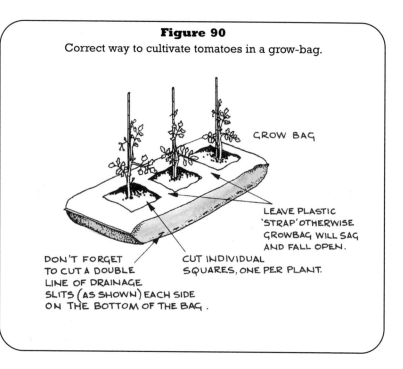

GROW BAG

LEAVE PLASTIC 'STRAP' OTHERWISE GROWBAG WILL SAG AND FALL OPEN.

DON'T FORGET TO CUT A DOUBLE LINE OF DRAINAGE SLITS (AS SHOWN) EACH SIDE ON THE BOTTOM OF THE BAG.

CUT INDIVIDUAL SQUARES, ONE PER PLANT.

Figure 91

Using French marigolds to deter whitefly in the greenhouse.

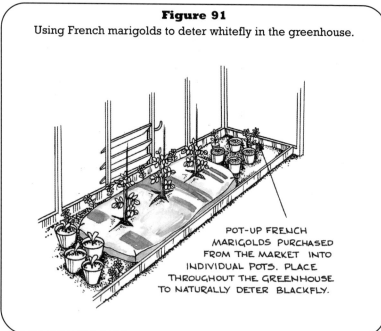

POT-UP FRENCH MARIGOLDS PURCHASED FROM THE MARKET INTO INDIVIDUAL POTS. PLACE THROUGHOUT THE GREENHOUSE TO NATURALLY DETER BLACKFLY.

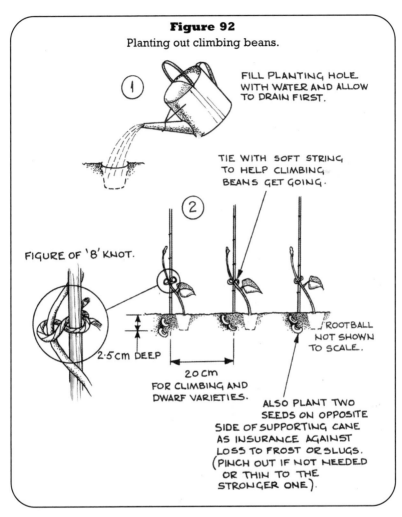

Figure 92

Planting out climbing beans.

① FILL PLANTING HOLE WITH WATER AND ALLOW TO DRAIN FIRST.

TIE WITH SOFT STRING TO HELP CLIMBING BEANS GET GOING.

②

FIGURE OF '8' KNOT.

2·5 cm DEEP

20 cm FOR CLIMBING AND DWARF VARIETIES.

ROOTBALL NOT SHOWN TO SCALE.

ALSO PLANT TWO SEEDS ON OPPOSITE SIDE OF SUPPORTING CANE AS INSURANCE AGAINST LOSS TO FROST OR SLUGS. (PINCH OUT IF NOT NEEDED OR THIN TO THE STRONGER ONE).

Peas & beans

102. RUNNER & FRENCH BEAN. Erect poles ready for runner beans **(Fig. 70, p. 85)**.

103. Apply organic fertilizer to soil around bean poles and hoe in as a preparation before planting (follow directions given with the product).

104. Acclimatize frost-tender French and runner beans by hardening off for a week to ten days **(Fig. 46, p. 63)**.

105. Plant out French and runner beans raised in pots at the bottom of already erected canes. They like rich soil so add a dollop of well-rotted manure to the bottom, fill with water and allow to soak down before snuggling the pot-grown root-ball into the ground. Sow a seed next to each one as insurance in case frost kills your charges (2.5cm deep). It can always be sacrificed at a later date if not needed **(Fig. 92, p. 109)**.

106. Gently and carefully train runner beans up their poles by tying loosely with soft string **(Fig. 92, p. 109)**.

107. Sow climbing or dwarf beans direct at 20cm intervals, two seeds per station, 2.5cm deep. Select the stronger and remove the other one after germination and emergence. Dwarf beans grow as a bush but still benefit from a few twiggy sticks to prop them up and keep subsequent pods clean. If sowing more than one row, allow 45cm between rows.

108. BROAD BEAN. Water autumn-sown broad beans generously at the roots as soon as flowers appear and continue giving extra rations into June as the pods swell **(Fig. 93, p. 110)**.

109. Use young broad bean plants, spring-sown as extras at the end of the row, to fill in gaps where plants have failed for some reason or seeds not germinated. Lift with a trowel and keep roots as intact as possible **(Mar 83)**.

110. Put supports around burgeoning broad beans: use a cane at each corner and lash string around the whole lot at the top, middle and bottom **(Fig. 93, p. 110)**.

111. Keep an eye out for blackfly on broad beans. Spray with weak dilution of biodegradable washing-up liquid or, preferably, pinch out tender growing tips. Burn or bury in the hot heart of a well-made compost heap **(Fig. 94, p. 111)**.

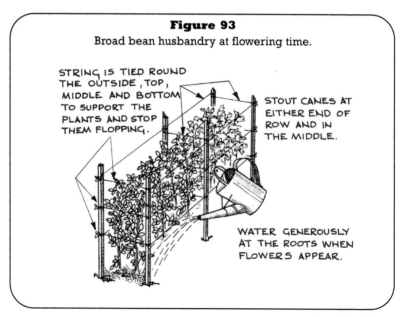

Figure 93
Broad bean husbandry at flowering time.

STRING IS TIED ROUND THE OUTSIDE, TOP, MIDDLE AND BOTTOM TO SUPPORT THE PLANTS AND STOP THEM FLOPPING.

STOUT CANES AT EITHER END OF ROW AND IN THE MIDDLE.

WATER GENEROUSLY AT THE ROOTS WHEN FLOWERS APPEAR.

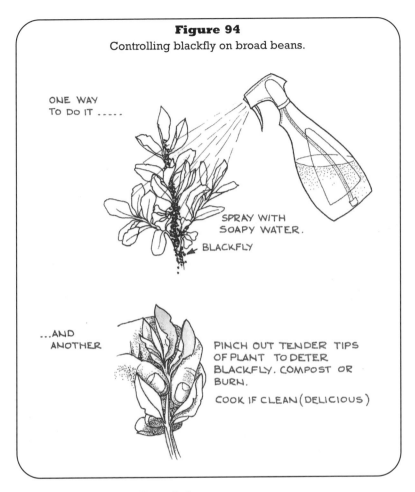

Figure 94
Controlling blackfly on broad beans.

ONE WAY
TO DO IT . . . . .

SPRAY WITH
SOAPY WATER.

BLACKFLY

...AND
ANOTHER

PINCH OUT TENDER TIPS
OF PLANT TO DETER
BLACKFLY. COMPOST OR
BURN.

COOK IF CLEAN (DELICIOUS)

112. PEA. Keep peas well weeded.

113. Continue to succession sow peas **(May 52/Fig. 71, p. 86)**.

114. Plant out peas grown in pots in rows or in deep, enriched containers with support supplied by netting or hazel 'pea sticks' **(Fig. 40, p. 54)**.

115. Check supports for peas are adequate as the heavy crop swells.

Edible flowers

116. NASTURTIUM. Plant out in odd places. 25cm apart is recommended for most varieties but sticking them in between cabbages, kale, Brussels sprouts or broccoli works well, looks fantastic later in the season and will go some way to hiding juicy 'greens' from keen-eyed pigeons. Just open a pocket of soil with hand or trowel, dangle the roots into it and press soil gently around.

117. SUNFLOWER. Pot on Giant Single, and place outside during the daytime to harden off **(Fig. 46, p. 63)**. Make sure a support is always in position to keep the stem upright. And, as ever with sunflowers, take precautions against slugs and snails. Ferric phosphate pellets are completely specific to molluscs, entirely safe for pets and wildlife, and will degrade into a soil-enhancing plant food. They're an acceptable alternative to beer traps **(Fig. 48, p. 64)** and decoy piles of wilting weeds.

118. Plant in their final positions. 30cm apart is adequate. Provide support from the off **(Fig. 73, p. 87)**.

119. GLOBE ARTICHOKE. Plant out pot-raised specimens. 90cm spacings all round in rich, weed-free soil is perfect. Keep moist until established **(Fig. 95, p. 112)**.

120. More weeding around established globe artichoke crowns!

121. POT MARIGOLD. Plant out pot marigolds or sow seeds along plot edges for a decorative and edible wildlife-friendly border **(Fig. 96, p. 113)**.

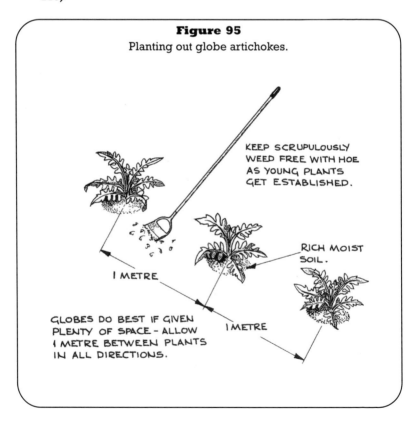

Figure 95
Planting out globe artichokes.

KEEP SCRUPULOUSLY WEED FREE WITH HOE AS YOUNG PLANTS GET ESTABLISHED.

RICH MOIST SOIL.

I METRE

GLOBES DO BEST IF GIVEN PLENTY OF SPACE - ALLOW I METRE BETWEEN PLANTS IN ALL DIRECTIONS.

I METRE

Cereals

122. SWEETCORN. Sow direct where it is to grow. Put two seeds together, each pair at 45cm spacings in a grid. This is important as they depend on wind for pollination. If planted in a single line the pollen can miss flowers. Remove the weaker of each pair when seedlings are up. At this stage they'll look like a luscious blade of thick grass.

123. Plant out pot-raised sweetcorn. Dig holes every 45cm in a grid, fill with water and allow to drain. Then slip your charges from their pots **(Fig. 54, p. 70)** and nestle them in so that the top of the compost is level with the soil. Canes, inserted at an angle so as not to spear the roots, and lashed around the plants with soft string, might help stabilize plants on exposed sites.

124. Erect a strong barrier around the sweetcorn to deter badgers (who love the stuff!). Urine-soaked rags will dissuade them for a while.

125. Plant dill seedlings amongst sweetcorn as a good companion.

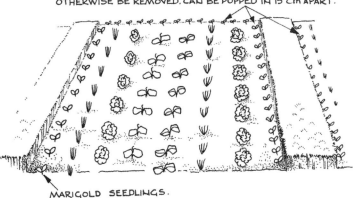

Figure 96

How to use pot marigolds as a decorative, edible and wildlife-friendly edge.

TRANSPLANT SEEDLINGS SOWN IN TRAYS SPECIALLY OR USE SELF SOWN SPECIMENS WHICH WOULD OTHERWISE BE REMOVED. CAN BE POPPED IN 15 cm APART.

MARIGOLD SEEDLINGS.

Fruit garden

126. APPLE & PEAR. Generous dose of water for fruit trees. A bucket per tree every fortnight will be worth the effort in the long run **(Fig. 74, p. 89)**.

127. Tie in new growth of apples and pears being trained in unusual 'restricted' shapes to a wire framework **(Feb 63/Jun 92)**.

128. Remove embryonic fruitlets from apples and pears in their first and second seasons after planting. Letting them produce fruits will sap their energy in subsequent years. Far better to exercise prudence and wait. Play the long game **(Fig. 97, p. 114)**.

129. BLACKCURRANT. Fasten netting over blackcurrants because birds might take a fancy to your crops as soon as berries commence to colour.

130. Cut down grasses and weeds around soft fruit bushes and from around the stems of apples and pears.

131. RASPBERRY. Keep cane fruits tied in to their supporting structures and wires **(Jan 49)**.

132. STRAWBERRY. Plant out Alpine strawberries in a shady bed (around a north-facing Morello cherry is ideal). Allow up to 30cm between individuals **(Feb 78/Apr 115)**.

133. Mulch strawberries when the soil is damp in late spring. Use decomposed leaves, dried bracken or straw. Lay it down as thick as

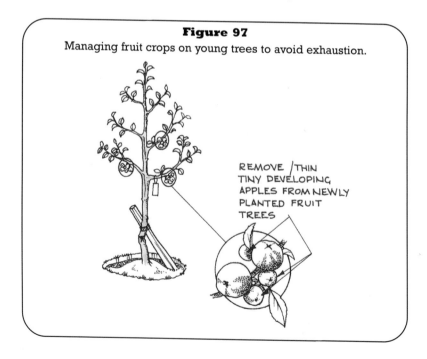

Figure 97

Managing fruit crops on young trees to avoid exhaustion.

REMOVE /THIN TINY DEVELOPING APPLES FROM NEWLY PLANTED FRUIT TREES

possible right around the plants and all along the row. This will conserve moisture in the soil.

134. Cover strawberries with netting to dissuade birds. Prop it up away from the crowns otherwise birds will just land on top and peck through the netting. Water liberally at this stage, but keep water off the leaves and fruits. Direct it to the root zone. Apply in the mornings only. Add a splosh of nettle and comfrey feed **(Fig. 78, p. 95)** every third watering.

JUNE

They say that simple things please simple minds. For genuine satisfaction, arguably, it does not come much simpler than broad beans with new potatoes fresh out of the garden and within half an hour, side by side, hot, with oil, salt and pepper on a plate.

If you over estimated lettuces then you might at times feel overwhelmed. The building explosion of summer growth is realised this month.

Dawn breaks before 5am in flaming June. Some gardeners like to rise with the lark and plunder fresh peas straight 'off the vine'. The world looks different during those early hours on a sunny blue-sky morn. Part of the magic is the fact that these special moments are so fleeting. It is easy to blink and miss them.

There is much to do in terms of caring for your charges and working towards a bountiful future. Use the time wisely.

With luck the first big harvest comes in for drying and storage on or around midsummer: shallots. If you planted them on winter solstice then this keeps you tuned in to the rhythm of the changing year.

Suddenly, as the season shifts again, gaps and bare earth appear amongst the rows of veg. Slower-growing crops like kale, winter cabbage and Brussels sprouts can fill the spaces. Or sow something which will grow thick and fast then, when cut down and turned in, maintain your soil in good heart – what we call a 'green manure'.

Remember, if you continually feed the soil in your garden then the soil will keep feeding you.

General jobs to do

1. Keep plants moist but not wet, especially seedlings in trays and pots **(Fig. 12, p. 22)**.
2. Water leafy salads and 'greens' direct by hand with a watering can to the base of crops; the roots **(Fig. 80, p. 97)**.
3. Keep the hoe busy whenever the soil surface is dry **(Fig. 98, p. 117)**.
4. Tend veggies and look over daily for signs of pests and disease. Keep a reference book handy so preventative measures can be employed swiftly **(Jun 58)**.
5. Keep bird-scaring devices in good working order, especially around the cabbage patch. Plastic toy snakes are one trick to try in an effort to keep the birds off, but be sure to flick them around with a stick every other day so it looks as though they are alive and moving **(Fig. 52, p. 68)**.
6. Make a fuss of the cat if rabbits are nibbling to encourage her to keep guard! Alternatively, erect rabbit-proof netting with a mesh size of 25mm maximum. Dig it in 30cm deep, angled outwards at the bottom to stop them burrowing underneath. The minimum height above ground must be 120cm to thwart the twitch-nosed rascals!
7. Cut back plot edges **(Fig. 49, p. 65)** regularly and mow grass paths **(Fig. 79, p. 96)** to keep a neat and tidy framework to your plot (other

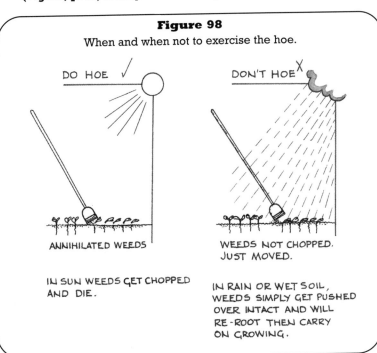

Figure 98
When and when not to exercise the hoe.

DO HOE ✓

DON'T HOE ✗

ANNIHILATED WEEDS

WEEDS NOT CHOPPED. JUST MOVED.

IN SUN WEEDS GET CHOPPED AND DIE.

IN RAIN OR WET SOIL, WEEDS SIMPLY GET PUSHED OVER INTACT AND WILL RE-ROOT THEN CARRY ON GROWING.

paths must be kept clear of clutter and swept).

8. Empty the nettle-and-comfrey bin. Use pulp as a hearty mulch around cabbages or fruit bushes. Decant and store remaining liquid. Refresh the bin with freshly-cut nettle and comfrey leaves **(Fig. 99, p. 118)**.

9. Hand weed here and there.

10. Mooch around the plot having a good look at the amazing world of vegetables, fruits and nature **(Fig. 100, p. 119)**.

11. Fix any leaky hoses immediately, don't leave these annoying jobs until tomorrow. 'A stitch in time' really does 'save nine' when it comes to maintaining the home and garden **(Fig. 101, p. 119)**.

12. Drench crops in pots weekly.

13. Import bags of manure and green waste from wherever possible for future use. This will be invaluable at some future point. Never turn down the opportunity to gather some in. When ripened manure is

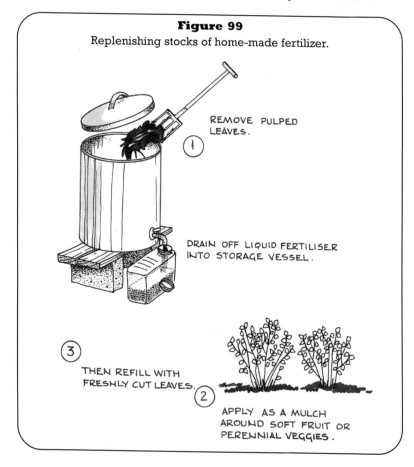

Figure 99

Replenishing stocks of home-made fertilizer.

REMOVE PULPED LEAVES.

(1)

DRAIN OFF LIQUID FERTILISER INTO STORAGE VESSEL.

(3)

THEN REFILL WITH FRESHLY CUT LEAVES.

(2)

APPLY AS A MULCH AROUND SOFT FRUIT OR PERENNIAL VEGGIES.

Figure 100
Taking time to think about something and nothing.

Figure 101
Fixing a leaky hosepipe.

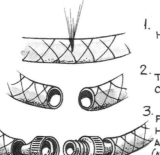

1. HOLE OR LEAK.

2. TURN OFF WATER. CUT OUT THE LEAKY SECTION.

3. FIX WITH NEW SECTION OF HOSE AND TWO SPECIALLY ADAPTED JOINERS (AVAILABLE FROM THE GARDEN CENTRE.)

teeming with worms it's ready to flop on your plot **(Fig. 102, p.120)**.

14. Hoe over open soil and seedbeds to keep them ready for sowing and planting **(Fig. 50, p. 66)**.

15. Sow seeds of a 'green manure' crop on open ground which won't be used for raising crops this season. Mustard provides bulky foliage to turn back in for adding humus to the soil; alfalfa and clover are leguminous plants which fix atmospheric nitrogen in their roots and this feeds subsequent crops; Phacelia provides lots of humus and will also attract pollinating insects if some are allowed to flower around the edges. Scatter it by the handful and rake in ('broadcast sow'). Let nature do the rest. There are other options too, so think about the needs of your plot and sow appropriately (see also Green Manures, **p. 6**).

16. Check over crops and remove any sickly-looking foliage to maintain health and vigour.

17. Ventilate greenhouse freely.

18. Water greenhouse crops daily.

19. Check over for signs of pests and diseases every day **(Jun 58)**.

20. Spot-weed horsetail and bindweed. This means pulling them out wherever seen. Don't expect the plants to give up – they won't – but with regular sessions you will get the upper hand **(Fig. 77, p. 94)**.

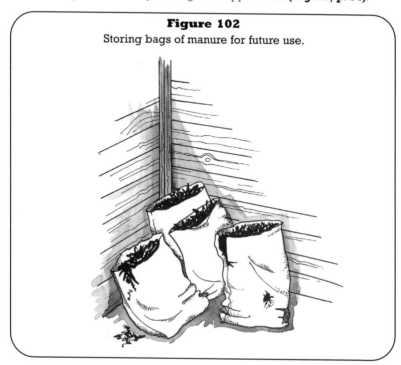

Figure 102
Storing bags of manure for future use.

Leaves & greens

21. BROCCOLI, CABBAGE, KALE, CALABRESE, BRUSSELS SPROUT. Pot on Nine Star Perennial broccoli **(Figs 54 and 55, p. 70)**.

22. Sow red cabbage and calabrese in trays of seed compost. 1.5cm deep and 4cm apart is perfect. Keep moist but not wet. Prick out **(Feb 27)** when large enough to handle **(Fig. 14, p. 25)**.

23. Plant out potted kale, sprouting broccoli, Savoy and January King cabbages in blocks or rows with 60cm between plants. Firm soil is essential so tread it down with the Gardener's Shuffle first **(Fig. 38, p. 53)**, then rake to a neat and tidy level. Use a trowel to dig a hole bigger than the root-ball, fill it with water and allow to drain. Then line with well-rotted manure or compost. Plant your brassicas deep and firm. Specimens should be planted deep, with the first set of leaves proud of the soil but no stem below these showing. Tread the sides carefully with a heel or thump with a fist. Fit a barrier of carpet underlay to thwart cabbage root flies who wreak much havoc on freshly planted-out brassicas **(Figs 58 and 81, pp. 73 and 98)**.

24. Plant out calabrese as above **(Jun 23)**, except 45cm apart.

25. Last chance to plant out Brussels sprout seedlings and be confident of a reliable crop. As for kale and cabbages, above **(Jun 23)**.

26. Stake Brussels sprout plants already established on the plot, especially if there is a threat of summer storms. Looseness at the roots is a cause of loose, or 'blown', buttons which is not what the Christmas kitchen wants **(Aug 23)**.

27. Check brassica plantings for signs of cabbage root fly. Any pale and limp seedlings will pull out of the ground easily and show maggot-eaten roots crawling with white grubs. Remove entire cabbage to the fire site **(Fig. 103, p. 122)**.

28. Fold outer leaves over developing cauliflower curds (the white florety heart) and tie them at the top with string. The aim is to keep sunlight off them so they remain white and tight rather than discolouring and loosening up.

29. ROCKET. Cut off flowering shoots of rocket to encourage new fresh growth. Eat the flowers **(Fig. 104, p. 122)**.

30. LETTUCE. Thin lettuces as and when leaves are touching those of their neighbours. Pull out every other one to use as baby salad leaves. Aim for final spacings of 20cm **(Fig. 105, p. 123)**.

31. Plant out lettuces which have been grown in pots. 20–30cm between plants will suffice. Keep them moist until established and thereafter **(Fig. 53, p. 69)**.

32. LEAF BEET. Cut back chard going to seed to encourage a new flush of growth. Chop any emerging flower stems right out.

Figure 103
Symptoms of attack by cabbage fly.

LIMP, DROOPING, YELLOWING STEM AND LEAVES.

FIT ONLY FOR BURNING. PLANT NO CABBAGES OR RELATIONS IN THIS SOIL FOR TWO YEARS.

MAGGOTS

NO ROOTS. EASY TO PULL UP (NO RESISTANCE). ALL EATEN BY MAGGOTS.

ADULT FLY RARELY SEEN

HEALTHY PLANT

SYMPTOMS OF CABBAGE ROOT FLY WHICH CAN AFFECT ALL MEMBERS OF THAT FAMILY.

Figure 104
The edible parts of rocket.

ROCKET FLOWERS AND BUDS ARE DELICIOUS! DONT COMPOST THEM – EAT THEM! THIS WILL ENCOURAGE NEW FRESH GROWTH.

NOTE: IF ROCKET IS ALLOWED TO SET SEED THE LEAVES BECOME TOO TOUGH FOR PLEASURABLE EATING.

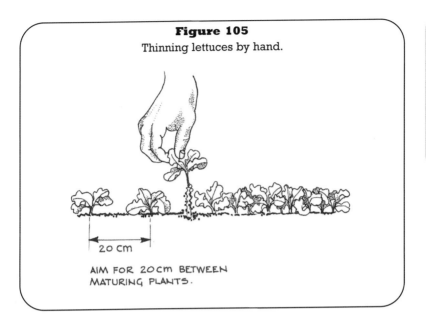

Figure 105
Thinning lettuces by hand.

20 CM

AIM FOR 20CM BETWEEN
MATURING PLANTS.

33. Pull out spinach which has flowered and re-sow if not done already
(Jun 34).
34. Sow Giant Winter spinach, 2.5cm deep in pre-moistened drills 30cm
apart (if more than one row) **(Fig. 34, p. 44)**.

Roots, tubers & stems

35. CELERIAC. Prick out seedlings into 9cm pots. Be careful of those
fibrous roots. Hold seedlings with leaf tips in one hand (fingers). Use a
flat spatula or lolly stick to ease them up and out of trays then guide
them in to compost-filled pots. Be sure to prick out to the same level as
they were in trays (no deeper).
36. Plant out celeriac when sturdy, and when roots show through pot
drainage holes. Take out a shallow, flat-bottomed drill with a draw hoe
in enriched soil. Allow 30cm between plants. Make sure the swelling at
the top of the stem is proud of the soil surface (don't bury it). Keep
moist, especially for a few days until established **(Fig. 83, p. 101)**.
37. POTATO. Earth up with a draw hoe. Might be necessary to do this on a
weekly basis as growth in June can be rampant. If possible, pat the
sides of your potato ridges with the back of a spade. If blight strikes
later in the season **(Jul 54)** spores in rainwater will be less likely to
soak in immediately onto tubers below. Instead, water will shed quickly
into the space between rows **(Fig. 106, p. 124)**.

Figure 106

Earthing up potatoes with a swan-necked (or 'draw') hoe.

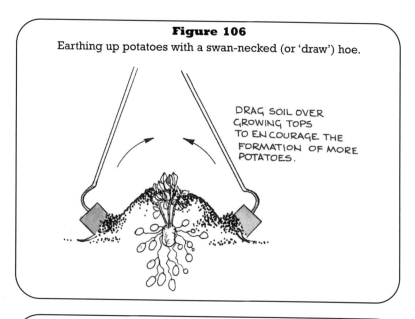

DRAG SOIL OVER
GROWING TOPS
TO ENCOURAGE THE
FORMATION OF MORE
POTATOES.

Figure 107

Midsummer Jerusalem artichoke management.

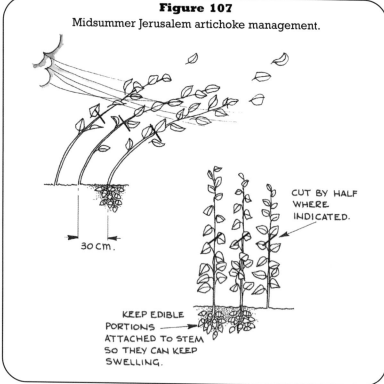

CUT BY HALF
WHERE
INDICATED.

30 cm.

KEEP EDIBLE
PORTIONS
ATTACHED TO STEM
SO THEY CAN KEEP
SWELLING.

38. Give a thorough drenching if conditions have been dry.

39. Commence digging First Early potatoes once they are in flower after the middle of the month. Insert fork tines well to the side but deeply, then lever up to avoid spiking any potatoes by accident. If possible, use a blunt-ended specially designed 'potato fork' **(Aug 35)**.

40. PARSNIP. Hoe between rows of 'snips, then hand weed between the plants. Take care not to nick the parsnip shoulders. No need to apply water – we want roots to plunge deeply in search of moisture **(Fig. 50, p. 66)**.

41. SWEDE. Hoe swede bed **(Fig. 50, p. 66)**.

42. Thin young plants to approximately 25cm spacings. Might take two thinning sessions. Less room equals smaller plants and is perfectly acceptable if this meets your requirements **(Fig. 105, p. 123)**.

43. Tie string criss-crossed over swedes to deter pigeons: insert canes around the bed and lash string between these canes to make an obstructive mesh.

44. RADISH. Succession sow **(May 52)** French Breakfast, in pre-moistened drills **(Fig. 35, pp. 4–7)**.

45. KOHLRABI. Succession sow **(Apr 43)**.

46. BEETROOT. Sow from now until early August. Try any of the cylindrical-rooted beets. 2.5cm deep in pre-moistened drills, with 30cm between drills if sowing more than one, is perfect. Thin gradually, aiming for 8cm between plants **(Figs 63 and 64, p. 77)**.

47. JERUSALEM ARTICHOKE. Cut tops off by half to lessen the likelihood of wind damage during summer storms **(Fig. 107, p. 124)**.

48. FLORENCE FENNEL. Thin Florence fennel and carrots. Thinnings from both veggies are perfectly edible so put on your plate not the compost! Weed thoroughly at the same time **(Fig. 65, p. 78)**.

49. CARROT. Replant rows of carrots where germination has failed or seedlings have been taken by slugs. Try growing them in pots of peat-free multi-purpose compost instead, with a ring of petroleum jelly around the rim to thwart molluscs **(Apr 45)**.

50. ASPARAGUS. Hand weed asparagus bed. Do it regularly to keep it easy **(Fig. 87, p. 104)**.

51. Put support system in for asparagus tops, which are liable to blow in the wind and could damage the crowns at ground level. Stout posts at either end of the rows with string tied tight in between should do the trick. Lash the ferny tops to this **(Fig. 108, p. 126)**.

52. Check asparagus for beetles/eggs and remove/destroy any found. Do this daily if possible. Beetles are under 1cm long, black and white at the head with six creamy white chequers against black on the back. Grubs are brown-grey maggots. Eggs are pinhead-sized cylinders, laid in rows or clusters. Crush all. Beetles drop off at first disturbance so cup hand below first to catch them **(Fig. 109, p. 126)**.

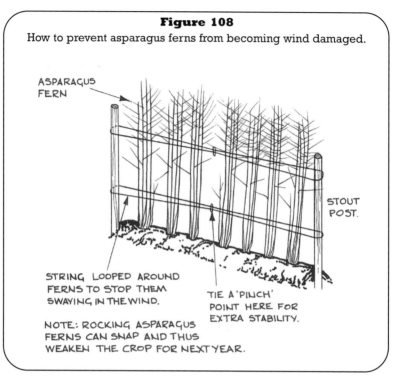

Figure 108

How to prevent asparagus ferns from becoming wind damaged.

ASPARAGUS FERN

STOUT POST.

STRING LOOPED AROUND FERNS TO STOP THEM SWAYING IN THE WIND.

TIE A 'PINCH' POINT HERE FOR EXTRA STABILITY.

NOTE: ROCKING ASPARAGUS FERNS CAN SNAP AND THUS WEAKEN THE CROP FOR NEXT YEAR.

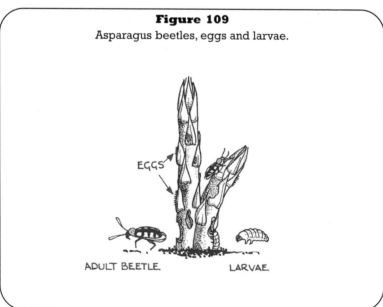

Figure 109

Asparagus beetles, eggs and larvae.

EGGS

ADULT BEETLE.

LARVAE.

Veg fruit

53. TOMATO, PEPPER, CUCUMBER. Water crops in pots and grow-bags daily. Keep moist but not wet.

54. Position supports for greenhouse cucumbers and tomatoes to climb up. Strings tied underneath the pots then lashed to the roof girders is one way. Another is to secure canes **(Fig. 110, p. 127)**.

55. On tomatoes, pinch out shoots between leaf and stem (side shoots) **(Fig. 111, p. 128)**.

56. Plant tomatoes for outdoor cultivation into enriched soil in the sunniest bed possible, early in the month. Liquid feed weekly. Use home-made nettle and comfrey feed **(Fig. 78, p. 95)**. Add just a drop to a can of water, enough to taint the colour. If using a proprietary product, mix and apply according to the manufacturer's instructions.

57. Cut off discoloured lower leaves from tomato plants.

58. Keep an eye out for pests and diseases in the greenhouse or conserva-

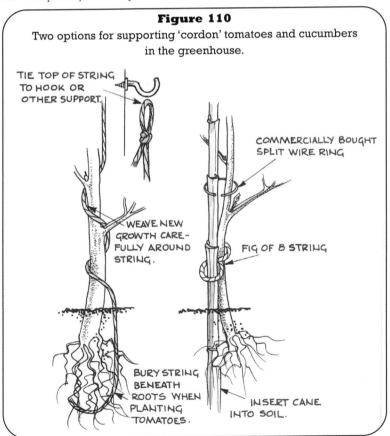

Figure 110
Two options for supporting 'cordon' tomatoes and cucumbers in the greenhouse.

TIE TOP OF STRING TO HOOK OR OTHER SUPPORT.

COMMERCIALLY BOUGHT SPLIT WIRE RING

WEAVE NEW GROWTH CARE- FULLY AROUND STRING.

FIG OF 8 STRING

BURY STRING BENEATH ROOTS WHEN PLANTING TOMATOES.

INSERT CANE INTO SOIL.

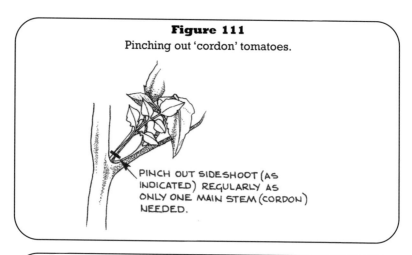

Figure 111

Pinching out 'cordon' tomatoes.

PINCH OUT SIDESHOOT (AS INDICATED) REGULARLY AS ONLY ONE MAIN STEM (CORDON) NEEDED.

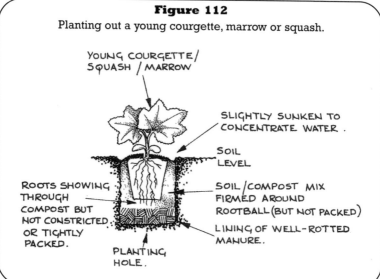

Figure 112

Planting out a young courgette, marrow or squash.

YOUNG COURGETTE/ SQUASH / MARROW

SLIGHTLY SUNKEN TO CONCENTRATE WATER.

SOIL LEVEL

ROOTS SHOWING THROUGH COMPOST BUT NOT CONSTRICTED OR TIGHTLY PACKED.

SOIL/COMPOST MIX FIRMED AROUND ROOTBALL (BUT NOT PACKED)

LINING OF WELL-ROTTED MANURE.

PLANTING HOLE.

tory, especially insects on leaves, discolouration or moulds. Remove affected foliage. A decent reference book is essential. It is Sod's Law that the ailment your plant is suffering from will be difficult to identify but keep trying. Dr Hessayon's *Be Your Own Veg Doctor* (1978) is a good one and cheap too. Track it down on Amazon.

59. Tie in outdoor tomatoes to supporting canes **(Jun 75)**.
60. Sprinkle a top dressing of wood ash amongst outdoor tomatoes and hoe into the soil **(Dec 6)**.
61. Plant out 'ridge' cucumbers outside on the open plot. Nestle into

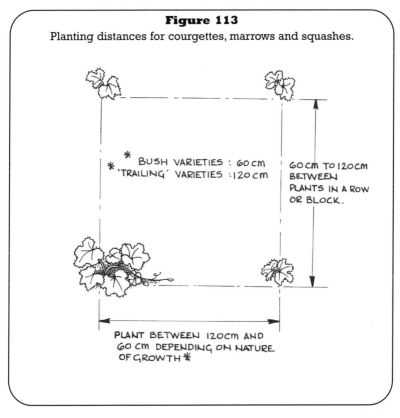

Figure 113

Planting distances for courgettes, marrows and squashes.

* * BUSH VARIETIES : 60 CM

* 'TRAILING' VARIETIES :120 CM

60 CM TO 120CM BETWEEN PLANTS IN A ROW OR BLOCK.

PLANT BETWEEN 120CM AND 60 CM DEPENDING ON NATURE OF GROWTH *

enriched mounds **(Fig. 89, p. 106)**. Be sure not to plant too deep. Keep water off leaves if at all possible. Cucumbers do not like this.

62. Keep tomatillos and 'ridge' cucumbers watered and weed free.

63. AUBERGINE. Plant aubergines in 28cm diameter pots or good quality grow-bags. Use JI Number 3 if using pots. It has all the nutrient requirements for a fruiting vegetable to succeed **(Figs 54 and 55, p. 70)**.

64. COURGETTE, MARROW, SQUASH. Plant out marrows, butternut and other squashes. Make a pocket in enriched soil and nestle them into this. Firm soil gently around the root-ball. Fashion a mounded ring around the plant. Apply a good dose of pure water into this. The ring will prevent run-off and concentrate water to the roots **(Figs 112 and 113, pp. 128 and 129)**.

65. Plant marrows at 60cm intervals amongst runner beans as a companion crop and to save space **(Fig. 114, p. 130)**.

66. Mulch around courgettes and squashes with straw. This preserves moisture, suppresses weeds and keeps the edible portions clean too.

67. Liquid feed for courgettes once weekly **(Jun 56)**.

Figure 114

Interplanting marrows and beans.

BEANS PLANTED AT
20 cm INTERVALS
IN DOUBLE ROWS 45cm
APART.

PLANT MARROWS BETWEEN CLIMBING
BEANS, THEY WILL THRIVE IN THE MOIST
SHADE AND GIVE YOU TWICE THE CROP
FROM THAT PIECE OF GARDEN.

Onion tribe

68. LEEK. Finish preparing a bed for the maincrops by clearing all weeds, turning soil over, digging in any well-rotted manure or compost (if available) and raking to a level.

69. When they are about the thickness of a pencil, ease young leeks from their nursery bed **(Apr 75)**, pop into a bucket of water to keep roots moist, and plant out in final resting places. Use a rounded-off broken spade handle or similar 'dibber' to make holes 15cm deep at 15cm intervals in parallel rows 30cm apart. Drop in one leek per hole. Ensure roots are well down at the bottom then fill the hole with water. Allow to drain naturally. Repeat watering ('puddling in') daily for a week until leeks are firmly established (two or three times a week might be more realistic!) **(Fig. 115, p. 131)**.

70. SHALLOT. Harvest shallots sown on the winter solstice **(Dec 29)**. Shallots are ripe when they lift easily (roots have shrivelled somewhat), tops have turned brown or died down. Break clusters into individual bulbs and place on a wire rack, elevated off the ground to allow circulation of air. Position in a sunny spot, keep rain off and store in trays when skins are dry like thin paper **(Fig. 116, p. 132)**.

71. ONION. Hand weed and hoe in the maincrop onion bed. Do not nick any bulbs with hoe blade **(Aug 60)**.

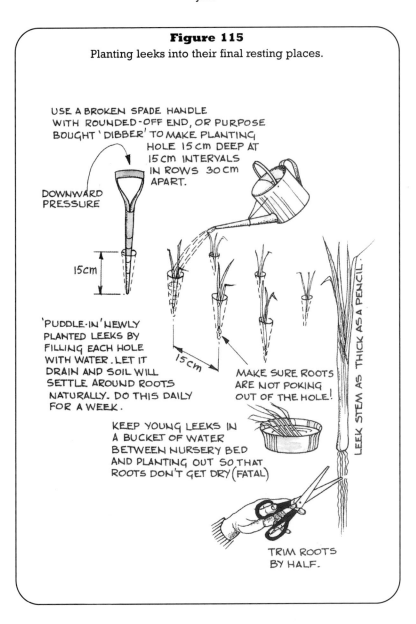

Figure 115

Planting leeks into their final resting places.

USE A BROKEN SPADE HANDLE WITH ROUNDED-OFF END, OR PURPOSE BOUGHT 'DIBBER' TO MAKE PLANTING HOLE 15 cm DEEP AT 15 cm INTERVALS IN ROWS 30 cm APART.

DOWNWARD PRESSURE

15cm

'PUDDLE-IN' NEWLY PLANTED LEEKS BY FILLING EACH HOLE WITH WATER. LET IT DRAIN AND SOIL WILL SETTLE AROUND ROOTS NATURALLY. DO THIS DAILY FOR A WEEK.

15cm

MAKE SURE ROOTS ARE NOT POKING OUT OF THE HOLE!

KEEP YOUNG LEEKS IN A BUCKET OF WATER BETWEEN NURSERY BED AND PLANTING OUT SO THAT ROOTS DON'T GET DRY (FATAL)

LEEK STEM AS THICK AS A PENCIL.

TRIM ROOTS BY HALF.

72. Remove and burn leaves from maincrop onions which are showing signs of downy mildew (looking mouldy).

73. Harvest winter onions. Tie in bunches and hang somewhere dry. They won't store for very many months, so eat between now and the maincrop harvest in August.

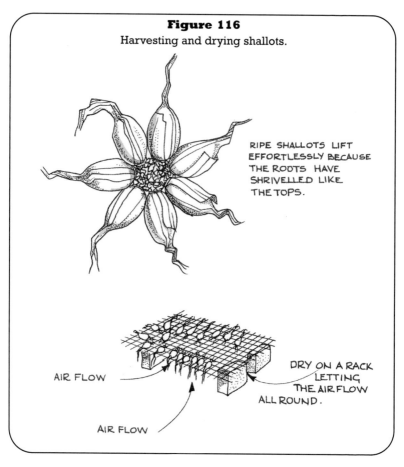

Figure 116
Harvesting and drying shallots.

RIPE SHALLOTS LIFT EFFORTLESSLY BECAUSE THE ROOTS HAVE SHRIVELLED LIKE THE TOPS.

AIR FLOW

DRY ON A RACK LETTING THE AIR FLOW ALL ROUND.

AIR FLOW

Peas & beans

74. RUNNER & FRENCH BEAN. Plant out into enriched soil at 20cm intervals **(Fig. 92, p. 109)**.

75. Support climbing beans with loose figure-8 knots tied around support and stem to train initially. Important to get plants climbing as quickly as possible to get them out of slug and snail danger zone (primarily at soil level) **(Fig. 117, p. 133)**.

76. Tend runner beans by checking supports, providing water direct to the roots and removing all competing weeds **(Fig. 80, p. 97)**.

77. Plant out dwarf French beans at 20cm intervals in double rows 30cm apart. Use twiggy sticks to keep leaves and bean pods up off the soil.

78. Liquid feed French and runner beans weekly **(Fig. 78, p. 95)**.

79. Weed close in amongst climbing French beans.

80. BROAD BEAN. Snip tops off broad beans to discourage blackfly. Sap-sucking pests prefer the tenderest tips of spring-sown crops. If these bits are clean, steam for delicious greens. Otherwise burn **(Fig. 94, p. 111)**.

81. Keep broad beans well watered as their pods swell **(Fig. 93, p. 110)**.

82. Test ripeness of broad beans by squeezing the plump pods to feel for bean development within. When the shapes of bulging beans are visible in the pod, they're ready.

83. Keep broad beans that are top-heavy with fat pods well supported with canes and string **(Fig. 118, p. 134)**.

84. Clear spent broad beans by cutting tops ('haulm') at ground level. Leave roots in the soil to slow-release nitrogen from the root nodules. A

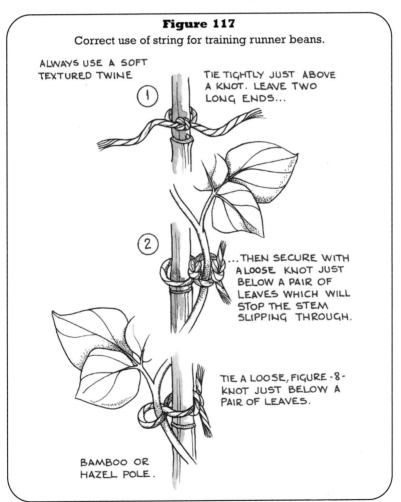

Figure 117
Correct use of string for training runner beans.

ALWAYS USE A SOFT TEXTURED TWINE

① TIE TIGHTLY JUST ABOVE A KNOT. LEAVE TWO LONG ENDS...

② ...THEN SECURE WITH A LOOSE KNOT JUST BELOW A PAIR OF LEAVES WHICH WILL STOP THE STEM SLIPPING THROUGH.

TIE A LOOSE, FIGURE -8- KNOT JUST BELOW A PAIR OF LEAVES.

BAMBOO OR HAZEL POLE.

follow-on crop of cabbages will benefit from this natural fertilizer **(Fig. 119, p. 134)**.

85. PEA. Remove and compost rows of spent peas. Cut the stems (haulm) but leave roots in the soil to rot down naturally and slow-release their locked-up supplies of nitrogen **(Fig. 119, p. 134)**.

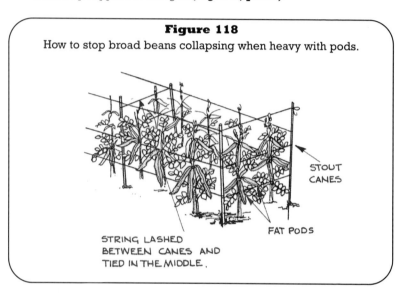

Figure 118
How to stop broad beans collapsing when heavy with pods.

STOUT CANES

FAT PODS

STRING LASHED BETWEEN CANES AND TIED IN THE MIDDLE.

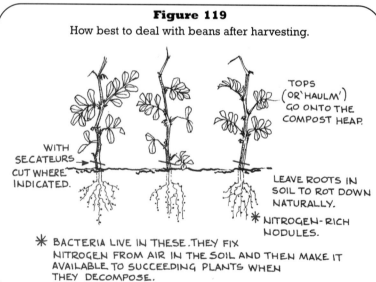

Figure 119
How best to deal with beans after harvesting.

TOPS (OR 'HAULM') GO ONTO THE COMPOST HEAP.

WITH SECATEURS CUT WHERE INDICATED.

LEAVE ROOTS IN SOIL TO ROT DOWN NATURALLY.

✳ NITROGEN-RICH NODULES.

✳ BACTERIA LIVE IN THESE. THEY FIX NITROGEN FROM AIR IN THE SOIL AND THEN MAKE IT AVAILABLE TO SUCCEEDING PLANTS WHEN THEY DECOMPOSE.

Edible flowers

86. SUNFLOWER. Tie sunflowers to supporting poles. Watch out for slugs **(Fig. 48, p. 64)**.

87. GLOBE ARTICHOKE. Weed and water thoroughly around the silver-green leaved 'crowns' **(Fig. 80, p. 97)**.

88. SALSIFY. Harvest salsify flower buds with about 5–10cm of stem. Steam bunches for a minute, serve with a knob of margarine as 'poor man's asparagus'.

89. NASTURTIUM. Commence picking nasturtium leaves for peppery saladings.

Cereal

90. SWEETCORN. Hoe amongst sweetcorn and dill (planted as companions).

Fruit garden

91. APPLE, PEAR, CHERRY & PLUM. Water all fruit trees with at least two good bucket-loads per tree. Pour it around the roots slowly so water has a chance to get into the ground and not run off.

92. Tie in restricted (trained) apple and pear trees to training wires **(Feb 63/Fig. 120, p. 135)**.

93. Prune established plums and other 'stone fruits' at the end of this month or beginning of next. Remove crossing, dead, dying, damaged

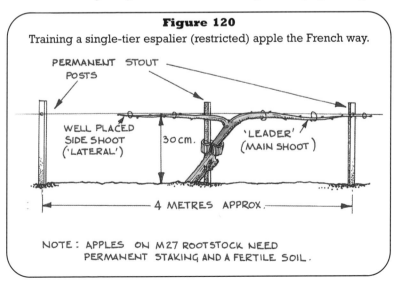

Figure 120

Training a single-tier espalier (restricted) apple the French way.

PERMANENT STOUT POSTS

WELL PLACED SIDE SHOOT ('LATERAL')

30 cm.

'LEADER' (MAIN SHOOT)

4 METRES APPROX.

NOTE: APPLES ON M27 ROOTSTOCK NEED PERMANENT STAKING AND A FERTILE SOIL.

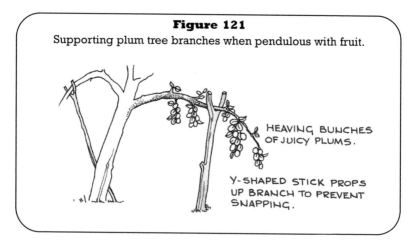

Figure 121
Supporting plum tree branches when pendulous with fruit.

HEAVING BUNCHES OF JUICY PLUMS.

Y-SHAPED STICK PROPS UP BRANCH TO PREVENT SNAPPING.

or diseased branches. Keep reduction to a minimum. No need to reduce leaders (main shoots). Also, tear shoots coming from around the trunk base. These are called 'suckers' and will multiply if cut with secateurs so always pull off by hand when small.

94. Formatively prune plums being grown as bushes or standards as for apples **(Mar 93a)**.

95. Thin developing plums by removing up to or over half in a good 'setting' year (when lots of plums hang heavy on the tree) to avoid potential snapping of over-laden branches. Cut them out with thin scissors. Consider propping up branches under pressure with Y-shaped sticks **(Fig. 121, p. 136)**.

96. MORELLO CHERRY. On specimens in their third year of being trained as a fan, select newly-produced leading main branches and tie them on to the horizontal wires with soft string. These will become the permanent framework of the tree. Take care not to damage the bark. Remove buds facing in or outwards by rubbing off with a thumb **(Feb 63, Jul 107)**.

97. Erect a bird-proof cage around fan-trained trees before the fruits commence to ripen.

98. RED & WHITE CURRANT. Net red and white currants to thwart birds (who will strip the berries given half a chance).

99. BLACKCURRANT. Net blackcurrants against birds **(May 129)**.

100. RASPBERRY. Water then mulch raspberries with grass mowings if available **(Nov 50)**.

101. STRAWBERRY. Pick strawberries when they are dry, fully coloured and before they go soft. Doing this pleasurable job in the heat of the day retains best flavour in the fruits. Retain the plug and a centimetre of stalk. Summer-fruiting varieties will bear once in early summer.

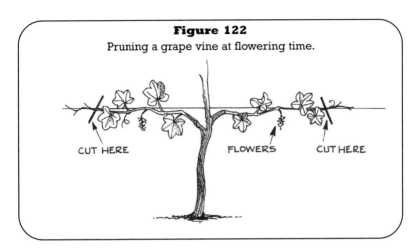

Figure 122

Pruning a grape vine at flowering time.

CUT HERE   FLOWERS   CUT HERE

Perpetual or Remontant strawberries crop on and off from summer until the first autumnal frosts.

102. GRAPE. Prune vines planted this year; cut back 'lateral' side-growths to five leaves. If there are any 'sub-laterals' coming off these then cut these back to one leaf. Allow the leader (main stem) to carry on. Tie it to a support cane if necessary.

103. Prune second-year vines; as above **(Jun 102)**. Cut out flowering 'trusses' for long-term vigour: they will produce now but a lot of energy is required and it's best to conserve this until the plant is stronger.

104. Prune established vines to within two leaves of each flower truss. Limit to one grape bunch per side branch ('lateral'). If no flower truss shows snip back beyond five leaves **(Fig. 122, p.137)**.

JULY

Strange though it may seem, early July often sees a lull in the edible garden. If all is going to plan, veggies should be developing and cropping nicely. The pressure of spring and that whoosh of early growth has passed again.

Relish the heat and long evenings. These are the glory days, and nights, of high summer.

Vegetable fruits will now be on the menu.

Continue digging potatoes and young roots, plucking peas and beans and picking great bowlfuls of dreamy salads. With a happy combination of luck and judgement there should be great choice of fruit and veg to eat fresh or take from store.

As well as spending more time, trug-in-arm, foraging for tonight's dinner and maybe even lunch tomorrow, weed and vegetation control remains a priority. Keep your hoe sharp and busy. Do a little-and-often to keep life easy. Get stuck in amongst your charges. While you toil peacefully, keep a caretaker's eye out for signs of pests and disease.

This could be the last chance to sow a few rows of family favourites and still have enough growing season left to secure a crop. A range of oriental leaves are appropriate, plus winter radishes such as Black Spanish Round and Mooli. They're bigger than their red-shouldered cousins, more spicy too. They'll be ready from autumn, stand through half the winter and be welcome additions to home-made stew.

Be prepared to share spoils from the fruit garden with birds if you choose not to protect berries with nets.

Carry out 'summer pruning' to induce formation of next year's fruit buds.

General jobs to do

1. Cut back comfrey and remove to the liquid manure bin or allow to wilt in the sun, then apply as a mulch around runner beans or in rows between crops **(Fig. 99, p. 118)**.

2. Cut nettles from around compost heaps. Getting stung when doing the right thing (i.e. composting) is no fun **(Fig. 123, p. 139)**.

3. Maintain tidy plot edges by cutting back all round. Maintain a neat frame for your horticultural picture, so to speak **(Fig. 49, p. 65)**.

4. Mow paths weekly **(Fig. 79, p. 96)**.

5. Cut back vegetation overflowing onto paths to remove any obstructions.

6. Keep on top of couch grass along plot edges. Remove and burn. Maintaining a 25cm 'kerb' at the edge will thwart this shallow-rooting invader **(Mar 11/Fig. 124, p. 141)**.

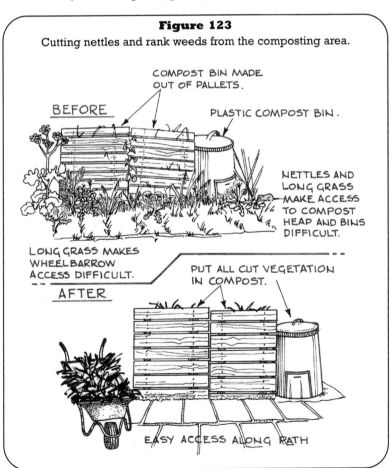

Figure 123

Cutting nettles and rank weeds from the composting area.

COMPOST BIN MADE OUT OF PALLETS.

BEFORE

PLASTIC COMPOST BIN.

NETTLES AND LONG GRASS MAKE ACCESS TO COMPOST HEAP AND BINS DIFFICULT.

LONG GRASS MAKES WHEELBARROW ACCESS DIFFICULT.

AFTER

PUT ALL CUT VEGETATION IN COMPOST.

EASY ACCESS ALONG PATH

7. Get busy with the hoe whenever possible when soil surface is dry and the sun is out **(Fig. 98, p. 117)**.

8. Weed as you harvest to keep on top of the workload and keep edible gardening fun **(Fig. 125, p. 141)**.

9. Remove any big weeds showing signs of flowering before seeds are set **(Fig. 76, p. 93)**.

10. Keep water butts topped up in dry weather (use a hose).

11. Keep recently sown seeds moist in the hot sun. Water with a rose on the can either in the morning first thing, or at night-time.

12. Water all leafy crops in dry weather direct to the roots. Moist but not wet is the key. A weekly drenching achieves this rather than daily dampening **(Fig. 80, p. 97)**.

13. All crops in containers need plenty of good water, probably daily.

14. If rain is not forthcoming give water to beans and cucurbits especially **(Fig. 126, p. 141)**.

15. Tidy up messy areas. Do it as you go along. It really is much easier than letting chaos develop and then having a big task looming when other, more urgent jobs (like weeding) need attention.

16. Sow green manure Phacelia in open soil where crops were harvested **(Jun 15)**.

17. Collect manure from outside sources in plastic bags and deliver to the plot for future use **(Fig. 102, p. 120)**.

18. Collect grass mowings wherever possible and add to the compost or mulch around crops (avoid any which have been chemically treated).

19. Allow time for savoured moments strolling around and looking over the veg patch with a keen eye; this is a great time of the year!

20. Get up early as often as possible to enjoy the dawn of each new day. There is an element of truth in the saying that one hour before lunchtime is worth two in the afternoon.

Leaves & greens

21. CABBAGE, BROCCOLI, KALE, CALABRESE (BRASSICAS). Start regular inspections of brassicas for cabbage white butterfly eggs, and rub out with thumb where found. Be sure to look on the underside of leaves as well.

22. Fix stout supports for all the brassicas if they are looking unstable. Alternatively, mound earth up around the stem with a draw hoe and pat firm **(Aug 23)**.

23. Pot on young red cabbages. Line the bottom of a larger pot with compost. JI Number 2 is ideal, or peat-free alternative. Knock cabbage plants from smaller pot **(Fig. 54, p. 70)** then sit in new container. Firm

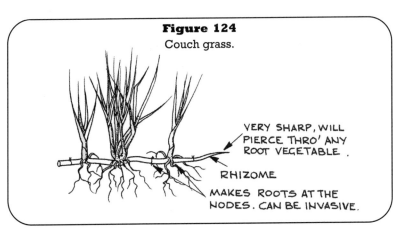

Figure 124
Couch grass.

VERY SHARP, WILL
PIERCE THRO' ANY
ROOT VEGETABLE.

RHIZOME

MAKES ROOTS AT THE
NODES. CAN BE INVASIVE.

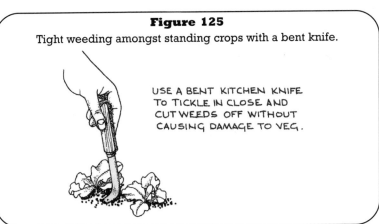

Figure 125
Tight weeding amongst standing crops with a bent knife.

USE A BENT KITCHEN KNIFE
TO TICKLE IN CLOSE AND
CUT WEEDS OFF WITHOUT
CAUSING DAMAGE TO VEG.

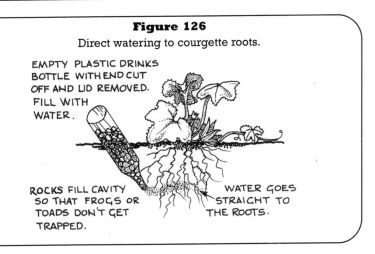

Figure 126
Direct watering to courgette roots.

EMPTY PLASTIC DRINKS
BOTTLE WITH END CUT
OFF AND LID REMOVED.
FILL WITH
WATER.

ROCKS FILL CAVITY
SO THAT FROGS OR
TOADS DON'T GET
TRAPPED.

WATER GOES
STRAIGHT TO
THE ROOTS.

July

more compost around the sides. Young cabbage can go in quite deep – up to first set of leaves is fine **(Fig. 81, p. 98)**.

24. Sow varieties of Spring cabbage in pots (e.g. Wintergreen, Myatt's Offenham). Sow two seeds 2cm deep and thin to the stronger. Keep in partial shade. Protect from butterflies with horticultural fleece **(Fig. 15, p. 25)**.

25. Plant out purple sprouting and calabrese if not already done **(Figs 81 and 82, pp. 98 and 99)**.

26. Weed amongst purple sprouting and kale with hoe and hand **(Figs 50 and 125, pp. 66 and 141)**.

27. Plant out Nine Star Perennial broccoli, firm and deep into fertile, moist soil. Allow 90cm between plants. Will require support from a stake **(Aug 23/Fig. 81, p. 98)**.

28. Tie shredded plastic bags to canes and insert the canes around Nine

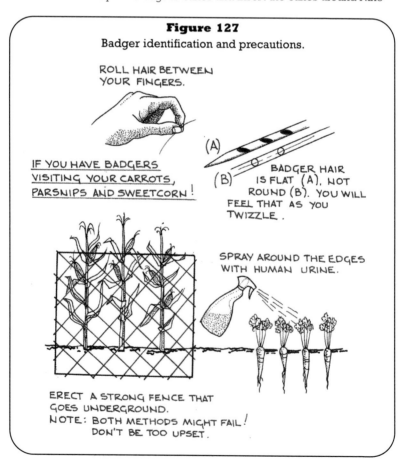

Figure 127

Badger identification and precautions.

ROLL HAIR BETWEEN YOUR FINGERS.

(A)

IF YOU HAVE BADGERS VISITING YOUR CARROTS, PARSNIPS AND SWEETCORN!

(B) BADGER HAIR IS FLAT (A), NOT ROUND (B). YOU WILL FEEL THAT AS YOU TWIZZLE.

SPRAY AROUND THE EDGES WITH HUMAN URINE.

ERECT A STRONG FENCE THAT GOES UNDERGROUND.
NOTE: BOTH METHODS MIGHT FAIL!
DON'T BE TOO UPSET.

Star Perennial broccoli to keep off pigeons **(Fig. 16, p. 26)**.

29. Apply mulch of well-rotted manure over bed where broad beans were (in preparation for spring cabbages).

30. Mulch all brassicas thickly with well-rotted manure **(Fig. 59, p. 73)**.

31. LETTUCE. Sow lines of lettuce. Make a straight, 1.5cm deep drill in fertile, weed-free soil. Flood it with water and allow to drain. Sow seeds thinly, directly into the drill, cover over and tamp firm with the flat end of a rake. Lettuce seed struggles to germinate when temperature exceeds 25°C so provide shade if possible. Or sow similarly in trays for pricking out later **(Aug 27/Fig. 14, p. 25)**.

32. Weed closely amongst lettuces. Remove tatty outer foliage to take away slug hidey-holes.

33. Clear lettuces going to seed.

34. LEAF BEET. Clear exhausted Swiss chard to the compost heap. Or place it at the bottom of a trench earmarked to take a late sowing of beans **(Apr 84)**.

35. Sow leaf beet and Swiss chard for winter and spring greens. 1cm deep in rows 30–45cm apart. Thin in stages, aiming for 20cm between plants. Will be more productive come the winter if protected with a cloche or horticultural fleece **(Figs 34 and 64, pp. 44 and 77)**.

36. Thin Giant Winter spinach sown last month so that neighbouring plants are not touching **(Fig. 86, p. 103)**.

37. Clear bolted spinach plants to compost.

38. Artificially drench the roots of all 'greens' weekly in a drought **(Fig. 80, p. 97)**.

Roots, tubers & stems

39. Take badger precautions if they are in your area at night by spraying human urine around their favourite crops (spuds, parsnips, carrots). Save and store this useful mammal repellent (and compost activator – just pour it on) in a discreet bucket **(Fig. 127, p. 142)**.

40. CARROT. Sow, either direct into a prepared seedbed or into pots and containers **(Mar 54/Fig. 60, p. 74)**.

41. Thin and earth up carrots. Drawing a little soil around the necks will prevent 'Green Top' (which is when exposed carrot shoulders lose their orange colour). Green Top is, however, only cosmetic **(Sep 54)**.

42. Thin container-grown carrots so there are no clumps, but let them fight for space. Roots will be thin but hopefully long, tender and very sweet. Water more often than those in the ground – every other day is ideal in hot, dry spells but can leave it longer if drenchings are thorough (make sure you have provided drainage holes in container bottoms!).

43. ASPARAGUS, RHUBARB. Hand weed asparagus bed. Show weeds no mercy. This is always a productive use of time. May need to get in between the rows on hands and knees by this stage of the summer, but do it anyway **(Fig. 87, p. 104)**.

44. Keep up the watering of asparagus and rhubarb.

45. Use stakes and string to support ferny asparagus tops and prevent wind damage **(Fig. 108, p. 126)**.

46. Control asparagus beetles by hand picking **(Jun 52/Fig. 109, p. 126)**.

47. BEETROOT. Thin latest sowings. Aim for between 10 and 15cm between the roots eventually but get there in stages. So maybe thin now and again when leaves are touching until desired distance apart is achieved. Hand weed at the same time. Keep moist **(Fig. 86, p. 103)**.

48. Sow cylindrical varieties of beetroot **(Jun 46)**.

49. KOHLRABI. Sow **(Apr 43)**.

50. TURNIP. Sow **(Apr 44)**.

51. SWEDE. Water swedes in dry conditions. Thoroughly drench weekly.

52. POTATO. Rake bed where First Early potatoes were level in preparation for sowing green manure or planting out the next crop **(Jun 15)**.

53. Spray Bordeaux Mixture on Second Early and Maincrop potatoes. This copper sulphate treatment is the only preventative measure which might stop blight. Mix according to manufacturer's instructions. Will only succeed if first applied before blight attack (i.e. end of June/beginning of July) and thereafter every three weeks until late August. Spray must coat all leaf and stem surfaces both top and bottom. This treatment is certified as organic but will prove harmful to soil creatures.

54. Cut down haulms of spuds showing any signs of blight. This serious fungal disease can strike whenever the weather is humid (warm and moist). In suitable conditions inspect daily if possible. Blight can flatten a potato crop overnight. Shows as brown patches on leaf tips and edges with white halo of fungal fluff on leaf undersides. Distinctive aroma in wet weather. No cure for domestic growers. Once spotted, cut and remove all tops ('haulm'). Burn immediately. Delay in doing so can lead to infection of potatoes under ground and complete loss of crop. Try cultivating blight-resistant maincrop varieties Sarpo Mira or Sarpo Axona. Alternatively only grow First Earlies which yield to harvest before blight season (if you're lucky!).

55. JERUSALEM ARTICHOKE. Weed around Jerusalem artichokes. Will still crop well if neglected but always happier with some TLC.

56. Cut tops off by a third to a half to reduce wind damage in summer storms **(Fig. 107, p. 124)**.

57. FLORENCE FENNEL. Hand weed. Keep fennel well watered to avoid early running to flower ('bolting').

Veg fruit

58. Keep all crops beginning to fruit consistently well watered. Add liquid feed once or twice weekly **(Fig. 78, p. 95)**.

59. TOMATO. Check tomatoes for signs of blight on foliage; remove any showing signs of discolouration immediately and burn. This is the same affliction which potatoes suffer from. Prevention with copper sulphate spray is the same as for potatoes **(Jul 53/54)**.

60. Keep tying in tomatoes to supporting canes and pinching out side shoots **(Fig. 111, p. 128)**.

61. Remove any tomato leaves which are obviously shading fruits **(Aug 51)**.

62. Remove oldest and lowest leaves from tomatoes if they are looking shabby and tired.

63. Carefully monitor greenhouse-grown plants, removing unhealthy foliage and keeping environment well ventilated. In very hot weather you might need to provide shading. Water daily.

64. TOMATILLO. Tie in tomatillo plants to supporting canes to keep plants upright and fruits clean off the soil **(Fig. 117, p. 133)**.

65. CUCUMBER. Train climbing cucumbers up their supports. Keep picking fruits when they are small and at their best, to encourage more production **(Fig. 128, p. 145)**.

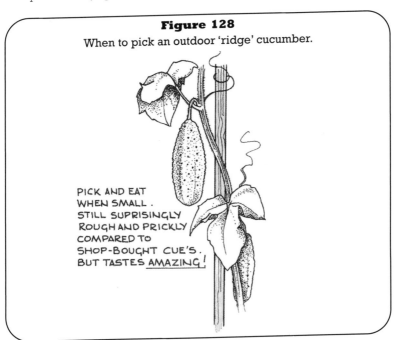

Figure 128
When to pick an outdoor 'ridge' cucumber.

PICK AND EAT WHEN SMALL. STILL SUPRISINGLY ROUGH AND PRICKLY COMPARED TO SHOP-BOUGHT CUE'S. BUT TASTES AMAZING!

66. SQUASH, MARROW, COURGETTE. Spot weed amongst the sprawling cucurbits. Their foliage will shade out most but occasionally a tall weed shoots up through. Pull it out before seed is set.

67. Give squashes, courgettes and marrows plenty to drink applied down at the roots. Take the sprinkler 'rose' attachment off the can spout. Aim water at the root zone rather than splashing it all over the leaves. In strong sunshine water droplets act like mini mirrors and can cause burns **(Fig. 126, p. 141)**.

Onion tribe

68. LEEK. Hoe through rows of leeks and anywhere else regardless of whether weeds are visible or not **(Fig. 50, p. 66)**.

69. Continue to puddle in leeks whenever time permits **(Jun 69)**.

70. Plant out last of the nursery bed leeks into prepared ground **(Jun 69)**.

71. ONION. Sow spring onions **(Mar 72)**.

72. Harvest over-wintered onions **(Sep 67)**. Ease from soil with a fork, pull and shake roots free. Tie in bunches, hang in a dry, airy place. Start to consume immediately. Use those with thick central stems first.

73. Do not weed the maincrop onions **(Mar 69)** from mid-month until harvesting in August. Too much water in the onion bulb can affect long-term storage. Be content to let weeds suck up much of it and enjoy firmer, flavoursome onions well into next year as a result.

74. SHALLOT. Harvest shallots when tops are brown and shrinking and bulbs lift easily from the soil **(Fig. 116, p.132)**.

75. GARLIC, ELEPHANT GARLIC. Lay out garlic, shallots and Elephant garlic on slatted pallets or chicken wire to dry in a sunny place **(Fig. 116, p. 132)**.

76. Harvest Elephant garlic when tops are browning. Dry and store as for garlic **(Fig. 116, p. 132)**.

77. Hand weed garlic before harvesting.

78. Sow green manure where onion family members have been cleared **(Jun 15)**.

Peas & beans

79. Weed thoroughly amongst all peas and beans with hoe and hand **(Figs 50 and 125, pp. 66 and 141)**.

80. Weekly liquid feed for all beans **(Jun 56)**.

81. FRENCH BEAN. Plant dwarf French beans (e.g. Royalty or Purple Teepee) for a late-season harvest (frost permitting) **(May 107)**.

82. Plant bush beans. These are runner beans which don't run! Perfect for a small garden. Plant now for a late crop. Or could use runner bean seeds and keep pinching out the leading shoots. Plant as for dwarf French beans **(May 107)**.

83. PEA. Cut and compost spent peas but leave roots in the soil to decompose naturally **(Fig. 119, p. 134)**.

84. BROAD BEAN. Clear the last of the broads but leave roots in the soil to rot down and release locked-up nitrogen for next crop. Maybe save some dried seeds in pods for sowing next year and save yourself a bit of money **(Fig. 119, p. 134)**.

Edible flowers

85. GLOBE ARTICHOKE. Weed around globe artichoke crowns and keep well watered.

86. SUNFLOWER. Tie sunflowers to supporting canes or posts. Guard against losing specimens of Giant Single, which can reach 3m plus, in high winds.

87. Admire the first Giant Single sunflower bloom of the season, if you're lucky.

88. SALSIFY. Collect salsify seeds to raise in pots or give to family and friends. Gather the hoary 'clocks' on a dry, sunny day. Rub them in your hands then lay on a plate. Gently blow to remove the beardy bits but retain heavier seeds (which are like long grains of rice). This process is called 'winnowing' **(Fig. 129, p. 147)**.

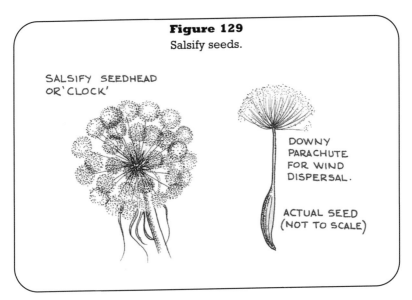

Figure 129
Salsify seeds.

SALSIFY SEEDHEAD OR 'CLOCK'

DOWNY PARACHUTE FOR WIND DISPERSAL.

ACTUAL SEED (NOT TO SCALE)

Cereals

89. SWEETCORN. With a draw hoe, earth up soil around the stem bottoms of sweetcorn to help stabilize them and do weeding at the same time.

90. Erect sturdy wire fence around sweetcorn to keep the badgers out (good luck!) **(Fig. 127, p. 142)**.

Fruit garden

91. APPLE, PEAR & PLUM. Assess apple bunches early in the month when they are shedding undersized fruitlets naturally. This is called the June Drop. If bunches still seem overcrowded then thin by hand. On apple trees, if the largest, most centrally-placed fruit (the so-called 'King Apple') is less than perfect then snip it out with slender scissors. Leaving two or three of the best pieces on each truss should result in better quality fruit **(Fig. 130, p. 148)**.

92. Thin clusters of young pears after the naturally occurring 'June Drop' (when the tree sheds fruitlets of its own accord). Remove up to half of all fruits on all clusters to promote healthier and heavier crops from those remaining. Retain the largest and most handsome **(Fig. 130, p. 148)**.

93. Late on, or in August, 'summer prune' restricted forms of apples and pears (those grown as bushes, espaliers, flat fans or other human-

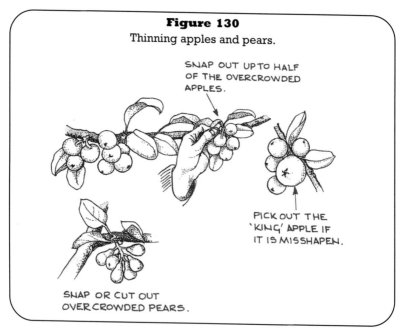

Figure 130
Thinning apples and pears.

SNAP OUT UP TO HALF OF THE OVERCROWDED APPLES.

PICK OUT THE 'KING' APPLE IF IT IS MISSHAPEN.

SNAP OR CUT OUT OVERCROWDED PEARS.

dictated shapes) then tie them in to training wires **(Feb 63/Fig. 117, p. 133)**. Identify laterals (side shoots) that are over 23cm long, then cut off this season's new growth (paler in colour and smoother of bark) as follows **(Fig. 131, p. 149)**:

- if growing from a 'lateral' or 'spur' **(Mar 93b)** prune to either 2.5cm or one leaf above the 'basal cluster' (the group of leaves at the base of a shoot);
- if coming straight out of a 'leader' (main branch) take down to three leaves above the 'basal cluster';
- leave anything less than 23cm or not ripened (i.e. still soft) until September or October.

94. Give fruit trees a generous amount of water if they have been planted within the last four years. Two buckets, emptied slowly at the roots, is

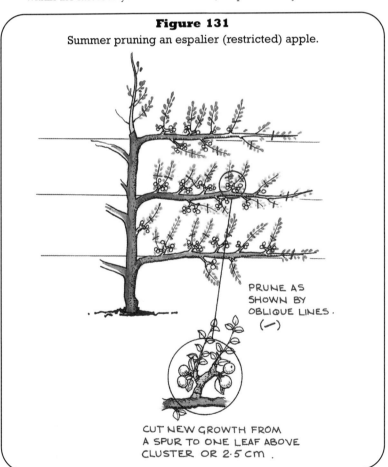

Figure 131
Summer pruning an espalier (restricted) apple.

PRUNE AS SHOWN BY OBLIQUE LINES. (╱)

CUT NEW GROWTH FROM A SPUR TO ONE LEAF ABOVE CLUSTER OR 2·5 cm .

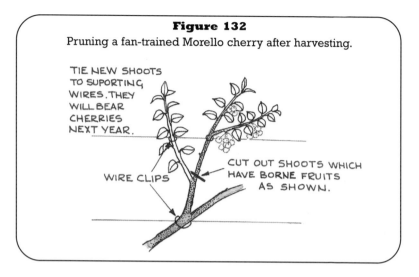

Figure 132

Pruning a fan-trained Morello cherry after harvesting.

TIE NEW SHOOTS TO SUPORTING WIRES. THEY WILL BEAR CHERRIES NEXT YEAR.

WIRE CLIPS

CUT OUT SHOOTS WHICH HAVE BORNE FRUITS AS SHOWN.

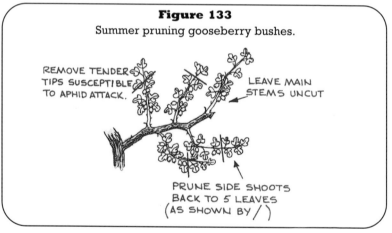

Figure 133

Summer pruning gooseberry bushes.

REMOVE TENDER TIPS SUSCEPTIBLE TO APHID ATTACK.

LEAVE MAIN STEMS UNCUT

PRUNE SIDE SHOOTS BACK TO 5 LEAVES (AS SHOWN BY /)

beneficial to their establishment **(Fig. 74, p. 89)**.

95. Second thinning of plum clusters if branches are struggling to bear the weight **(Jun 95)**.

96. Harvest plums from month's end to October, depending on variety. Should be delightfully soft but not squashy when perfectly ripe.

97. MORELLO CHERRY. Prune fan-trained specimens soon after harvesting. Cut out all shoots which have yielded fruits back to the main framework of branches. Tie in the current season's shoots as replacements: the Morello cherry yields this year on wood produced the summer before. It is this new growth which will be productive next time around **(Feb 63/Fig.132, p. 150)**.

98. GOOSEBERRY. Early in the month, 'summer prune' established gooseberry bushes. This means snipping all newly-produced side shoots (the 'laterals') back to five leaves. This not only thins out a congested bush but also removes the tender tips which are attractive to insect pests. Don't touch the main stems ('leaders') **(Fig. 133, p. 150)**.

99. RED & WHITE CURRANT. Net red and white currants against birds. Harvest the dangling 'strigs' before they do!

100. Early in month, 'summer prune' red and white currant cordons **(Feb 73)** by nipping this season's side shoots back to four leaves from the main stem. If further side shoots (or 'sub laterals') have developed nip these back to one leaf. Do not prune the main stem at all in the early years. Only when the cordon is established should the 'leader' be summer pruned back to four leaves on new, current season's growth.

101. BLACKCURRANT. Net blackcurrants to keep birds off.

102. RASPBERRY. Prune summer raspberries. This involves removing all the canes which have yielded fruit in this season. Cut them off at ground level. Leave no stubs. New canes, which have grown since the spring, should be tied to the wires **(Jan 49)** as replacement canes – they will fruit next year. Weave the tops of canes along the top wire or tie and

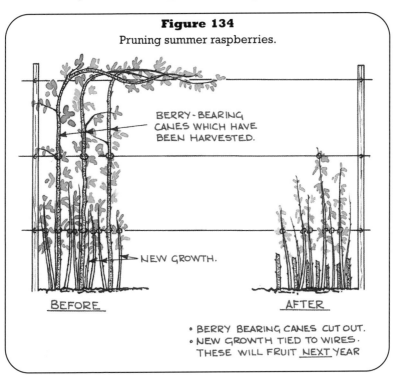

Figure 134
Pruning summer raspberries.

BERRY-BEARING
CANES WHICH HAVE
BEEN HARVESTED.

NEW GROWTH.

BEFORE

AFTER

• BERRY BEARING CANES CUT OUT.
• NEW GROWTH TIED TO WIRES.
  THESE WILL FRUIT NEXT YEAR

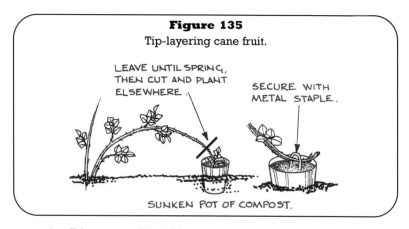

Figure 135
Tip-layering cane fruit.

LEAVE UNTIL SPRING,
THEN CUT AND PLANT
ELSEWHERE.

SECURE WITH
METAL STAPLE.

SUNKEN POT OF COMPOST.

snip off the excess **(Fig. 134, p. 151)**.

103. BLACKBERRY, TAYBERRY, LOGANBERRY & RELATIONS. Commence the propagation of new plants by 'tip layering'. Just bend down and bury a cane tip in about 10cm of soil. Secure with a wire staple if desired and leave until spring **(Fig. 135, p. 152)**.

104. STRAWBERRY. Propagate strawberry runners early in the month. Choose a healthy plant which bears fruit well. Sink a 9cm-diameter pot filled with a 50:50 soil/compost mix into the ground beneath a strong 'runner' – that is, a young strawberry plant which has grown on a stem away from the parent but is still attached. Select a runner near to the parent plant as those further away are liable to be weaklings. Press the young plant into the growing medium and secure with a bent wire staple. Do not sever it from the parent but do cut away all runners beyond this first one. Allow four to six weeks to take root and become established before snipping free and planting out August to October **(Aug 81/Fig. 136, p. 152)**.

105. End of the month, tidy harvested strawberry plants: scrape back any

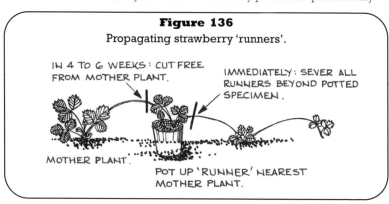

Figure 136
Propagating strawberry 'runners'.

IN 4 TO 6 WEEKS: CUT FREE
FROM MOTHER PLANT.

IMMEDIATELY: SEVER ALL
RUNNERS BEYOND POTTED
SPECIMEN.

MOTHER PLANT.

POT UP 'RUNNER' NEAREST
MOTHER PLANT.

mulching material, remove all runners and weeds plus tatty leaves. Cut back to about 10cm above the crowns. Burn everything instead of composting to prevent spread of viruses and disease.

106. In a strawberry bed which is in its second year, you may allow rooted runners to remain in the rows. Distance between plants is reduced, fruits will be smaller but the overall weight of crop will increase. Retain bare soil between the rows by hoeing **(Fig. 50, p. 66)**.

107. FIG. Tie fan-trained fig tree to supporting framework of canes. Prune out branches growing at right angles to the flat fan, plus anything dead, diseased and congested or crossing new growth **(Fig. 137, p. 153)**.

108. GRAPE. Cut back all fruit-bearing branches on vines to two leaves beyond last bunch of grapes **(Fig. 122, p. 137)**.

Figure 137
Tying branches of a fan-trained fig to supporting framework of canes.

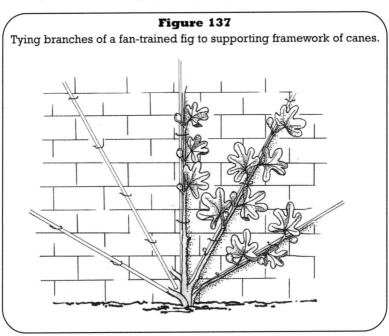

AUGUST

Unless you can find keen and reliable friends or neighbours, August is possibly not the best month for going on holiday!

Vegetable fruits plus peas and beans rely on regular, consistent harvesting to keep them youthful and productive. Letting the pods on runners become woody actually causes changes within the plant which prompt them to cease flowering. Sweet and tender courgettes develop into bloated monsters seemingly overnight. Harvesting, preparing and storing veg can feel like a full-time job.

Give away whatever your family can't eat. Offering the cream of your spoils to others who can't grow their own due to lack of garden, time or good health is beneficial to your soul. This is something which should not be taken for granted. Kind gestures can make a person's day, including yours.

Watch the weather this month. Gather maincrop onions when conditions are settled fine and dry. Sort a place for storage in the shed. Organise your clutter. The season of plenty lies ahead.

In the fruit garden, good fortune willing, you'll be inundated with juicy plums. Early apples and pears come into ripeness now.

Some folk will be sick of the sight of raspberries already, but not many! Just as well. The autumn-fruiting varieties get into full swing during August.

Remember that fruits on tree, bush, cane and vine are perennial. This means they'll come back year after year. They produce their bounty with or without human interference. A nip and tuck here and there is designed simply to increase their delicious potential.

General jobs to do

1. Check for pests and diseases. Do this both by day with a caretaker's eye and at night with a torch and bucket. Identify any problems and act accordingly **(Jun 58/Fig. 47, p. 64)**.
2. Keep potted or tray-grown seedlings moist. Do not water in the hot daytime because the sun is magnified through water droplets and can burn the leaves or scorch tender foliage. Do the watering in the early morning or evening instead **(Fig. 12, p. 22)**.
3. Water/feed crops in pots. Thoroughly soak weekly **(Jun 56)**.
4. Hoik out weeds manually. If you do it at the same time as harvesting certain crops nothing gets too out of hand!
5. Keep the hoe busy in the mornings **(Fig. 98, p. 117)**.
6. Remove perennial weeds such as bindweed and horsetail wherever they're appearing on the plot.
7. Tidy the shed in preparation for veg as produce comes in to store **(Nov 2)**.
8. Tidy and potter round the plot to keep everything ship-shape.
9. Cut nettles around compost heaps to allow easy access. Compost the nettles or replenish the liquid feed nettle and comfrey bin **(Figs 78 and 123, pp. 95 and 139)**.
10. Cut comfrey and top up the large plastic bin used to make nettle and comfrey tincture (liquid manure) **(Fig. 99, p. 118)**.
11. Trim plot edges to maintain a tidy work space. Ongoing but important **(Fig. 49, p. 65)**.
12. Hoe open soil to keep weeds under control, then broadcast sow a green manure if the space is not needed for a few months. This simply

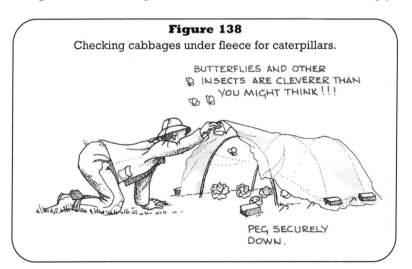

Figure 138

Checking cabbages under fleece for caterpillars.

BUTTERFLIES AND OTHER INSECTS ARE CLEVERER THAN YOU MIGHT THINK !!!

PEG SECURELY DOWN.

involves scattering the seeds by hand over the soil surface in the same way as one might chuck down grain to feed chickens. Then rake it in and let nature do the rest **(Jun 15)**.

13. Wash accumulating dirty pots, which tend to litter the place, in mild soapy water. Doing a few at regular intervals makes this an easy task to keep on top of. Some high-profile gardeners pooh-pooh the idea of washing pots, believing it to be unimportant. Certainly, if your pots are made of clay, washing is essential to prevent the potential spread of fungus or other diseases, but even with plastic pots it is arguably much more pleasant to start each job with clean equipment which you are confident has been disinfected. This job is mellow and relaxing on a warm summer's evening as opposed to a chilly, dark winter's night **(Nov 20)**. Hint, hint!

14. Have a look at veggies under horticultural fleece for unseen signs of pests and diseases. It is easy to not bother, thinking your charges are safe… This may not be the case! Check regularly and act accordingly **(Fig. 138, p. 155)**.

15. Collect and deliver manure. Store it to season for use in a few months' time **(Fig. 102, p. 120)**.

16. Have a fire to dispose of rubbish and stuff which is unsuitable for composting (like woody waste). Always save dry wood ash before it has been rained on as the goodness is quickly washed out ('leached') **(Dec 6)**.

Leaves & greens

17. Constantly check brassicas for caterpillar eggs under the leaves; rub out any patches or individuals with a thumb.

18. Remove caterpillars from brassicas to sacrificial crops of nasturtiums cultivated for this purpose elsewhere, or squash with thumb and first finger.

19. CABBAGE. Plant out Spring and red cabbages sown last month **(Fig. 81, p. 98)** and sow some more now **(Jul 24)**. Spring cabbages can go in at 45cm spacings for harvesting tightly-packed heads next April/May. Or, put them in at half that distance, take every other cabbage for loose leaves ('collards'), and let the others form a head.

20. Secure horticultural fleece over cabbages to keep off butterflies. They will find even the smallest gap so don't underestimate their ability to get under or through a poorly secured barrier.

21. BROCCOLI. Weed amongst purple sprouting broccoli and other brassicas (the cabbage family) with hoe and hand **(Figs 50 and 125, pp. 66 and 141)**.

22. CALABRESE. Compost early-season calabrese plants; bash the stalks with a hammer to aid swift decomposition **(Fig. 17, p. 27)**.

23. BRUSSELS SPROUT. Tie Brussels sprouts plants to stout stakes to keep their roots firm **(Fig. 139, p. 157)**.

24. Mulch Brussels sprouts with well-rotted manure. Flop it thickly around the stems as what is called a 'top dressing' **(Fig. 59, p. 73)**.

25. WINTER PURSLANE. Sow seeds in a tray **(Figs 25 and 26, pp. 36 and 37)**. Seeds are tiny shiny things, impossible to handle singly without the aid of tweezers. Inserting into moist seed compost to a depth of 2 or 3mm is perfect. They can be pricked out into pots **(Feb 27)** when large enough to handle. Potted purslane may then be nurtured over the winter months in a greenhouse or on a bright window sill and planted out the following spring. Alternatively, scatter them thinly on bare soil, rake in and allow to grow by themselves. Easier, but more risky.

26. LETTUCE. Prick out lettuces sown outside in trays during July **(Jul 31)** into pots for culture in a protected environment **(Feb 27)**. Alternatively, plant them into open soil at 20cm intervals for hearting, or half that distance if planning to forage a few leaves at regular intervals. Will require protection from the weather later in the season **(Fig. 53, p. 69)**.

27. Into a tray, sow lettuces suitable for over-wintering (e.g. Enya, Montel, Winter Density). Put in a cool, partially-shaded place to germinate (lettuce seeds fail in temperatures exceeding 25°C) **(Figs 14 and 140, pp. 25 and 158)**.

Figure 139

Staking Brussels sprouts (or other cabbages) to keep roots firm.

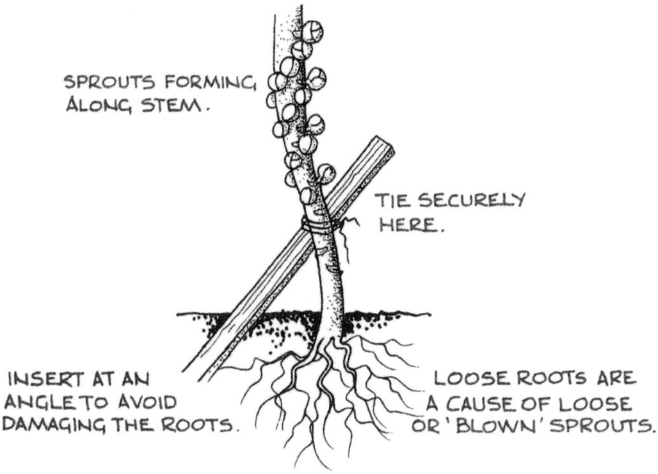

SPROUTS FORMING ALONG STEM.

TIE SECURELY HERE.

INSERT AT AN ANGLE TO AVOID DAMAGING THE ROOTS.

LOOSE ROOTS ARE A CAUSE OF LOOSE OR 'BLOWN' SPROUTS.

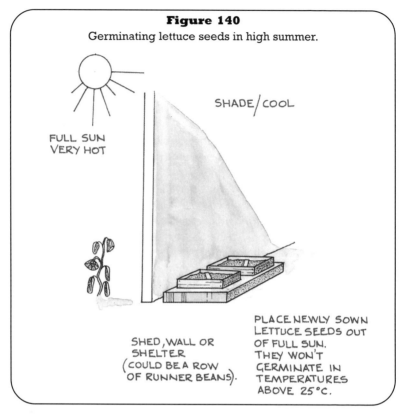

Figure 140
Germinating lettuce seeds in high summer.

SHADE/COOL

FULL SUN
VERY HOT

PLACE NEWLY SOWN
LETTUCE SEEDS OUT
OF FULL SUN.
THEY WON'T
GERMINATE IN
TEMPERATURES
ABOVE 25°C.

SHED, WALL OR
SHELTER
(COULD BE A ROW
OF RUNNER BEANS).

28. Thin lettuce seedlings, and use thinnings either to plant elsewhere or to enjoy as baby leaf salad **(Fig. 105, p. 123)**.

29. LEAF BEET. Cut down all the Swiss chard and leaf beet to about 5cm to encourage fresh new tender growth.

Roots, tubers & stems

30. Inspect the plot for badger damage if they live in your area. Take nightly badger precautions by spraying around roots and tuber beds with human urine **(Fig. 127, p. 142)**.

31. JERUSALEM ARTICHOKE. Cut a third off the tops of Jerusalem artichokes to prevent wind damage **(Fig. 107, p. 124)**.

32. POTATO. Keep a sharp eye on potatoes for signs of blight. Apply Bordeaux mixture or similar preventative spray before mid-month **(Jul 53)**.

33. Cut down and burn potato haulms if necessary **(Jul 54)**.

34. Completely weed soil and ridges in potato bed before starting to harvest. This delay will allow time for the potato skins to 'cure' slightly underground. Lifting is much easier and more fun if you are not fighting for the edible portions through a tangle of weeds.

35. Dig Second Early potatoes for both immediate use and storage. Wipe clean with great care by hand in bucket of water to avoid damaging fragile skin. Allow to dry for a day in the sun then store in plastic fruit trays, keeping potatoes completely dark until wanted for the kitchen (lay blankets, old coats or similar over the top) **(Fig. 141, p. 159)**.

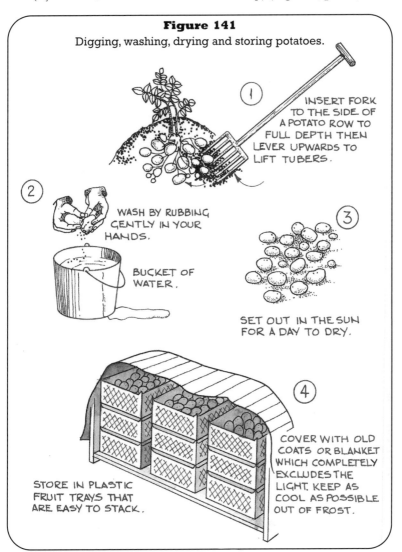

Figure 141
Digging, washing, drying and storing potatoes.

① INSERT FORK TO THE SIDE OF A POTATO ROW TO FULL DEPTH THEN LEVER UPWARDS TO LIFT TUBERS.

② WASH BY RUBBING GENTLY IN YOUR HANDS.

BUCKET OF WATER.

③ SET OUT IN THE SUN FOR A DAY TO DRY.

④ STORE IN PLASTIC FRUIT TRAYS THAT ARE EASY TO STACK.

COVER WITH OLD COATS OR BLANKET WHICH COMPLETELY EXCLUDES THE LIGHT. KEEP AS COOL AS POSSIBLE OUT OF FROST.

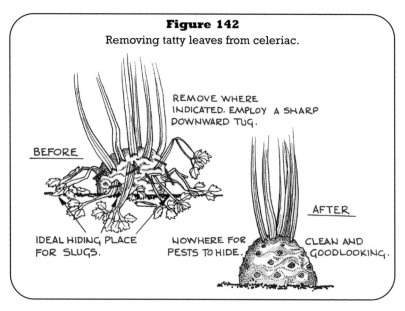

Figure 142
Removing tatty leaves from celeriac.

REMOVE WHERE INDICATED. EMPLOY A SHARP DOWNWARD TUG.

BEFORE

AFTER

IDEAL HIDING PLACE FOR SLUGS.

NOWHERE FOR PESTS TO HIDE.

CLEAN AND GOODLOOKING.

36. Start to dig salad potatoes, as for Second Earlies **(Aug 35)**.

37. CELERIAC. Remove tatty lower leaves on celeriac. Keeps the crop clean and removes hiding places for slugs and snails. Keep crop moist. Liquid feed once or twice **(Jun 56/Fig. 142, p. 160)**.

38. ASPARAGUS. Hand weed asparagus bed **(Fig. 87, p. 104)**.

39. BEETROOT. Clean rows of cylindrical beetroot completely of weeds.

40. SCORZONERA. Cut off any flowers shooting from salsify and scorzonera plants to concentrate energy into the roots.

41. RADISH. Sow winter radishes (e.g. China Rose, Black Spanish Round and Mooli) early in the month. Do this as for summer radishes **(Mar 60)**. Cropping will commence late September/October and can continue until late into the season. Winter radishes are excitingly spicy. They tend to grow bigger and tougher. Thin gradually, aiming eventually for up to 5–10cm between roots **(Fig. 143, p. 161)**.

42. Water container-grown carrots regularly to avoid compost drying out **(Fig. 60, p. 74)**.

43. PARSNIP. Remove old leaves from parsnips which can provide hiding places for slugs and snails **(Dec 25)**.

44. SWEDE. Check over and hand weed amongst swedes.

45. FLORENCE FENNEL. Harvest bulbous Florence fennel. Pull up and compost plants which have bolted (gone to seed) through lack of water, or allow to set seed, harvest and collect them in paper bags for winter stew flavouring **(Fig. 144, p. 162)**.

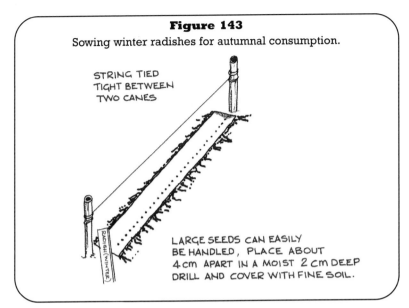

Figure 143
Sowing winter radishes for autumnal consumption.

STRING TIED
TIGHT BETWEEN
TWO CANES

RADISH (WINTER)

LARGE SEEDS CAN EASILY
BE HANDLED, PLACE ABOUT
4 cm APART IN A MOIST 2 cm DEEP
DRILL AND COVER WITH FINE SOIL.

Veg fruit

46. Water all indoor crops daily.

47. In the greenhouse, keep providing adequate ventilation in hot weather.

48. Liquid feed twice weekly this month for veggies producing a crop **(Jun 56)**.

49. Be alert for pests and diseases **(Jun 58)**.

50. TOMATO. Pick tomatoes as they come into ripeness. Try to keep the green 'knuckle' intact by lifting and snapping/twisting rather than pulling the tomato away.

51. Remove leaves from tomatoes that are shading fruits. Let the sunshine in **(Fig. 145, p. 163)**.

52. Remove diseased tomato leaves and stalks (burn, do not compost).

53. Tie outdoor 'cordon' tomatoes in pots to supporting canes, and water daily **(Fig. 110, p. 127)**.

54. MARROW, SQUASH, COURGETTE. Water all cucurbits generously **(Fig. 126, p. 141)**.

55. Pinch out rampant squash shoots to contain the bushy growth if it is smothering other veggies, or pin the stems down with wire staples in the direction(s) that you are happy for them to grow in **(Fig. 146, p. 163)**.

56. Cut and remove shading leaves from squashes and marrows to let sunlight onto fruits and encourage ripening **(Fig. 147, p. 164)**.

57. Harvest the largest marrows.

58. Position flat stones (roofing slates are ideal) under squashes to lift them

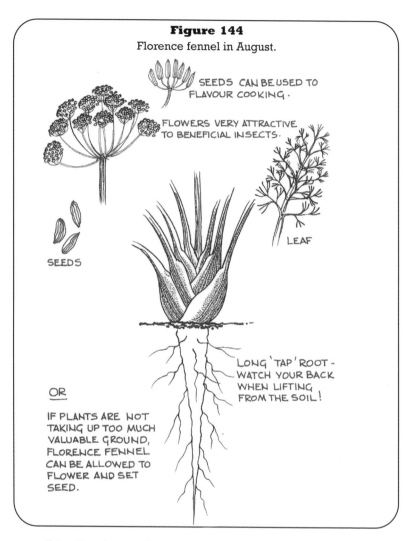

Figure 144
Florence fennel in August.

SEEDS CAN BE USED TO FLAVOUR COOKING.

FLOWERS VERY ATTRACTIVE TO BENEFICIAL INSECTS.

LEAF

SEEDS

LONG 'TAP' ROOT - WATCH YOUR BACK WHEN LIFTING FROM THE SOIL!

OR

IF PLANTS ARE NOT TAKING UP TOO MUCH VALUABLE GROUND, FLORENCE FENNEL CAN BE ALLOWED TO FLOWER AND SET SEED.

off the dirty, damp soil and assist ripening (unless a thick bed of straw has been laid down at planting time) **(Fig. 148, p. 164)**.

59. CUCUMBER. Liquid feed cucumbers twice weekly **(Jun 56)**.

Onion tribe

60. LEEK. Carefully hoe along lines of leeks, then hand weed between the plants **(Fig. 149, p. 165)**.

61. ONION. Harvest onions early in the month if the August forecast is dodgy. Lift and allow to dry in the sunshine for a few days. Then tie in

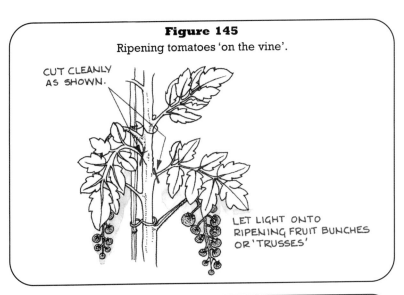

Figure 145

Ripening tomatoes 'on the vine'.

CUT CLEANLY AS SHOWN.

LET LIGHT ONTO RIPENING FRUIT BUNCHES OR 'TRUSSES'

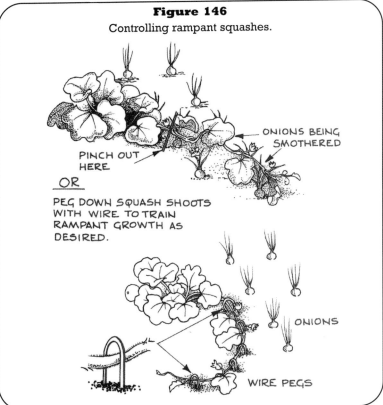

Figure 146

Controlling rampant squashes.

ONIONS BEING SMOTHERED

PINCH OUT HERE

OR

PEG DOWN SQUASH SHOOTS WITH WIRE TO TRAIN RAMPANT GROWTH AS DESIRED.

ONIONS

WIRE PEGS

Figure 147

Removing leaves from a marrow to ripen fruit.

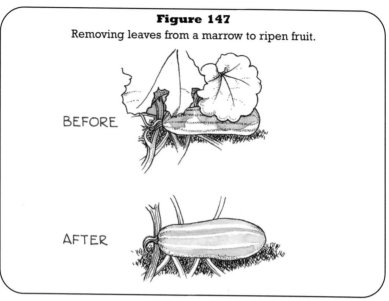

BEFORE

AFTER

Figure 148

Using flat crocks to keep squashes off damp soil.

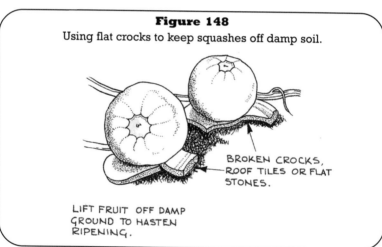

BROKEN CROCKS,
ROOF TILES OR FLAT
STONES.

LIFT FRUIT OFF DAMP
GROUND TO HASTEN
RIPENING.

bunches and hang in a sheltered but airy place to become thoroughly dry and crispy. Do not hurry this process. If the month is set fair onions can be left standing in the ground until early September if need be **(Fig. 150, p. 165)**.

62. Prepare a bed for winter onion sets by applying wood ash, raking to a crumbly tilth, treading firm with the Gardener's Shuffle **(Fig. 38, p. 53)**, and repeating the process. Make sure onions, garlic, shallots and leeks have not been grown here in the last two years. If the fungal disease

Figure 149
Hoeing and hand weeding leeks.

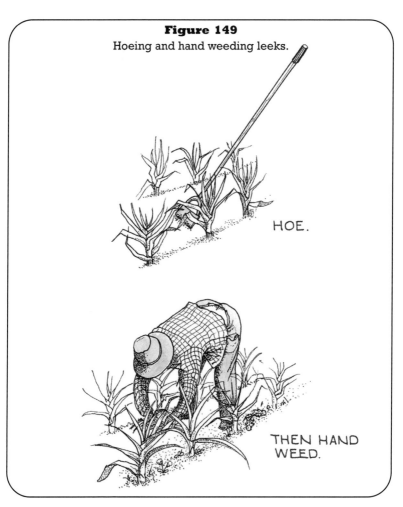

HOE.

THEN HAND
WEED.

Figure 150
Hanging onions on a wire to dry.

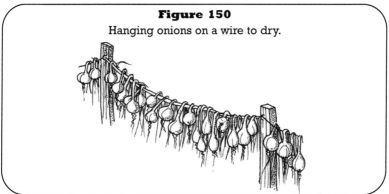

'white rot' has been noted, ground must be clear of the onion family for at least eight years **(Mar 68 and 69/Jun 58)**.

63. Water leeks but not the onions.

64. GARLIC, SHALLOT. Sort and store previously harvested and dried garlic and shallots **(Fig. 116, p. 132)**. Snip stems from garlic with scissors. Roots should be dried by now but these can be trimmed too. Rub papery outer skin off. Do the same with shallots. Place in plastic fruit trays which stack easily on top of each other. Keep in a cool corner of the shed away from rodents.

Peas & beans

65. PEA. Clear away pea sticks no longer in use. Put aside as kindling for future fires.

66. RUNNER & FRENCH BEAN. Water beans consistently and thoroughly at the roots.

67. Liquid feed all beans once weekly **(Jun 56)**.

68. Keep harvesting beans. If pods are allowed to get tough and swollen the plants will stop producing more flowers (and subsequent beans). Pick meticulously even if the woodiest beans end up on the compost heap **(Fig. 151, p. 166)**.

69. The exception to this is borlotti beans. They're grown for the dried crop at season's end. Leave the pods to swell and dry 'on the vine' (as gardeners say).

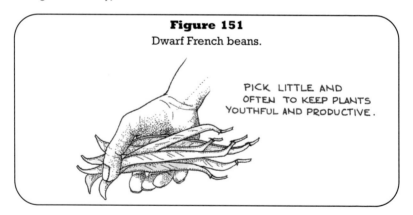

Figure 151
Dwarf French beans.

PICK LITTLE AND OFTEN TO KEEP PLANTS YOUTHFUL AND PRODUCTIVE.

Edible flowers

70. SUNFLOWER. Tie sunflowers to strong supports to prevent them keeling over under their own weight.

71. GLOBE ARTICHOKE. Keep crowns moist and weed free.

72. Dig up and split crowns. Side growths are called 'chards'. Those with roots attached can be potted up for the next generation of edible flower buds **(Fig. 152, p. 167)**.

73. Keep young potted globes moist.

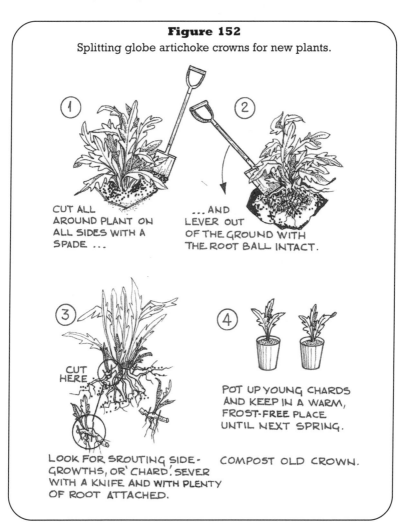

Figure 152
Splitting globe artichoke crowns for new plants.

① CUT ALL AROUND PLANT ON ALL SIDES WITH A SPADE ...

② ...AND LEVER OUT OF THE GROUND WITH THE ROOT BALL INTACT.

③ CUT HERE

LOOK FOR SROUTING SIDE-GROWTHS, OR 'CHARD'. SEVER WITH A KNIFE AND WITH PLENTY OF ROOT ATTACHED.

④ POT UP YOUNG CHARDS AND KEEP IN A WARM, FROST-FREE PLACE UNTIL NEXT SPRING.

COMPOST OLD CROWN.

Cereals

74. SWEETCORN. Help the wind to fertilize sweetcorn when flowers and tassels are showing by tapping the plants to release the pollen. Do this job daily, morning and night **(May 122)**.

Fruit garden

75. APPLE, PEAR & PLUM. Tie in branches of restricted (trained) apples to training wires **(Feb 63/Figs 120 and 137, pp. 135 and 153)**.

76. On apple and pear trees grown as bushes, 'summer prune' by snipping back side growths (laterals) by half of the current season's growth **(Jul 93)**.

77. Summer prune restricted apples (and pears) **(Feb 63/Jul 93)**.

78. Give every young fruit tree a bucket of water each, applied slowly and steadily so it all soaks down to the roots **(Fig. 74, p. 89)**.

79. Formatively prune young gages and plums by nipping back all this year's shoots to five or six leaves beyond the older, previous year's growth. Remove prunings to the fire site.

80. MORELLO CHERRY. Prune if not already done **(Jul 97)**.

81. STRAWBERRY. Prepare, then, a fortnight later, plant strawberries: ideally any time from August until early October at the latest. Use your own potted runners **(Jul 104)** or purchase certified disease-free stock. Select full sun if at all possible. Prepare the ground in advance so that it has time to settle, as for raspberries **(Jan 49)**. Tread firm with the Gardener's Shuffle **(Fig. 38, p. 53)**. Allow 45cm between individual plants and 75cm betwixt rows if planning to establish more than one row. Insert the plants into a trowel-dug hole, retaining as much soil around the root-ball as possible. Nestle into the holes so that the crown

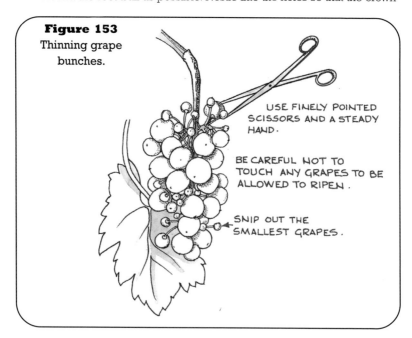

Figure 153
Thinning grape bunches.

USE FINELY POINTED SCISSORS AND A STEADY HAND.

BE CAREFUL NOT TO TOUCH ANY GRAPES TO BE ALLOWED TO RIPEN.

SNIP OUT THE SMALLEST GRAPES.

of the plant is level with the soil surface. Planting either too deep or too shallow (i.e. with bare roots showing) is detrimental, causing rotting or drying. Firm with your fingers and water generously. If purchased bare-rooted stock arrives dry prior to this operation then soak them in a bucket for two hours in advance. At planting time, use your fingers to ensure the roots are fully extended – use a trowel to make the hole and slip them in. Keep well watered until new growth is visible. Beds prepared and planted thus may remain viable for up to four years, whereupon another bed should have been established in a different part of the garden. Fruiting will commence the following season.

82. FIG. Train branches of young fig tree growing against the shed into a fan-shaped framework of bamboo canes **(Nov 55a, b, c/Fig. 137, p. 153)**.

83. GRAPE. Start to thin grapes when berries are pea-sized by snipping out the tiniest ones from within the bunches. Don't handle the bunches; use a Y-shaped twig to manipulate the stem and employ very narrow, pointed scissors. Avoid brushing the powdery 'bloom' off the grapes which have been selected to remain. Removing the smallest grapes now produces bigger and better bunches at harvest time. Aim for about 1cm between those retained. Damaged berries can become diseased **(Fig. 153, p. 168)**.

84. COBNUT & FILBERT. Clear a path by cobnuts and filberts so you can spy and admire the lovely nut clusters, in preparation for harvesting.

85. 'Brut' bushes. Look at the laterals (side branches). On any which are more than 30cm long, snap them about half way so they hang down but are not broken off. This is called 'brutting' and it stimulates the production of flowers which will become next season's nuts – we hope **(Fig. 154, p. 169)**.

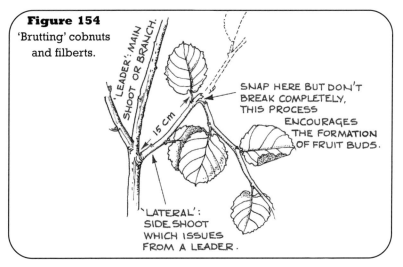

Figure 154
'Brutting' cobnuts and filberts.

'LEADER': MAIN SHOOT OR BRANCH.

15 cm

SNAP HERE BUT DON'T BREAK COMPLETELY, THIS PROCESS ENCOURAGES THE FORMATION OF FRUIT BUDS.

'LATERAL': SIDE SHOOT WHICH ISSUES FROM A LEADER.

SEPTEMBER

Something happens in September. You can smell it in the air, feel it on the breeze, see it in the mists which swirl around our hilltops and linger along river valleys and low-lying plains.

All around, creatures which share our space are feasting on the naturally-occurring country larder. Robin finds his watery, sad-but-sweet voice again; blackbirds and other thrushes flock to the heaving boughs of elder and, alongside greedy pigeons, strip the berries bare; squirrels and foxes dig and bury supplies in secret stashes; the skies are thick with tiny spiders and their silken threads; swallows and martins plunder the soft-bodied fare and by month's end are gone again; daddy-long-legs rise forth from lawns and pasture by the million with a gangly urge to mate, while starlings dash back and forth in a mesmerized feeding frenzy, like sharks diving amongst a shoal of fish.

In the edible garden, now's the time to feast on fruit, gather nuts and harness the ripening power of the sun. Cut back lolling vegetation so the rays can bathe your crops.

Keep the hoe busy, as ever. Sow green manures, plant onion sets, keep picking beans and courgettes.

Lift squashes up off damp soil on a flat piece of stone or slate but don't harvest pumpkins yet. As long as the frosts don't come, your veg patch will remain productive for some weeks still.

September is a fine month. Rest your hands on your hips, arch your back, turn your face to the sky, close your eyes, heave a sigh. It hasn't been such a bad season after all!

General jobs to do

1. Keep the hoe busy between standing crops **(Fig. 50, p. 66)**.
2. Hand weed here and there as required.
3. Cut back encroaching brambles (harvest the fruits) **(Fig. 51, p. 67)**.
4. Weed plot edges, especially removing the invasive white wiry threads of couch grass **(Fig. 32, p. 43)**.
5. Cut back nettles and grasses around compost bins. Ongoing, and keeps access routes to important places clear **(Fig. 123, p. 139)**.
6. Water crops if the weather continues dry.
7. Mow paths. Trim the edges with shears. Keep on top of these little tasks. Approaching the autumn/winter seasons with the plot looking pukka rather than letting it go will give you an emotional lift as the nights draw in **(Figs 49 and 79, pp. 65 and 96)**.
8. Thoroughly clean soil where crops have been harvested then sow with green manure such as Phacelia **(Jun 15)** or field beans if not needed in the immediate future. Field beans look like broads. They can be planted 5cm deep at 10–15cm intervals in rows 30cm apart.
9. Construct new bins for leaf mould with wooden pallets lashed together using wire to make an open-topped, four-sided box. A cinch to make and virtually free as well. Look especially elegant on an allotment in a make-do-and-mend kind of way. There really is no need to purchase expensive ready-made versions.
10. Collect and deliver tree leaves from wherever they can easily be gathered and deposit into a leaf mould bin. Avoid busy roadsides (they may be polluted) and woodlands (where falling leaves are part of the natural recycling process). Try parks, country lanes, people's gardens – maybe offer a leaf-sweeping service.
11. Mix grass mowings with leaves in the bin where possible, to balance the 'green' and 'brown' ingredients and achieve a faster result. Avoid grass from lawns which has been treated with weedkiller.
12. Empty contents of compost bin strategically in places on the plot. Small beds can be covered with an even layer, ideally 5–10cm thick. Alternatively, piles may be positioned in places convenient for future targeted cultivations **(Nov 10)**.
13. Collect molehills for home-made potting compost. The soil is generally finely textured without stones in. Use a shovel to scoop molehills up from pasture. Combine with leaf mould to make a free alternative to proprietary products **(Jan 1)**.
14. Paint wooden sheds with preservative. Unless you enjoy painting, 'nuff said!!
15. Repair broken panes of glass in the shed. 'A stitch in time saves nine' applies to all those little DIY jobs which can be attended to between now and the spring **(Fig. 13, p. 23)**.

16. Maintain order in the shed. With veggies coming in to store over the next few weeks, hygiene and organization are of utmost importance to save time and avoid disappointment.

17. Regularly sniff stored veg (especially potatoes) and check for rotting articles. Remove anything which is showing signs of being 'on the turn'.

18. Potter about and enjoy the mellowness of autumn. A very important job to do, this one!

19. On (heavy) clay soils, commence digging over vacant ground to allow natural forces of the weather to break it down to a crumbly tilth over the winter (light, sandy soils are best left until late winter) **(Nov 13)**.

20. Clear and sweep paths. Now is a good time to make adjustments and/or widen if desired. Straight paths are easier to negotiate than winding ones on a veg patch. Must be wide enough for easy wheelbarrow access **(Fig. 31, p. 42)**.

21. Wash pots to prevent a massive job later. A large bucket of soapy water and a toilet brush are all you need to do this. At the mellow tail-end of September it can actually be a pleasure rather than a chore **(Nov 20)**.

22. Tidy away unused bamboo canes and sticks. Some will be useable next season, others will be perfect kindling to start winter bonfires. Either way, keep in the dry.

23. Ensure adequate ventilation in the greenhouse. Days can still be hot.

24. In the greenhouse, as crops come to a productive finish, completely clear out and sweep.

25. Dismantle shelving in preparation for cleaning and disinfecting.

26. Construct log piles in uncultivated corners to provide shelter for hibernating frogs and toads **(Fig. 75, p. 92)**.

Leaves & greens

27. Put up shredded plastic bags on sticks to deter pigeons around brassicas (the cabbage family) including swedes **(Fig. 16, p. 26)**.

28. Check brassicas every other night for butterfly eggs and caterpillars. Crush the eggs. Crush caterpillars or remove to a sacrificial bed of nasturtiums elsewhere.

29. CABBAGE. Keep cabbages moist but not wet. Those that are hearting can have water poured into the middle of the crown in dry weather.

30. Lift fleece from red and Spring cabbages to facilitate weeding, then replace **(Fig. 138, p. 155)**.

31. Plant out Savoy and Spring cabbages into enriched (with well-rotted manure or compost) ground **(Fig. 81, p. 98)**.

32. Mulch ground between cabbages with newspaper and grass clippings.

33. BROCCOLI, BRUSSELS SPROUT, KALE. Tie purple sprouting and Nine

Star Perennial broccoli, Brussels sprouts and kale to stakes to prevent wind damage this coming winter **(Fig. 139, p. 157)**.

34. Tend Brussels sprouts by removing tatty, yellowing lower leaves. Hoe amongst the crop to stir up the soil and slice off weeds **(Nov 28)**.

35. Check over the leaves of curly kale for snails and slugs hiding away in the leaf folds.

36. Mulch strap-leaved kale plants with mature manure (i.e. manure that's choc full of worms). This will give them a boost for November/December harvesting. Withhold manure from curly-leaved types aimed at producing in late winter or early spring as it will encourage sappy growth which could be ruined in harsh weather. Best to wait until late January or February for these crops **(Fig. 59, p. 73)**.

37. WINTER PURSLANE. Sow a tray of winter purslane, also known as Miner's lettuce **(Aug 25)**.

38. CORN SALAD. Sow corn salad directly into the soil **(Apr 41)**.

39. LETTUCE. Sow varieties suitable for over-winter cultivation (e.g. Winter Density and All-Year-Round) in a protected greenhouse or cloche-covered bed. Start them off in trays **(Fig. 14, p. 25)** then prick out into 9cm pots **(Feb 27)**. Grow on in their pots on a sunny windowsill or greenhouse shelf, or plant into the soil at 20cm intervals when roots are showing from the drainage holes **(Fig. 53, p. 69)**. Plant out pot-raised lettuces, such as Tiger, with some protection **(Apr 20)**.

40. Ensure newly-sown seeds are kept moist if the month is particularly lacking in precipitation. Dribble water along the rows carefully and softly (but generously, to moisten thoroughly) **(Fig. 12, p. 22)**.

41. LEAF BEET. Strip off tough outside leaves from Swiss chard and perpetual spinach to encourage fresh growth.

42. ROCKET. Clear spent rocket to the compost heap.

Roots, tubers & stems

43. POTATO. If not blighted and cut already, clear all top growth ('haulm') from Maincrop spuds in the ground and burn **(Jul 54)**.

44. Commence to dig and prepare Maincrops for storing **(Fig. 141, p. 159)**.

45. CELERIAC. Liquid feed. Use nettle and comfrey tincture – just a capful, enough to taint the water in your can **(Jun 56)**.

46. Remove tatty lower leaves **(Fig. 142, p. 160)**.

47. ASPARAGUS. Hand weed the bed **(Fig. 87, p. 104)**.

48. Cut top third off ferns to lessen risk of wind rock. Don't remove more than this until late October, by which time they will have gone yellow and reabsorbed all the goodness back into the roots (essential for next year's growth).

49. RHUBARB. Compost dead and dying stalks. Just pull them when they yield without any effort and sling on the compost heap.

50. FLORENCE FENNEL. Compost fennel that has bolted unless saving for edible seeds **(Fig. 144, p. 162)**.

51. JERUSALEM ARTICHOKE. Reduce height of Jerusalems by half to avoid damage by wind-rock in stormy weather **(Fig. 107, p. 124)**.

52. PARSNIP. Clean through parsnips, Hamburg parsley and other root crops. Remove all weeds in preparation for harvesting (in the case of parsnips, best wait until after the first frost so that starches in the roots naturally convert to sweet sugars).

53. SWEDE. Keep moist at the roots – plenty of swelling time left for this staple winter fare which is ready to harvest from now on.

54. CARROT. Earth up crops grown in open soil **(Fig. 155(a), p. 174)**.

55. Keep container carrots moist but not wet. Pull as required from different places in the pot or box to allow remaining roots room to grow bigger **(Fig. 155(b), p. 174)**.

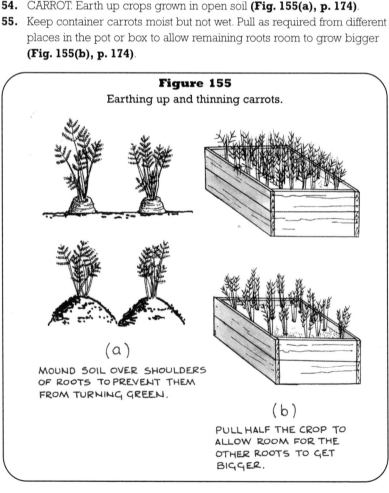

Figure 155
Earthing up and thinning carrots.

(a)

MOUND SOIL OVER SHOULDERS OF ROOTS TO PREVENT THEM FROM TURNING GREEN.

(b)

PULL HALF THE CROP TO ALLOW ROOM FOR THE OTHER ROOTS TO GET BIGGER.

Veg fruit

56. SQUASH. In dry conditions give plenty of water to the roots before the foliage collapses.

57. Harvest squashes. Leave as long as possible but do it before the first frost (so keep an ear to the weather forecast – October, hopefully). For longer storage potential, keep the stem attached between fruit and branch. Cut either side of where it joins the vine so it is like a T **(Fig. 156, p. 175)**.

58. CUCUMBER. Carefully clear spent cucumbers and any other plants showing signs of disease such as grey mould (Botrytis). Burn (preferably) or bury in the centre of a hot heap to kill fungal spores.

59. TOMATO, PEPPER, AUBERGINE. Keep watering potted tomatoes, peppers, aubergines and other crops still bearing sparingly. Add nettle and comfrey **(Jun 56)** once weekly.

60. Place newspapers under and around outdoor 'cordon' tomato plants such as Ailsa Craig. Untie from their supporting canes and lay them on the paper for fruits to ripen but stay clean **(Fig. 157, p. 176)**.

61. Remove and burn spent tomato and pepper plants to check any chance of spreading disease.

62. De-leaf lower foliage from tomatoes to let the sun in to hasten ripening.

63. Clear outdoor tomato plants once the harvest is over.

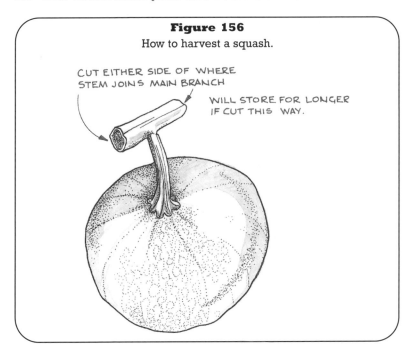

Figure 156
How to harvest a squash.

CUT EITHER SIDE OF WHERE
STEM JOINS MAIN BRANCH

WILL STORE FOR LONGER
IF CUT THIS WAY.

64. COURGETTE. Keep harvesting courgettes and marrows as long as the plants are producing.

65. PEST CONTROL. Remove spent French marigold plants from the greenhouse to the compost.

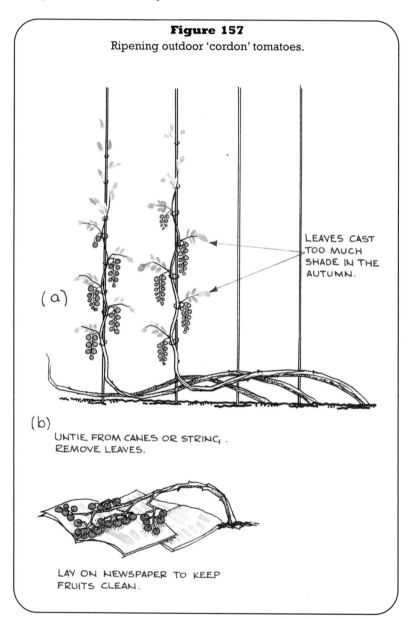

Figure 157

Ripening outdoor 'cordon' tomatoes.

LEAVES CAST TOO MUCH SHADE IN THE AUTUMN.

(a)

(b)

UNTIE FROM CANES OR STRING.
REMOVE LEAVES.

LAY ON NEWSPAPER TO KEEP
FRUITS CLEAN.

Onion tribe

66. LEEK. Hoe leeks **(Fig. 149, p. 165)**.

67. ONION, SHALLOT. Plant winter onion sets. Any time this month will do, but when schools go back and house martins are gathering before flying south for winter is as good a time as any. Prepare ground and plant as for maincrop onions **(Mar 68/69)**. Remember to check daily until roots have taken anchor **(Fig. 7, p. 15)**.

68. Hoe and hand weed through winter onions **(Figs 50 and 125, pp. 66 and 141)**.

69. Hang maincrop onions and shallots in the shed or store in trays **(Aug 64)**.

Peas & beans

70. RUNNER & FRENCH BEAN. Pick beans regularly, every day if possible **(Aug 68)**.

71. Compost spent beans. Cut at ground level. Remove the tops but let the roots rot down naturally over time and release their accumulated store of nitrogen **(Fig. 119, p. 134)**.

Edible flowers

72. GLOBE ARTICHOKE. Harvest the last bud if you are lucky!

73. Weed amongst globe artichoke crowns to keep perennial weeds at bay **(Fig. 95, p. 112)**.

74. POT MARIGOLD. Continue to collect flower seeds in fine dry weather for sowing next year.

Cereals

75. SWEETCORN. Harvest sweetcorn **(Fig. 158, p. 178)**.

76. Clear spent sweetcorn plants to the compost heap.

Fruit garden

77. APPLE, PEAR & PLUM. Harvest pears (depending on the variety) when pieces come away with gentle pressure applied. Gather carefully, as pears bruise easily **(Fig. 159, p. 179)**.

78. Clear encroaching vegetation from around fruit trees carefully with a hand-fork, water generously and mulch with bark chippings or well-rotted manure.

79. Generously water young fruit trees **(Fig. 74, p. 89)**.

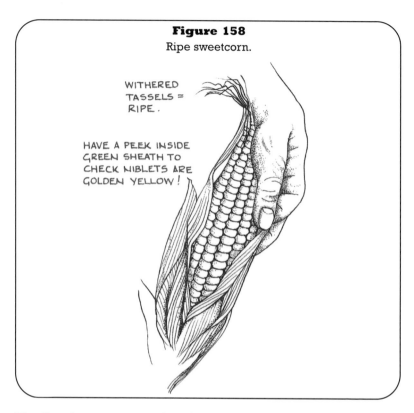

Figure 158
Ripe sweetcorn.

WITHERED
TASSELS =
RIPE.

HAVE A PEEK INSIDE
GREEN SHEATH TO
CHECK NIBLETS ARE
GOLDEN YELLOW!

80. Complete summer pruning of restricted apples and pears early on in the month **(Feb 63, Jul 93/Fig. 131, p. 149)**.
81. BLACKBERRY, TAYBERRY, LOGANBERRY & RELATIONS. Cut out the oldest fruited canes at ground level and train new growth in their place to fruit next year. More old canes may be retained and be fruitful if space allows or you want a permanent screen.
82. STRAWBERRY. Drench strawberries in pots.
83. FIG & GRAPE. Generously water fig trees and vines.
84. GRAPE. Prepare a planting pit for grape vine **(Feb 81)**.
85. COBNUT & FILBERT. Gather nuts when brown and effortlessly slip out of their husk. Filberts generally have a husk which covers the nut (hence the alternative name 'full-beard'). Husks on cobnuts are usually shorter. Use as a guide only; the Kentish Cob is a filbert!
86. Propagate to raise new stock of named varieties. Bend a lowly-positioned shoot of new growth and peg its end down into a 12cm deep hole. Firm soil with a boot heel. Leave for a year to establish roots. Then cut free of the parent plant and position as desired **(Fig. 160, p. 179)**.

Figure 159

Checking the ripeness of apples and pears.

1. CRADLE FRUIT IN HAND.
2. LIFT SLIGHTLY
3. IF RIPE, WILL COME AWAY EFFORTLESSLY

(IF NOT, RESIST THE TEMPTATION AND WAIT!)

Figure 160

Propagating new nut trees.

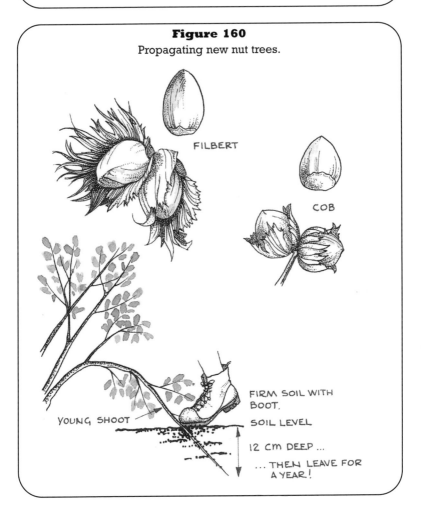

FILBERT

COB

FIRM SOIL WITH BOOT.

SOIL LEVEL

12 cm DEEP ...

... THEN LEAVE FOR A YEAR!

YOUNG SHOOT

OCTOBER

The colour which best describes October is brown. Think ploughed fields and golden hedgerows; an allotment or kitchen garden freshly turned; the glistening range of earthy hues in home-made chutney dolloped on a hunk of crusty bread; a cup of tea being nursed in your cradled hands outside the back door as a new morning is just waking up.

Most parts of the country will be visited by frost this month. A daily ear to the forecast is a must.

Vegetable fruits require careful harvesting and storing, alongside potatoes, the onion tribe and individually wrapped fruit.

You may decide to let the edible garden slacken at the edges around now. The pace of life is slowing down. The natural world, like shortening daylight hours, is drawing in.

Of course, you cannot keep taking from the land without giving something back. Your garden is a living system which, like a bank account, must receive deposits occasionally or else go bust. In October, an afternoon invested in the gathering of leaves, manures and composts is time well spent. It is nigh-on impossible to have too much!

This month, and right through until March, begins the season for planting woody species to secure a supply of future fruits.

Keep clearing, digging, picking, nipping and tucking. Make long- and short-term plans but never forget to live in the precious present.

General jobs to do

1. Continue to clear crops as plants become exhausted.
2. Tidy pots, bags and accumulated rubbish.
3. Keep on collecting leaves from elsewhere. Deposit in a pile in an out-of-the-way place to decompose for a year **(Sep 10)**.
4. Check over all crops.
5. Keep cleaning and turning vacant ground if your soil is heavy **(Dec 8)**. Light soils may be left until February. On sloping light soils, winter erosion may be lessened by actually allowing a surface mat of weeds or a green manure crop **(Jun 15)** to establish. Foliage will buffer the rain and roots will bind the soil.
6. Collect and store horse manure in bags **(Fig. 102, p. 120)**.
7. Dig out compost heap and apply the good stuff as a mulch or in piles **(Nov 10)**.
8. Keep paths clear and grass paths mown in an Indian summer **(Fig. 79, p. 96)**.
9. Empty and store away hosepipes safely and tidily in a frost-free place.
10. Potter and observe the slowing of the season.
11. Cut back plot edges **(Fig. 49, p. 65)**.
12. Carry out hedge trimming between now and early February **(Fig. 3, p. 11)**.
13. Tidy all vegetable debris which could harbour pests and spread disease to the compost heap, or burn.
14. If the soil is wet, either keep off it or work from wooden boards to minimize damage to the structure **(Nov 3)**.
15. Have a big bonfire to get rid of all the non-compostable rubbish. There's nothing quite as satisfying!
16. Keep the hoe busy if conditions are dry, otherwise do a bit of hand weeding at every opportunity to keep on top of this ongoing chore **(Figs 50 and 125, pp. 66 and 141)**.
17. Cut comfrey bed and stuff foliage in old wormery to make liquid manure **(Fig. 78, p. 95)**.
18. Compost spent pot marigolds. They make useful bulky additions to the compost heap.
19. Check all veg and fruit in store. Do this weekly if you are really good **(Nov 16)**.
20. In the greenhouse, clean the gutters of fallen leaves.
21. Remove entire greenhouse contents onto wooden pallets to keep them clean, then clean the windows and sweep the floor. Wash the insides thoroughly with biodegradable detergent **(Nov 20)**.
22. Carry out essential maintenance and repairs while it is empty **(Fig. 13, p. 23)**.

October

181

23. Clean the glass well.

24. Keep ventilated in mild weather **(Fig. 29, p. 41)**.

Leaves & greens

25. Keep potted salads moist but not wet **(Fig. 12, p. 22)**.

26. LETTUCE, WINTER PURSLANE, CORN SALAD. Prick out winter purslane and corn salad into individual pots **(Feb 27)**.

27. Plant out winter purslane and lettuces with protection. A tunnel cloche of horticultural fleece **(Fig. 23, p. 32)** or plastic bottles with their bottoms cut off and placed over individual plants are options. Select a warm and sunny position for early saladings next spring **(Fig. 53, p. 69)**.

28. BROCCOLI, BRUSSELS SPROUT, KALE. Tidy round crops by removing dead and dying lower leaves and weeding in the vicinity **(Nov 28)**.

29. Stake brassicas and earth up the roots with topsoil or compost **(Nov 23/Fig. 139, p. 157)**.

30. Ensure that bird-scarers around the cabbage patch are in good order **(Fig. 16, p. 26)**.

31. CAULIFLOWER. Compost remaining cauliflowers which have gone past their best (are showing yellow curds).

Roots, tubers & stems

32. SWEDE. Remove caterpillars from swedes in an extended warm season.

33. PARSNIP. Tend crops by removing dead leaves and keeping the crowns tidy **(Dec 25)**.

34. Hand weed amongst the root veg.

35. ASPARAGUS. Cut down asparagus ferns when they are dry and brown/yellow. Burn to destroy pests.

36. Prepare a new asparagus bed. Incorporate every bit of bulky organic matter you can find. Space-wise, each row you plant will be 30cm wide. Budget for 40cm between individual plants within the row. Allow 75cm betwixt rows.

37. Spread a thick layer of compost onto asparagus bed; 5cm or more if you have the bulky organic matter to spare.

38. CARROT. Earth up all carrots **(Fig. 155, p. 174)**.

39. POTATO. Finish digging maincrop varieties **(Mar 47)**. Wash and dry before storing one-deep in plastic fruit trays **(Fig. 141, p. 159)**.

40. CELERIAC. Clean outside leaves off celeriac plants **(Dec 21)**.

41. RHUBARB. Mulch rhubarb crown with a thick layer of well-rotted manure and insert a cane to mark the spot where fresh growth will appear from in spring **(Fig. 161, p. 183)**.

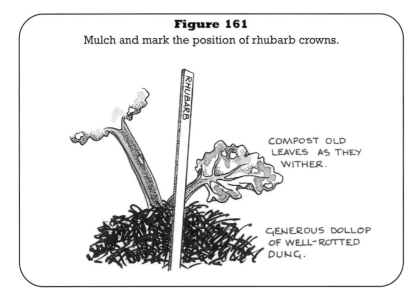

Figure 161
Mulch and mark the position of rhubarb crowns.

RHUBARB

COMPOST OLD
LEAVES AS THEY
WITHER.

GENEROUS DOLLOP
OF WELL-ROTTED
DUNG.

Veg fruit

42. PEPPER. Harvest the last hot chillis (e.g. Ring o Fire) and remove spent plants to fire site.

43. AUBERGINE. Keep harvesting aubergines before the purple fruits lose their shine then compost or burn spent plants.

44. SQUASH. Harvest and store all squashes if not already done **(Fig. 156, p. 175)**.

45. COURGETTE. Clear hardworking plants to refuse heap.

46. TOMATO. Take down outdoor tomato plants. Burn the stems and leaves (haulm) to prevent any over-wintering of disease.

47. TOMATILLO. Harvest tomatillos. Remove the green or purple fruits from their papery husks. Use in salsa and stir-fry dishes. Then remove and compost plants.

Onion tribe

48. LEEK, ONION. Weed amongst leeks and winter onions. It's easiest to do this as and when plants are harvested.

49. Hang maincrop onions and shallots in the shed or store in trays **(Aug 64)**.

50. Check over all stored onions weekly.

51. SHALLOT. Plant shallots this month, as for spring-planted **(Mar 73)**.

52. GARLIC. Plant garlic – a variety like Germidour is perfect for autumn planting **(Mar 75/Fig. 22, p. 31)**.

Peas & beans

53. BROAD BEAN, PEA. Sow broads, as for spring-sown **(Feb 58, Mar 77)** except maybe 3cm deeper just to give a bit of added protection. Aquadulce varieties are tops for planting now. The idea is they'll grow some before the solstice, then rest, and start into growth again sooner after New Year. Thus, come early summer when blackfly are about these broads will be unattractively tough in the tip and escape their predations. A 'cultural control' that really does work. Plus, you get a harvest about three weeks earlier than March-sown broad beans, and so extend the season. Plants might need some protecting with a horticultural fleece or cloche in really cold winters.

54. Alternatively, plant broads and Early peas (e.g. Feltham First) 5cm deep in compost-filled toilet roll tubes and grow on in a greenhouse over the winter months **(Feb 52)**.

55. RUNNER & FRENCH BEAN. Clean ground where runner and French beans were after collecting seeds for next year and storing in paper bags, but leave the roots to rot down and release ample supplies of stored nitrogen for the next crop **(Fig. 119, p. 134)**.

56. Harvest borlotti beans. Thoroughly dry before sorting the beans from crispy pods. Store beans in glass kilner jars for future use in winter stews. Then compost plants and dismantle canes.

57. Take down poles used as a climbing frame for beans. Disinfect if you are really keen. Store in a dry place ready to use next year.

Edible flowers

58. GLOBE ARTICHOKE. Put potted up globe artichoke chards (off-shoots) in the greenhouse for the winter.

Fruit garden

59. RED & WHITE CURRANT. From toward month's end, and then any time until March, when the ground is neither frosted nor waterlogged, plant red and white currants. Choose a warm site, one not prone to frost. Incorporate plenty of rotted dung or compost into the top 'spit' of soil (approximately 25cm) to make it rich and suitable for your plants. Ensure the fibrous roots have soil worked in amongst them well. Firm carefully with boot heel. Match the depth of planting at this stage to the darker showing 'soil mark' on the stem **(Oct 62)**. Can be grown as a bush (allow 1.2 to 1.5m between specimens) in exactly the same way as gooseberries **(Mar 95)**, or as a single-stemmed cordon with plants grown 30cm apart **(Oct 60)**.

60. Formatively prune newly-planted red and white currants to be grown as single-stemmed 'cordons': tie main stem to a vertical cane or stake. Canes might need the extra reinforcement of wires strained horizontally between two posts. Remove any growths sprouting from below 10cm to create a clear stem, or so-called 'leg'. Prune the leading shoot ('leader') on main stem by half, flush above a strong bud **(Fig. 44, p. 58)**. Prune all 'lateral' side growths to a bud about 2.5cm from main stem. Ideally, aim for about 15cm of stem between each lateral **(Fig. 162, p. 185)**.

61. Feed red and white currants by applying a 5cm thick mulch of well-rotted manure in a 45cm circumference around the plants.

62. BLACKCURRANT. Plant blackcurrants any time between late October and mid-March, whenever the soil is easily workable; neither frozen, lumpy, nor sticking to your tools. Blackcurrants are more tolerant of moist soils than other soft fruits such as gooseberries and red currants, but waterlogged ground must be drained or otherwise made drier. Dips and hollows which are prone to collecting frost are wisely avoided too, as blackcurrants flower early in the season and are easily nipped in the bud – with consequent failure of satisfactory crops. Some shelter is advantageous to the activities of pollinating insects, perhaps offered by a hedge. This applies to all soft fruits. Incorporate as much bulky organic matter as is available into the top 25cm of soil as blackcurrants enjoy a rich living. Allow a minimum of 1.5m between plants being grown as bushes, possibly more if soil is especially fertile. Spread roots well. Insert deep and firm with the heel of your boot. If you can see the old soil mark, a discolouration showing what was above and below the soil surface when propagated, make sure this is 5cm underground now.

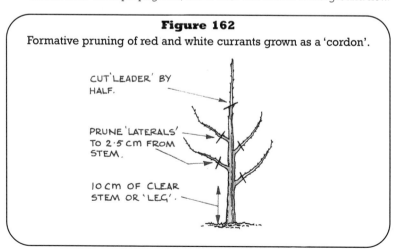

Figure 162
Formative pruning of red and white currants grown as a 'cordon'.

CUT 'LEADER' BY HALF.

PRUNE 'LATERALS' TO 2·5 CM FROM STEM.

10 CM OF CLEAR STEM OR 'LEG'.

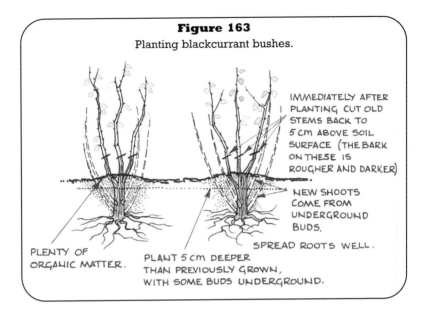

Figure 163
Planting blackcurrant bushes.

IMMEDIATELY AFTER PLANTING, CUT OLD STEMS BACK TO 5 CM ABOVE SOIL SURFACE (THE BARK ON THESE IS ROUGHER AND DARKER)

NEW SHOOTS COME FROM UNDERGROUND BUDS.

SPREAD ROOTS WELL.

PLENTY OF ORGANIC MATTER.

PLANT 5 CM DEEPER THAN PREVIOUSLY GROWN, WITH SOME BUDS UNDERGROUND.

Stems will sprout from underground buds and make the bush 'legless', which means there is no single main stem. Immediately after planting, cut old stems back to 5cm above the soil surface. The bark on older wood is darker and rougher. Water well **(Fig. 163, p. 186)**.

63. Prune blackcurrants any time from late in the month until March. Second year plants should not be pruned at all, to allow fruiting. From the third year, get rid of anything that is spindly, dead, diseased or crossing. On established bushes, cut out about a third of all the branches which have yielded fruit in previous years. Cut right down at soil level. This makes space for new growth (which should bear fruit in its second summer). Nothing should be retained that is older than four years. Old wood has much darker bark than that on younger branches **(Fig. 164, p. 187)**.

64. Propagate blackcurrant cuttings. Best practice dictates this is done during October and November, but actually blackcurrants will root, or 'strike', in virtually any month of the year so don't be averse to having a go in late winter or even March. All you need do is take a length of about 25cm from strong wood, as thick as a pencil, that was ripened in the previous summer. Snick the tender tip off flush above a bud, at an angle **(Fig. 44, p. 58)**. The bottom is cut straight across immediately below a bud. There are root-producing hormones in the bud area and the different angled cuts help you avoid accidentally popping it in upside-down. Leave all buds intact. In heavy soils, make a slit with a spade and line this with coarse sand to assist drainage. Insert cuttings

Figure 164

Autumnal pruning of a blackcurrant bush.

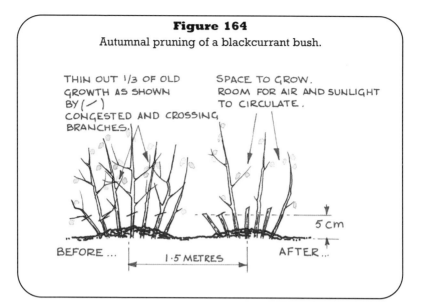

THIN OUT 1/3 OF OLD GROWTH AS SHOWN BY (⟋) CONGESTED AND CROSSING BRANCHES.

SPACE TO GROW. ROOM FOR AIR AND SUNLIGHT TO CIRCULATE.

5 cm

BEFORE ... | 1·5 METRES | AFTER...

15cm apart. Allow 45cm between rows if nurturing more than one. Two buds only should be showing above the surface. Firm the slit shut with a boot. If there is a lot of frost then further firming will be needed throughout the winter. Leave for a whole growing season. The following November, or February/March, lift and transplant into final resting places for hopefully ten years or more of productive life **(Fig. 165, p. 188)**.

65. BLACKBERRY, TAYBERRY, LOGANBERRY & RELATIONS. Ideally, plant this month (or early spring as an alternative). Most fertile, well-drained soils will suffice though wetter sites will be acceptable to a blackberry. Bulky organic matter mixed in with the soil at planting time is always appreciated by your charges. Choose any aspect, although a south-facing blackberry will ripen before one planted on an easterly or northerly location. Ensure roots are well spread out in the hole and that the soil mark, as identified low down on the stem **(Oct 62)**, is the same at planting now as it was in the nursery. Allow up to four metres between individuals, though closer spacing is acceptable.

66. FIG. Pinch out all figs on the tree which are larger than pea-sized, as they are most unlikely to survive the winter **(Fig. 166, p. 188)**.

67. Especially in northerly areas, secure horticultural fleece over fan-trained fig trees. Extra swaddling could be provided by packing straw or dry bracken between the branches. Leave in place until March.

68. GRAPE. Plant bare-rooted grape vine. Ensure roots are covered with about 10cm of soil, or do it in March/April **(Mar 109)**.

Figure 165
Propagating blackcurrant cuttings.

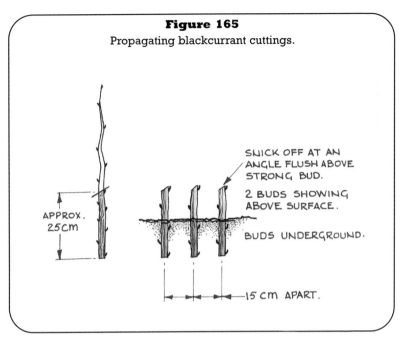

APPROX.
25 cm

SNICK OFF AT AN ANGLE FLUSH ABOVE STRONG BUD.

2 BUDS SHOWING ABOVE SURFACE.

BUDS UNDERGROUND.

15 cm APART.

Figure 166
Autumnal fig management.

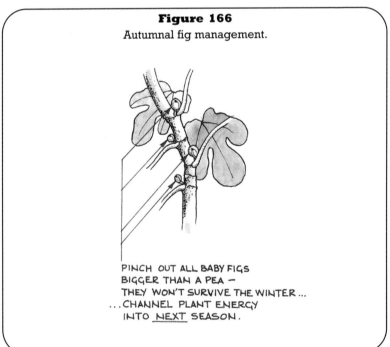

PINCH OUT ALL BABY FIGS
BIGGER THAN A PEA —
THEY WON'T SURVIVE THE WINTER...
...CHANNEL PLANT ENERGY
INTO NEXT SEASON.

NOVEMBER

If you grow food on heavy clay then commence turning it roughly on its head this month. Getting this job completed before New Year will pay dividends. But be sensible. Half an hour of strenuous digging is enough before taking a break. Do something else then have another stint.

Arguably, your back is your most important, hardest-working asset. Look after it and it will look after you.

Don't be fooled into thinking that in November's edible garden there is little else to do. There most certainly is, should you choose.

The fruit-growing area is a hive of activity in terms of pruning, training, planting and general husbandry. Keep vegetation clear from immediately around bushes and tree trunks. Maybe sprinkle down a little plant food or flop a layer of nutritious mulch.

The dinnertime menu changes. Parsnips taste much sweeter after a good frosting and are a vastly under-rated veg. Think kale, celeriac, leeks, Brussels sprouts.

Keep an eye on leaves and greens. Pigeons can spoil an outside crop if it is unprotected.

In the greenhouse or tunnel, hygiene is of utmost importance lest fungal diseases take hold. If you have not yet finished cleaning and disinfecting equipment, do it now!

Escape into the shed. Keep a weekly eye (and nose) to all that lovely stored fruit and veg. Discard anything showing signs of going off.

If you've no electricity supply then consider connecting one – all that tidying and pottering is so much more of a pleasure if there is decent light to work by.

General jobs to do

1. Check over all plants.
2. Avoid a build-up of clutter by finding a place for everything and keeping everything in its place **(Fig. 167, p. 190)**.
3. Store thick wooden planks somewhere handy for use as walking boards to protect the soil structure. They are really useful but will rot over time if left exposed to the elements, so store somewhere dry when not in use **(Fig. 168, p. 191)**.
4. Sweep paths. Think health and safety.
5. Snip round plot edges to keep neat and tidy **(Fig. 49, p. 65)**.
6. Use a garden fork to weed close to the edges and remove couch grass. Stamp the prongs down, lever up to loosen and tease out unwanted vegetation **(Fig. 32, p. 43)**. Don't compost couch grass and thick-rooted perennial weeds like dandelion and dock. They can be drowned in a bucket of water, weighted under a half-brick, or burned. If drowned, in a few weeks slop the dead stuff on the compost heap but

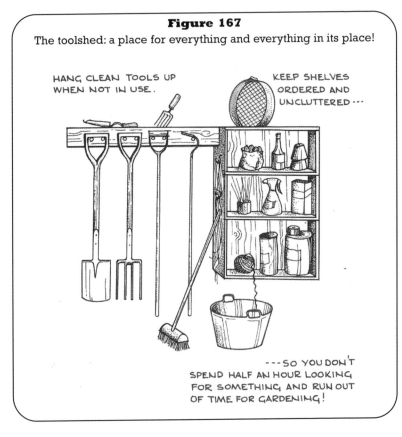

Figure 167

The toolshed: a place for everything and everything in its place!

HANG CLEAN TOOLS UP WHEN NOT IN USE.

KEEP SHELVES ORDERED AND UNCLUTTERED ···

··· SO YOU DON'T SPEND HALF AN HOUR LOOKING FOR SOMETHING AND RUN OUT OF TIME FOR GARDENING!

save the water as it'll be full of goodness and perfect to dilute as a
liquid feed in the growing season.

7. Cut back and compost comfrey **(Fig. 78, p. 95)**.

8. Shovel up and store wood ash from bonfires. Keep safe (i.e. in a metal
container) and dry. Can be profitably used to sprinkle around fruit
trees and bushes in early spring, or dusted between rows of winter
onions sometime before solstice **(Dec 6)**.

9. Turn the compost heap onto its head. The idea is to have two heaps
next to each other. One is rotting away and the other being filled. When

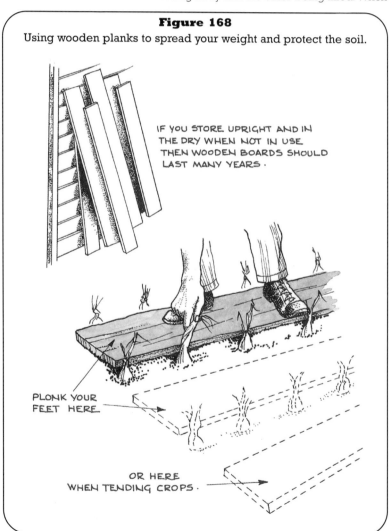

Figure 168

Using wooden planks to spread your weight and protect the soil.

IF YOU STORE UPRIGHT AND IN
THE DRY WHEN NOT IN USE
THEN WOODEN BOARDS SHOULD
LAST MANY YEARS.

PLONK YOUR
FEET HERE

OR HERE
WHEN TENDING CROPS.

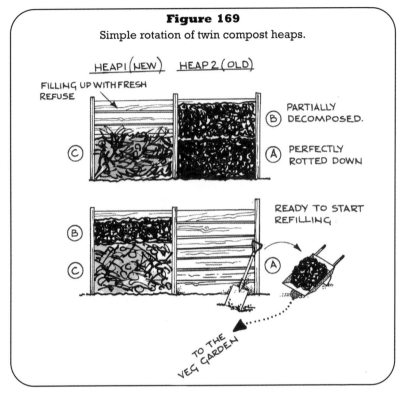

Figure 169
Simple rotation of twin compost heaps.

HEAP 1 (NEW)   HEAP 2 (OLD)

FILLING UP WITH FRESH
REFUSE

Ⓒ

Ⓑ PARTIALLY
DECOMPOSED.

Ⓐ PERFECTLY
ROTTED DOWN

READY TO START
REFILLING

Ⓑ

Ⓒ

Ⓐ

TO THE
VEG GARDEN

the ripe heap is emptied it leaves a void. So turn the other heap into
this ('on its head' so to speak), and leave to complete the process. In
the six-month meantime, start filling the other side. In due course
repeat, and so on **(Fig. 169, p. 192)**.

10. Rake level piles of leaf mould and compost on the plot as a mulch
where needed, either around crops still standing or to protect light soil
on a slope **(Fig. 170, p. 193)**.

11. Take time to enjoy the sights and sounds of the veg patch. This is still
rather a beautiful month in terms of wildlife and weather. Cast a caring
and thoughtful eye over the plot, noting jobs to do and planning in your
mind's eye for next year. These ideas will change, but it is not a bad
idea to start thinking into the future now **(Dec 2)**.

12. Cut down and dig in green manures grown on a heavy soil to add
valuable humus **(Jun 15)**.

13. Do a bit of digging on heavy, clayey soils. If soil is sandy, it is better to dig
in the late winter/early spring **(Figs 171 and 172, pp. 194 and 195)**.

14. Use woody cuttings to make sticks for marking rows of seeds sown in
the spring. Doing it now, when there is no pressure of time, will steal a

November

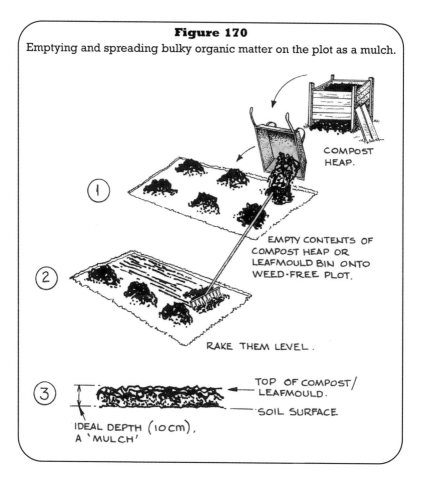

Figure 170

Emptying and spreading bulky organic matter on the plot as a mulch.

① COMPOST HEAP.

EMPTY CONTENTS OF COMPOST HEAP OR LEAFMOULD BIN ONTO WEED-FREE PLOT.

②

RAKE THEM LEVEL.

③ TOP OF COMPOST/ LEAFMOULD. SOIL SURFACE.

IDEAL DEPTH (10 cm), A 'MULCH'

march come the hectic weeks of next March/April/May.

15. Swaddle wormeries with bubble wrap if the forecast is for freezing weather. Make sure the worms can still breathe but don't let your hard-working wrigglers freeze or else they'll die.

16. Check stored veg; reject anything that is not keeping well **(Fig. 173, p. 195)**.

17. Trim hedges **(Fig. 3, p. 11)**.

18. Tidy the shed **(Nov 2)**.

19. In the greenhouse, continue attending to essential maintenance jobs **(Fig. 13, p. 23)**.

20. Replace washed and disinfected pots, shelves and accessories **(Fig. 174, p. 196)**.

21. Ventilate for a few hours in the morning if not too cold **(Fig. 29, p. 41)**.

22. After dark, with the aid of a torch, remove lurking snails **(Fig. 47, p. 64)**.

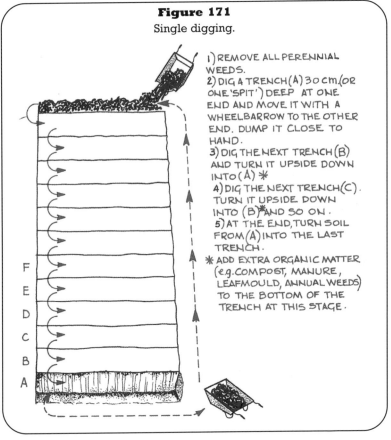

Figure 171
Single digging.

1) REMOVE ALL PERENNIAL WEEDS.
2) DIG A TRENCH (A) 30 cm (OR ONE 'SPIT') DEEP AT ONE END AND MOVE IT WITH A WHEELBARROW TO THE OTHER END. DUMP IT CLOSE TO HAND.
3) DIG THE NEXT TRENCH (B) AND TURN IT UPSIDE DOWN INTO (A) ✳
4) DIG THE NEXT TRENCH (C). TURN IT UPSIDE DOWN INTO (B) ✳ AND SO ON.
5) AT THE END, TURN SOIL FROM (A) INTO THE LAST TRENCH.
✳ ADD EXTRA ORGANIC MATTER (e.g. COMPOST, MANURE, LEAFMOULD, ANNUAL WEEDS) TO THE BOTTOM OF THE TRENCH AT THIS STAGE.

Leaves & greens

23. Earth up brassicas. Use a swan-necked, or 'draw', hoe to mound soil around the stem bases. It makes them more secure against rocking winter winds. Members of the cabbage tribe do best with a firm roothold **(Fig. 175, p. 197)**.

24. CABBAGE. Sprinkle lime on beds planned for brassicas. Don't worry about being too technical – about one handful per square metre is fine.

25. Uncover fleeced cabbages to do a thorough weeding job, then secure fleece back over **(Fig. 138, p. 155)**.

26. Tickle around amongst brassicas with a hoe **(Fig. 50, p. 66)**.

27. Keep removing cabbage white butterfly caterpillars from brassicas in mild weather. They can be active right up until solstice some years.

28. BRUSSELS SPROUT. Snap off 'blown' Brussels sprouts so that only tight buttons remain on the stems **(Fig. 176, p. 197)**. Steam them and eat as delicious 'greens'. Waste nothing!

Figure 172
Double digging of virgin ground.

THIS IS ALSO KNOWN AS 'BASTARD TRENCHING' BECAUSE IT
CAN BE SUCH HARD WORK (NOT A JOKE!)
DOUBLE DIGGING REALLY BENEFITS VIRGIN CLAY SOIL AND
MAKES IT MUCH EASIER TO WORK SUBSEQUENTLY.
DOUBLE OR SINGLE DIG CLAY SOILS BEFORE CHRISTMAS SO
THAT THE WIND, RAIN AND FROST CAN WORK THEIR
WEATHERING MAGIC BEFORE SPRING.

① COMMENCE WORK AS FOR SINGLE DIGGING.
② BUT... BEFORE TURNING TRENCH 'B' INTO 'A', 'C' INTO 'B'
AND SO FORTH, USE A FORK TO THOROUGHLY BREAK UP
THE NEXT SPIT OF CLAY AND LINE
IT AT THE BOTTOM WITH
TURF OR ORGANIC MATTER.

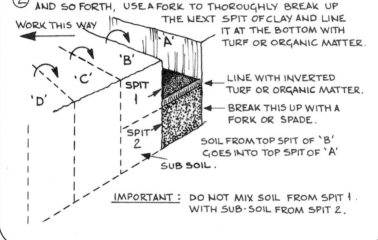

WORK THIS WAY

LINE WITH INVERTED
TURF OR ORGANIC MATTER.

BREAK THIS UP WITH A
FORK OR SPADE.

SOIL FROM TOP SPIT OF 'B'
GOES INTO TOP SPIT OF 'A'

SUB SOIL.

IMPORTANT: DO NOT MIX SOIL FROM SPIT 1.
WITH SUB-SOIL FROM SPIT 2.

Figure 173
Checking potatoes in store.

BAD SMELL = ROTTING SOMEWHERE
SO EXAMINE CAREFULLY.
DO NOT DELAY !!
DO IT WEEKLY.

POTATOES STORED
IN A TRAY IN THE
DARK.

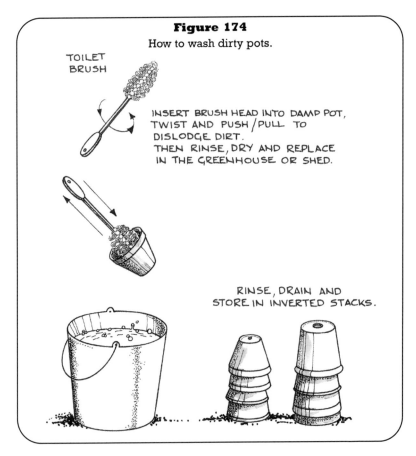

Figure 174
How to wash dirty pots.

TOILET BRUSH

INSERT BRUSH HEAD INTO DAMP POT, TWIST AND PUSH/PULL TO DISLODGE DIRT.
THEN RINSE, DRY AND REPLACE IN THE GREENHOUSE OR SHED.

RINSE, DRAIN AND STORE IN INVERTED STACKS.

29. KALE. Tidy yellowing leaves from kale and other members of the cabbage tribe. It looks shoddy and provides shelter for slugs and snails.

30. BROCCOLI. Tidy away and compost spent Chevalier calabrese plants. As with all brassicas, pulp stems with a hammer before composting to assist the process **(Fig. 17, p. 27)**.

31. LETTUCE. Remove browning leaves from potted lettuces in the greenhouse. Cut carefully with scissors rather than just tugging and ripping **(Fig. 177, p. 198)**.

32. CORN SALAD. Plant out corn salad plants under a protective covering. Use horticultural fleece or plastic drinks bottles with the bottoms cut off. Position plants with 15cm of space in all directions for best results.

33. LEAF BEET. Strip leaves from Swiss chard down to the fresh hearts and cover with cloches to stimulate new growth.

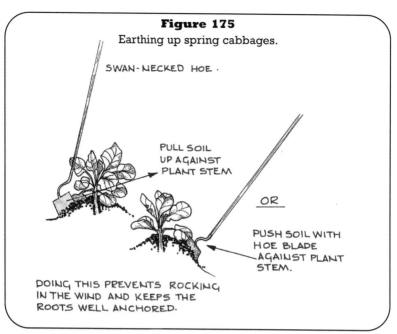

Figure 175

Earthing up spring cabbages.

SWAN-NECKED HOE.

PULL SOIL UP AGAINST PLANT STEM

OR

PUSH SOIL WITH HOE BLADE AGAINST PLANT STEM.

DOING THIS PREVENTS ROCKING IN THE WIND AND KEEPS THE ROOTS WELL ANCHORED.

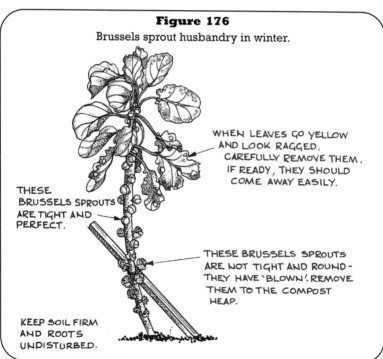

Figure 176

Brussels sprout husbandry in winter.

WHEN LEAVES GO YELLOW AND LOOK RAGGED, CAREFULLY REMOVE THEM. IF READY, THEY SHOULD COME AWAY EASILY.

THESE BRUSSELS SPROUTS ARE TIGHT AND PERFECT.

THESE BRUSSELS SPROUTS ARE NOT TIGHT AND ROUND - THEY HAVE 'BLOWN'. REMOVE THEM TO THE COMPOST HEAP.

KEEP SOIL FIRM AND ROOTS UNDISTURBED.

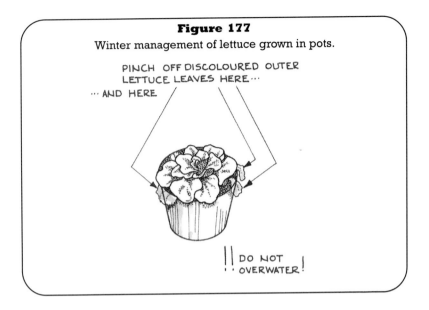

Figure 177

Winter management of lettuce grown in pots.

PINCH OFF DISCOLOURED OUTER
LETTUCE LEAVES HERE···

··· AND HERE

DO NOT
·· OVERWATER!

Roots, tubers & stems

34. JERUSALEM ARTICHOKE. Cut down tops to just above ground level.
Edible tubers can be left underground until needed in the kitchen **(Fig. 178, p. 198)**.

35. SCORZONERA. Hand weed amongst the scorzonera and other roots.

36. PARSNIP, SWEDE. Clear dead top growth from parsnips and swedes.
Both crops will sit quite happily in the ground until called upon to

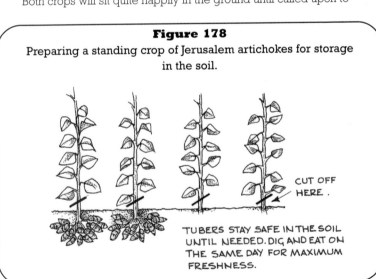

Figure 178

Preparing a standing crop of Jerusalem artichokes for storage in the soil.

CUT OFF
HERE.

TUBERS STAY SAFE IN THE SOIL
UNTIL NEEDED. DIG AND EAT ON
THE SAME DAY FOR MAXIMUM
FRESHNESS.

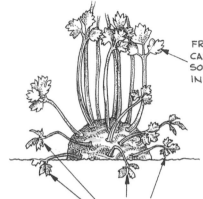

Figure 179
Celeriac husbandry to keep the crop clean.

FRESH GREEN LEAVES CAN BE USED TO FLAVOUR SOUPS - REMOVE INDIVIDUALLY.

DISCOLOURED LOWER LEAVES SHOULD BE PULLED SMARTLY DOWN AND OFF TO KEEP THE SWOLLEN STEM CLEAN AND REMOVE SLUG HIDEY-HOLES.

nourish family and/or friends. A mulch of dry bracken or straw might be prudently applied before temperatures are forecast to plummet at any stage through the winter **(Dec 25)**.

37. BEETROOT. Harvest the last of the beetroot. Remember, don't cut the leaves off – twist (as though giving the leaves a Chinese Burn) about 5cm up the stalks to prevent bleeding of red juice in the cooking pot.

38. CELERIAC. Pull off oldest lower leaves from celeriac to keep them clean, tidy and free from pests **(Fig. 179, p. 199)**.

39. ASPARAGUS. Thoroughly weed and mulch with leaf mould or well-rotted manure.

40. Burn up old tops if not already done to get rid of the unwanted vegetation and destroy over-wintering beetles **(Dec 6)**.

Onion tribe

41. LEEK. Hand weed leeks whilst harvesting.

42. ONION. Tend winter onions with a little hand weeding.

43. GARLIC. Hand weed amongst sprouting shoots of garlic planted last month.

44. Plant more garlic cloves **(Mar 75/Fig. 22, p. 31)**.

45. ELEPHANT GARLIC. Plant Elephant garlic. Pop individual cloves into fertile soil, 5cm below the surface at 15–20cm spacings, in rows 30cm apart.

Peas & beans

46. BROAD BEAN, PEA. Cover autumn-sown broads with fleece if cold weather demands it.

47. Sow broad beans Aquadulce Claudia and Early peas into prepared ground **(Oct 53/54)**.

Edible flowers

48. GLOBE ARTICHOKE. Cut down leafy 'crowns' and mulch with leaf mould **(Fig. 6, p. 14)**.

49. Ensure that compost in pots with globes and other plants is moist but not wet.

Fruit garden

50. APPLE, PEAR, CHERRY & PLUM. Mulch around fruit trees with rotted bark chippings **(Fig. 180, p. 201)**.

51. Plant bare-rooted apple trees any time from now until late February, except when the ground is waterlogged or frosty **(Fig. 43, p. 58)**.

52. Fit protective plastic coils around the bottom of fruit tree trunks to protect from nibbling rabbits and voles **(Fig. 181, p. 201)**.

53. Apply potash from fires as a top dressing around fruit trees. Just sprinkle a handful or two around the root zone and let natural rainfall wash it in **(Dec 6)**.

54. Cut down and clear rank vegetation amongst the fruit trees. Keep the bases immediately around the trunks weed free.

55. MORELLO CHERRY. Plant trees for fan-training **(Feb 63)** any time from early this month until early March when the ground is neither frosted nor waterlogged. Prepare the ground well. Cherries prefer a chalky subsoil so incorporate half a bucket of crushed chalk in advance. Heavy clay soils should be rendered more free-draining. Applications of rubble and grit as well as the chalk, deeply dug into the root zone, will assist enormously. Obtain a year-old 'maiden whip' from a reputable source and plant as described for other 'top fruits' **(Fig. 43, p. 58)**. Morellos do fertilize themselves so can be grown singly, but heavier crops will result if two or more trees are grown in the area. They thrive in a shaded, north-facing aspect, thus are especially suitable for fan-training against a shed, fence or wall which faces in that direction, where little else prospers. However, avoid areas prone to frost which might damage early blossom. Be prepared to wait four years before harvesting begins. Underplant with Alpine strawberries for maximum returns **(May 132)**.

November

Figure 180
Mulching fruit trees with bulky organic matter.

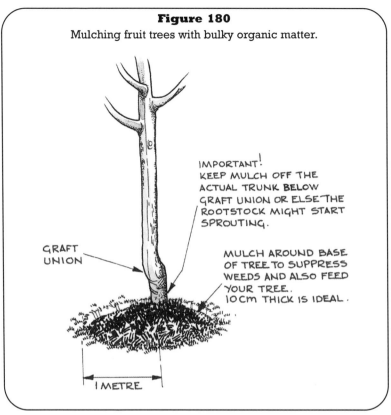

IMPORTANT!
KEEP MULCH OFF THE ACTUAL TRUNK BELOW GRAFT UNION OR ELSE THE ROOTSTOCK MIGHT START SPROUTING.

GRAFT UNION

MULCH AROUND BASE OF TREE TO SUPPRESS WEEDS AND ALSO FEED YOUR TREE.
10 cm THICK IS IDEAL.

1 METRE

Figure 181
Protecting fruit trees from rabbits and voles.

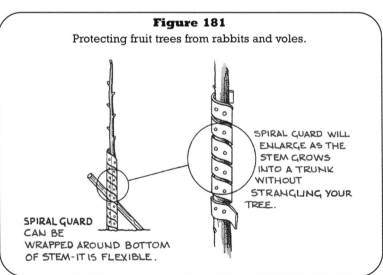

SPIRAL GUARD WILL ENLARGE AS THE STEM GROWS INTO A TRUNK WITHOUT STRANGLING YOUR TREE.

SPIRAL GUARD CAN BE WRAPPED AROUND BOTTOM OF STEM - IT IS FLEXIBLE.

55a. *Formative pruning of a maiden whip*:

Initially, cut the main stem back to about 45cm high with at least three healthy buds below the cut. Secure a cane either side at 45 degrees, tied on to strong horizontal wires, for future training **(Fig. 182, p. 203)**.

55b. *Second year formative pruning*:

Select two strong stems, one either side, and remove all others. Prune the selected stems by two-thirds to an upwards-facing bud **(Fig. 44, p. 58)**. Secure on to the angled canes for training.

55c. *Third year formative pruning*:

New growth should make the fan-trained tree look like it has three fingers on each side. Snip them all back by one-third to an upwards-facing bud.

56. 'Top dress' ground beneath established cherry trees with a couple handfuls of hydrated lime or crushed chalk scattered around the base of the trunk every other year.

57. GOOSEBERRY. Plant gooseberry bushes now, or do it in the spring **(Mar 95)**.

58. If gooseberry bushes have completed their second year of growth (one in the nursery, see **Mar 96**, and one on the plot) cut main stem 'leaders' back by half, most commonly to an inwards and upwards-facing bud. Treat strong side branches ('laterals') similarly, so that eight or nine branches in total form the main framework of the bush. Completely cut out any others which are crowding the centre or growing up from the stem base.

59. 'Winter prune' established gooseberries. Cut all overcrowded and crossing shoots from centre of the bushes back to one bud **(Fig. 44, p. 58)**, to allow light and air to circulate. Nip new wood (last season's growth; pale and smooth) on main stems ('leaders') by half, to an inwards and upwards-facing bud. On laterals which were 'summer pruned' **(Jul 98)**, cut back to two buds.

60. Propagate gooseberry bushes from cuttings before the soil gets too cold. Use healthy lengths removed during pruning operations. Ideally they will be about 30cm long, pencil-thick and of wood grown and ripened in the previous season. Remove the tender tip with a slanting cut flush above a bud **(Fig. 44, p. 58)**. Then use a knife to nick out all buds and the biggest thorns except the top four or five. The bottom of the 'cutting' is identified with a straight cut. In heavy soils, use a spade to make a V-shaped slit and line this with sand to assist drainage. Then insert the cutting(s) at 15cm spacings along this nursery. Allow 45cm between rows if making more than one. Ensure that the bottom bud is no less than 5cm proud of the soil surface. Press gently shut with the

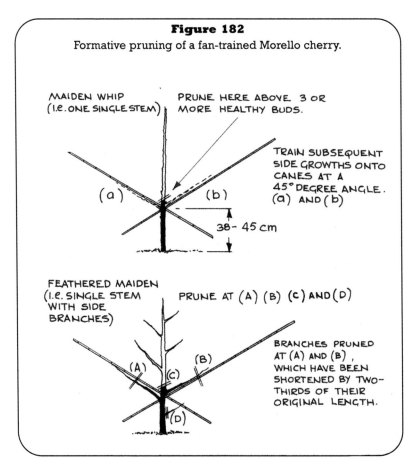

Figure 182
Formative pruning of a fan-trained Morello cherry.

MAIDEN WHIP
(I.e. ONE SINGLE STEM)

PRUNE HERE ABOVE 3 OR
MORE HEALTHY BUDS.

TRAIN SUBSEQUENT
SIDE GROWTHS ONTO
CANES AT A
45° DEGREE ANGLE.
(a) AND (b)

(a)   (b)

38- 45 cm

FEATHERED MAIDEN
(I.e. SINGLE STEM
WITH SIDE
BRANCHES)

PRUNE AT (A) (B) (C) AND (D)

(A)
(C)
(B)

(D)

BRANCHES PRUNED
AT (A) AND (B),
WHICH HAVE BEEN
SHORTENED BY TWO-
THIRDS OF THEIR
ORIGINAL LENGTH.

sole of your boot and leave until the following dormant season
(Nov–March) when rooted cuttings may be lifted and transplanted
(Mar 95). In lighter soils cuttings may simply be pushed into the
ground as described.

61. BLUEBERRY. Prune established bushes in the same way as for gooseberries **(Nov 59)**. Now is the time to feed with a balanced, all-round
fertilizer according to the manufacturer's specification.

62. STRAWBERRY. Cut alpine strawberry plants down to their crowns and
mulch with compost in between **(Jul 105)**.

63. GRAPE. After leaves have fallen, prune one-year-old, single stem
'cordon' vines planted in March **(Mar 109)**; reduce the leader by up to
two-thirds into ripe, brown (not green) stem. Nip alternately placed
side shoots to two good-looking buds from their base. These will
become the knuckle-like 'fruiting spurs'.

64. Prune second year vines as above **(Nov 63)**. Ensure the leader is cut back to a strong bud **(Fig. 44, p. 58)**.

65. Prune established cordon vines. Cut side branches ('laterals') to two buds. Cut leader back to same height as the fence or wall if it has filled the allotted space. Reduce congested knuckle-like fruiting 'spurs' by half with a penknife saw.

66. Propagate new grape vines from cuttings made whilst pruning. Insert a 10cm long piece of woody stem into light, sandy soil with one bud, or 'eye', at soil level. Nick the bark at the bottom of the inserted end to facilitate rapid root formation. Protect over winter and plant 'bare-rooted' the following autumn **(Oct 68)**.

67. COBNUT & FILBERT. Plant bare-rooted hazel trees **(Feb 62)** any time between now and late February. A deep, moist soil in a sheltered spot is preferred. Light shade is tolerated. Allow four metres between specimens when grown as bushes but only 75cm if lined out for a hedge. For training as a bush, follow the same principles as for apples **(Mar 93a)**.

DECEMBER

In a mild December raspberries might be picked throughout most of this month.

But, don't be sad if conditions are harsh and temperatures low. Lots of soil-borne pests will get exposed by ongoing clearing and digging. They'll either be killed off or provide valuable rations for birds.

If you planned ahead and grew your crops without too many hitches, there should be a pleasantly surprising assortment of fresh veg to choose from as we approach the festival of midwinter feasts. Keep the home-fires burning with roasts and mashes and hearty soups.

On the shortest day plant some shallots. Keep your fingers crossed that they'll be ready to harvest in precisely six months' time. Shallots represent the emergence of new life just when the seasonal pendulum swings towards the light again.

Also, with daily checking for a week or so essential to make sure they're happily bedded in, shallots provide a legitimate reason to excuse yourself from festivities indoors and enjoy priceless quiet time with fresh air in your lungs and honest dirt beneath your fingernails.

This final week of the calendar year can be quite mellow weather-wise. We must all hope, however, that it's not too sunny and warm. By late December spring bulbs might well be pushing through. But bumblebees on the wing are a bad sign. There remains little in the way of flowering action and conse-quently, for these busy and very important insects, precious little by way of food.

General jobs to do

1. Keep a fatherly (or motherly) eye on your charges.
2. Work out a planting plan for next year. Base this on your previous experiences, successes and failures, what the family likes to eat, what you enjoy growing, available space, pests and diseases, etc. Do it both in your head and on paper **(Fig. 183, p. 206)**.
3. Cut lanky vegetation and continue the job of weeding (which is far less hectic compared with six months ago!).
4. Clear and sweep paths.
5. Have a warming bonfire by burning woody bits and bobs.

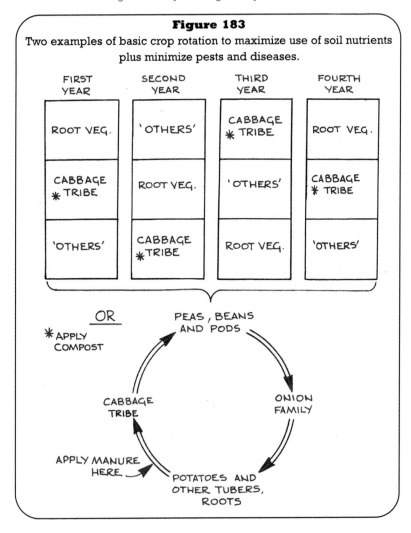

Figure 183

Two examples of basic crop rotation to maximize use of soil nutrients plus minimize pests and diseases.

6. Store wood ash from fires in a dry container for later use **(Fig. 184, p. 207)**.
7. Move pigeon-scarers to where they are needed most. This is usually around cabbages and their relations when winter conditions turn cold **(Fig. 52, p. 68)**.
8. On heavy soils, dig over any neglected areas planned for cultivation **(Figs. 171 and 172, pp. 194 and 195)**.
9. Keep plot edges weed free and neat **(Fig. 32, p. 43)**.
10. Repair and revamp bird-scaring devices **(Fig. 16, p. 26)**.
11. Harvest selections of veggies to make presents for family and friends.

December

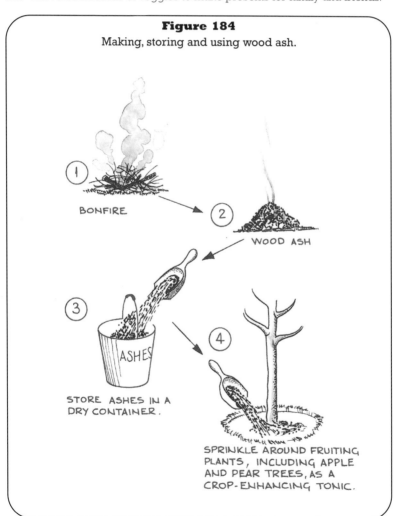

Figure 184
Making, storing and using wood ash.

BONFIRE

WOOD ASH

STORE ASHES IN A DRY CONTAINER.

ASHES

SPRINKLE AROUND FRUITING PLANTS, INCLUDING APPLE AND PEAR TREES, AS A CROP-ENHANCING TONIC.

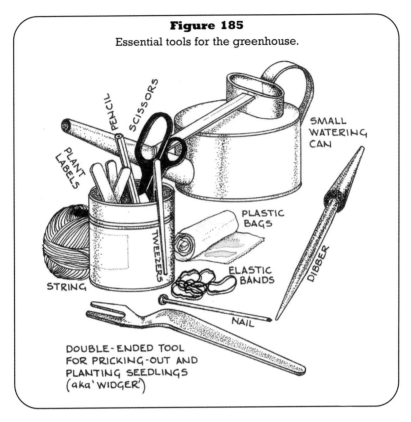

Figure 185
Essential tools for the greenhouse.

12. Ventilate greenhouses in mild weather, keep clean and in good repair **(Fig. 29, p. 41)**.

13. If you have not yet finished cleaning and disinfecting the greenhouse get it done and dusted as soon as possible **(Fig. 174, p. 196)**.

14. Find a place for all those little essentials like tweezers, dibber and plant identification labels ready for seed sowing in the future **(Fig. 185, p. 208)**.

15. Order up seed catalogues for pleasant winter reading!

Leaves & greens

16. SALAD. Check on potted up salad plants, but they're unlikely to need watering **(Fig. 177, p. 198)**.

17. CABBAGE FAMILY. Remove yellowing lower foliage from members of the cabbage tribe and firm soil around their stem bases **(Fig. 176, p. 197)**.

18. Harvest Brussels sprouts for feast-time. Pick lowest sprouts first then

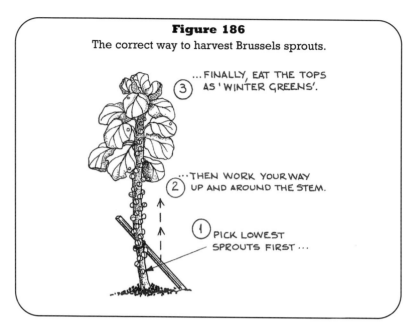

Figure 186

The correct way to harvest Brussels sprouts.

...FINALLY, EAT THE TOPS
③ AS 'WINTER GREENS'.

...THEN WORK YOUR WAY
② UP AND AROUND THE STEM.

① PICK LOWEST
SPROUTS FIRST ...

December

work your way up **(Fig. 186, p. 209)**.

19. Protect greens (especially Nine Star Perennial broccoli) from pigeons, with plastic netting **(Fig. 187, p. 210)**.

20. Tie kale plants securely to stout stakes to prevent wind-rock and firm those Brussels sprouts **(Fig. 188, p. 210)**.

Roots, tubers & stems

21. CELERIAC. Tear off old, tough leaves from celeriac **(Fig. 179, p. 199)**.

22. CARROT. Tend carrots still in the ground by checking for rot. Scrape soil away from the 'shoulders' at the surface and see they're (hopefully) still orange and clean.

23. Move container-grown carrots into a frost-free place **(Fig. 189, p. 211)**.

24. JERUSALEM ARTICHOKE. Prepare a fresh planting site by digging a trench one spit deep and lining with a mix of well-rotted manure and spent potting compost.

25. SWEDE. Remove any rank or decaying foliage to the compost heap **(Fig. 190, p. 212)**.

Veg fruit

26. SQUASH. Sort through squashes in store. Discard any going off, although usually the bad bits can be cut out and the remainder used immediately.

Figure 187
Protecting the cabbage patch from pigeons.

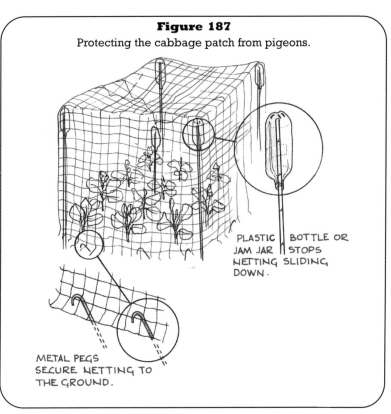

PLASTIC BOTTLE OR JAM JAR STOPS NETTING SLIDING DOWN.

METAL PEGS SECURE NETTING TO THE GROUND.

Figure 188
Firming in Brussels sprouts.

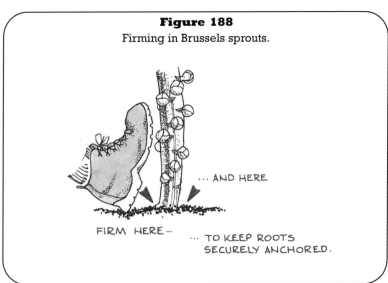

... AND HERE

FIRM HERE...

... TO KEEP ROOTS SECURELY ANCHORED.

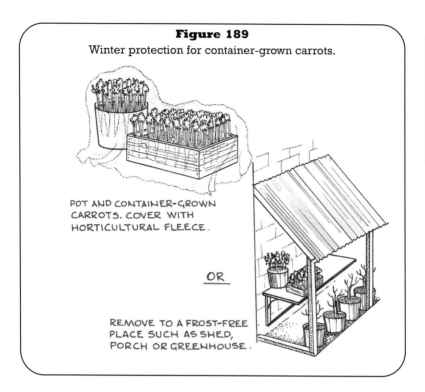

Figure 189
Winter protection for container-grown carrots.

POT AND CONTAINER-GROWN CARROTS. COVER WITH HORTICULTURAL FLEECE.

OR

REMOVE TO A FROST-FREE PLACE SUCH AS SHED, PORCH OR GREENHOUSE.

Onion tribe
27. LEEK. Weed as you harvest leeks.
28. SHALLOT. Sort through shallots in store and select the firmest and best-looking for replanting around midwinter.
29. Plant shallots on the winter solstice (shortest day). Prepare and plant as for onions **(Mar 68/69)**, except plant at 23cm intervals. Check daily until roots have securely taken anchor **(Fig. 191, p. 213)**.

Peas & beans
30. Sow peas, Feltham First, in pots or cardboard tubes **(Feb 52, Oct 54)**.

Edible flowers
31. GLOBE ARTICHOKE. Apply a protective mulch of dry bracken to globe artichoke crowns **(Fig. 6, p. 14)**.

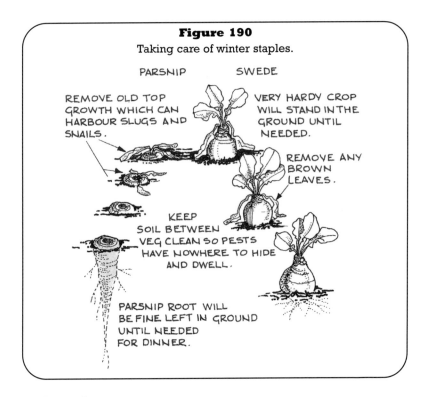

Figure 190

Taking care of winter staples.

PARSNIP   SWEDE

REMOVE OLD TOP
GROWTH WHICH CAN
HARBOUR SLUGS AND
SNAILS.

VERY HARDY CROP
WILL STAND IN THE
GROUND UNTIL
NEEDED.

REMOVE ANY
BROWN
LEAVES.

KEEP
SOIL BETWEEN
VEG CLEAN SO PESTS
HAVE NOWHERE TO HIDE
AND DWELL.

PARSNIP ROOT WILL
BE FINE LEFT IN GROUND
UNTIL NEEDED
FOR DINNER.

Fruit garden

32. APPLE, PEAR & PLUM. Hand weed around plum trees, gages, apples and pears. Mulch each tree with well-rotted manure to a distance of one metre all round the base, but keep the mulch free from touching the trunk **(Fig. 180, p. 201)**.

33. Tie in branches of fan-trained Morello cherry to supporting framework against a north-facing shed wall **(Fig. 137, p. 153)**.

34. GRAPE. Pot up vine cuttings if to be raised in the greenhouse **(Nov 66)**.

35. Scrape loose bark from woody stems of established grape vines to remove pest hidey-holes. It should come up beautifully smooth.

36. GOOSEBERRY. Top dress gooseberries with wood ash. Use whatever you can spare, which has been stored in the dry **(Fig. 184, p. 207)**.

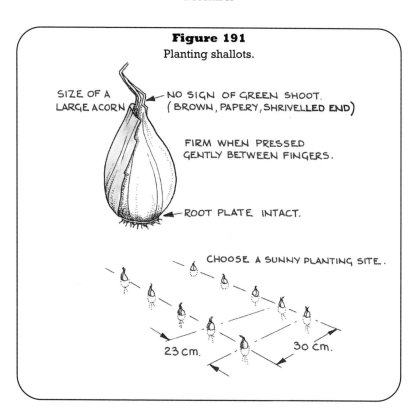

Figure 191
Planting shallots.

SIZE OF A LARGE ACORN

NO SIGN OF GREEN SHOOT.
(BROWN, PAPERY, SHRIVELLED END)

FIRM WHEN PRESSED GENTLY BETWEEN FINGERS.

ROOT PLATE INTACT.

CHOOSE A SUNNY PLANTING SITE.

23 cm.

30 cm.

INDEX

The Index directs you to salient entries on various topics. However, please note that reference is made to the following throughout the text, sometimes frequently.